— The Unofficial Guide to
Walt Disney World®
& EPCOT® —

Also available from Prentice Hall Press:

The Unofficial Guide to Disneyland, by Bob Sehlinger

The Unofficial Guide to
Walt Disney World ®
& EPCOT ®

1991 Edition

Bob Sehlinger

PRENTICE
HALL
PRESS

New York • *London* • *Toronto* • *Sydney* • *Tokyo* • *Singapore*

Produced by Menasha Ridge Press
Published by Prentice Hall Press
   A division of Simon & Schuster Inc.
   15 Columbus Circle
   New York, New York 10023
PRENTICE HALL PRESS and colophons
are registered trademarks
of Simon & Schuster Inc.

Manufactured in the United States of America

Library of Congress Cataloging-in-Publication Data
Sehlinger, Bob, 1945–
   The unofficial guide to Walt Disney World & EPCOT /
   Bob Sehlinger.—New and rev. 1991 ed.
      p.   cm.
   Includes index.
   ISBN 0–13–931619–1 : $9.95
   1. Walt Disney World (Fla.)—Guide-books.   2. EPCOT
(Fla.)—Guide-books.   I. Title.
GV1853.3.F62W3468   1991
791'.06'875924—dc20   90-47034
                                                  CIP

10 9 8 7 6 5 4 3 2 1

ISBN: 0–13–931619–1

Declaration of Independence

The author and researchers of this guide specifically and categorically declare that they are and always have been totally independent of Walt Disney Productions, Inc., of Disneyland, Inc., of Walt Disney World, Inc., and of any and all other members of the Disney corporate family not listed.

The material in this guide originated with the author and researchers and has not been reviewed, edited, or in any way approved by Walt Disney Productions, Inc., Disneyland, Inc., or Walt Disney World, Inc.

Trademarks

The following attractions, shows, components, entities, etc., mentioned or discussed in this guide are registered trademarks of Walt Disney Productions, Inc.:

> Adventureland
> AudioAnimatronics
> Captain EO
> Disneyland
> EPCOT
> Fantasyland
> Magic Kingdom
> New Orleans Square
> PeopleMover
> Space Mountain
> Walt Disney
> Walt Disney World

New trademarks are applied for almost continuously. These will be recognized as and when appropriate in subsequent editions of this guide.

Contents

—— *Acknowledgments* ——

Special thanks to our field research team who rendered a Herculean effort in what must have seemed like a fantasy version of Sartre's *No Exit* to the tune of *It's a Small World*. We hope you all recover to tour another day.

Ray Westbrook
Joan W. Burns
Cyril C. Sehlinger
Pid Rafter
Karin Zachow
Trent Sehlinger
Mary Mitchell

Many thanks also to Barbara Williams and Charles Ellertson for design and production, and to Alexa Dilworth for editorial work on this book. Tseng Information Systems, and especially Giovanna de Graaff, earned our appreciation for their fine work and for keeping tight deadlines in providing the typography. Cartography was provided by Tim Krasnansky.

Finally, some of John Finley's comments and descriptions, which originally appeared in *Central Florida Attractions* (co-authored by Finley and Bob Sehlinger, Menasha Ridge Press, 1983), are reproduced in this guide.

— The Unofficial Guide to
Walt Disney World®
& EPCOT® —

How Come "Unofficial"?

This guidebook represents the first comprehensive *critical* appraisal of Walt Disney World. Its purpose is to provide the reader with the information necessary to tour Walt Disney World with the greatest efficiency and economy, and with the least amount of hassle and standing in line. The authors of this guide believe in the wondrous variety, joy, and excitement of the Disney attractions. At the same time, we recognize realistically that Walt Disney World is a business, with the same profit motivations as businesses the world over.

In this guide we have elected to represent and serve you, the consumer. Its contents were researched and compiled by a team of evaluators who were, and are, completely independent of Walt Disney World and its parent corporation. If a restaurant serves bad food, or a gift item is overpriced, or a certain ride isn't worth the wait, we can say so, and in the process, hopefully make your visit more fun, efficient, and economical.

How This Guide Was Researched and Written

While much has been written concerning Walt Disney World, very little has been comparative or evaluative. Most guides simply parrot Disney World's own promotional material. In preparing this guide, however, nothing was taken for granted. Each theme park was visited at different times throughout the year by a team of trained observers. They conducted detailed evaluations and rated each theme park with all its component rides, shows, exhibits, services, and concessions according to a formal, pretested rating instrument. Interviews with attraction patrons were conducted to determine what tourists—of all age groups—enjoyed most and least during their Disney World visit.

While our observers were independent and impartial, we do not claim special expertise or scientific background relative to the types of exhibits, performances, or attractions. Like you, we visit Walt Disney World as tourists, noting our satisfaction or dissatisfaction. We do not believe it necessary then to be an agronomist to know whether we enjoyed the agricultural exhibits in the EPCOT Center Land pavilion. Disney offerings are marketed to the touring public, and it is as the public that we have experienced them.

The primary difference between the average tourist and the trained evaluator is in the evaluator's professional skills in organization, preparation, and observation. The trained evaluator is responsible for much more than simply observing and cataloging. While the tourist seated next to him is being entertained and delighted by the *Tropical Serenade* (*Enchanted Tiki Birds*) in the Magic Kingdom, the professional is rating the performance in terms of theme, pace, continuity, and originality. He or she is also checking out the physical arrangements: Is the sound system clear and audible without being overpowering; is the audience shielded from the sun or from the rain; is seating adequate; can everyone in the audience clearly see the staging area? And what about guides and/or performers: Are they knowledgeable, articulate, and professional in their presentation; are they friendly and engaging? Does the performance begin and end on time; does the show contain the features described in Disney World's promotional literature? These and many other considerations figure prominently in the rating of any staged performance. Similarly, detailed and relevant checklists were prepared and applied by observer teams to rides, exhibits, concessions, and to the theme parks in general. Finally observations and evaluator ratings were integrated with audience reactions and the opinions of patrons to compile a comprehensive quality profile of each feature and service.

In compiling this guide, we recognize the fact that a tourist's age, sex, background, and interests will strongly influence his or her taste in Walt Disney World offerings and will account for a preference of one ride or feature over another. Given this fact we make no attempt at comparing apples with oranges. How indeed could a meaningful comparison be made between the priceless historic artifacts in the Mexican pavilion of EPCOT Center and the wild roller coaster ride of the Magic Kingdom's Space Mountain? Instead, our objective is to provide the reader with sufficient description, critical evaluation, and pertinent data to make knowledgeable decisions according to individual tastes.

The essence of this guide, therefore, consists of individual critiques and descriptions of each feature of the Magic Kingdom, EPCOT Center, and Disney-MGM Studios, along with detailed Touring Plans to help you avoid bottlenecks and crowds. Also included are in-depth descriptions and Touring Plans for Typhoon Lagoon and Pleasure Island.

The Attraction that Ate Florida

Before Walt Disney World, Florida was a happy peninsula of many more-or-less equal tourist attractions. Distributed around the state in great proliferation, they constituted the most perennially appealing vacation opportunity in the United States. There was the Monkey Jungle, the Orchid Jungle, venerable Marineland, the St. Augustine Alligator Farm, Silver Springs, the Miami Wax Museum, the Sunken Gardens, the Coral Castle, and the Conch Train Tour. These, along with Cypress Gardens, Busch Gardens, and others, were the attractions that ruled Florida. Now like so many dinosaurs, those remaining survive precariously on the droppings of the greatest dinosaur of them all, Walt Disney World. With doors still open, the old standbys continue to welcome tourists, thank you, but when was the last time you planned your vacation around a trip to Jungle Larry's Safari Park?

When Walt Disney World arrived on the scene, Florida tourism changed forever. Before Disney (BD), southern Florida was the state's and the nation's foremost tourist destination. Throngs sunned on the beaches of Miami, Hollywood, and Fort Lauderdale and patronized such nearby attractions as the Miami Serpentarium and the Parrot Jungle. Attractions in the Ocala and St. Augustine area upstate hosted road travelers in great waves as they journeyed to and from their southern Florida destinations. At the time, Orlando was a sleepy little central Florida town about an hour's drive from Cypress Gardens, and with practically no tourist appeal whatsoever.

Then came Disney, and it was not as if Walt had sneaked up on anyone. To the contrary, he came openly and bargaining hard, asking for improved highways, tax concessions, bargain financing, and community support. So successful had been his California Disneyland that whatever he requested, he received.

Generally approving, and hoping for a larger aggregate market, the Florida attractions industry failed to discern the cloud on the horizon. Walt had tipped his hand early, however, and all the cards were on the table. When Disney bought 27,500 central Florida acres, it was fairly evident that he did not intend to raise cattle.

The Magic Kingdom opened on October 1, 1971, and was immediately successful. Hotel construction boomed in Orlando and Kissimmee and around Walt Disney World. Major new attractions popped up along recently completed Interstate 4 to cash in on the wellspring of tourists arriving to tour Disney's latest wonder. Walt Disney World became a destination, and suddenly nobody cared as much about going to the beach. The Magic Kingdom was good for two days, and then you could enjoy the rest of the week at Sea World, Cypress Gardens, Circus World, Gatorland Zoo, Busch Gardens, the Stars Hall of Fame Wax Museum, and the Kennedy Space Center.

These various satellite attractions, all practically new and stretching from east coast to west coast, formed what would come to be called the Orlando Wall. No longer did tourists pour into Miami and Fort Lauderdale. Rather, they held up at the Orlando Wall and exhausted themselves and their tourist dollars in the shiny modern attractions arrayed between Cape Canaveral and Tampa. In southern Florida venerable old attractions held on by a parrot feather and more than a few closed their doors. Flagship hotels on the fabled Gold Coast went bust or were converted to condominiums for legions of retirees.

When Walt Disney World opened, the very definition of a tourist attraction changed. Setting standards for cleanliness, size, scope, grandeur, variety, and attention to detail, Walt Disney World relegated overnight the majority of Florida's headliner attractions to positions of comparative insignificance. Newer attractions such as Sea World and the vastly enlarged Busch Gardens strove successfully to achieve the new standard. Cypress Gardens, Weeki Wachi, and Silver Springs expanded and modernized. Most other attractions, however, slipped into a limbo of diminished status from which they never recovered. Far from being headliners or tourist destinations, they plugged along as local diversions, pulling in the curious, the bored, and the sunburned for two-hour excursions.

Many of the affected attractions were and are wonderful places to spend a vacation day, but even collectively, as has been sadly demonstrated, they do not command sufficient appeal to lure many tourists beyond the Wall. We recommend them, however, not only for their variety of high quality offerings, but as a glimpse of Florida's golden age, a time of less sophisticated, less plastic pleasures, before the

Mouse. Take a day or two and drive three and one-half hours south of Orlando. Visit the Miami Seaquarium or Ocean World, try Vizcaya, Fairchild Tropical Gardens, and Lion Country Safari. Drive Collins Avenue along the Gold Coast. You'll be glad you did.

When EPCOT Center opened in Walt Disney World on October 1, 1982, another seismic shock reverberated through the Florida attractions industry. This time it was not only the smaller and more vulnerable attractions that were affected, but the newer large-scale attractions along the Orlando Wall. Suddenly, with EPCOT Center, Walt Disney World had swallowed up another one to two days of each tourist's vacation week. When the Magic Kingdom stood alone, most visitors had three or four days remaining to sample other attractions. With the addition of EPCOT Center, that available time was cut to one or two days.

Disney ensured its market share by creating the multi-day admission passes which allow unlimited access to both the Magic Kingdom and EPCOT Center. More cost-efficient than a one-day pass to a single park, these passes had the effect of keeping the guest on Disney turf for three to five days.

The Kennedy Space Center and Sea World, by virtue of their very specialized products, continued to prosper following the opening of EPCOT Center. Most other attractions, however, were forced to focus more of their energy on local markets. Some, like Busch Gardens, did very well, with increased local support replacing the decreased numbers of Walt Disney World destination tourists coming over for the day. Others, like Cypress Gardens, suffered badly but worked diligently to improve their product. Some, like Circus World and the Hall of Fame Wax Museum, passed into history.

Though long an innovator, Disney turned in the mid-80s to copying existing successful competitor attractions, except that copying is not exactly the right word. What Disney did was to take a competitor's product concept, improve it, and reproduce it in Disney style on a grand scale.

The first competitor to feel the heat was Sea World when Disney added The Living Seas pavilion to the Future World section of EPCOT Center. Sea World, however, had killer whales, the Shark Encounter, and sufficient corporate resources to remain preeminent among marine exhibits. Still, many Walt Disney World patrons willingly substituted a visit to The Living Seas for a visit to Sea World.

Disney had one of its own products threatened when the Wet 'n

Wild water theme park took a shot at the older, smaller, but more aesthetically pleasing River Country. Never one to take a challenge sitting down, Disney responded in 1989 with the opening of Typhoon Lagoon, the largest swimming theme park in the world.

Also in 1989 Disney opened Pleasure Island, a one-admission multi-nightclub entertainment complex patterned on Orlando's successful Church Street Station. While the jury is still out, odds are that Pleasure Island will strip Church Street Station of much of its destination tourist traffic.

Finally, and most significant of all, in 1989 Walt Disney World opened the Disney-MGM Studios, a combination working motion picture and television production complex and theme park. Copying from the long-heralded Universal Studios tour in southern California, the Disney-MGM Studios were speeded into construction and operation after Universal had announced its plans for a central Florida park.

This newest of the Walt Disney World theme parks, however, affects much more than Universal's plans. With the opening of Disney-MGM, the 3-Day World Passport was discontinued. Instead, Disney patrons are offered either a single-day pass or the more economical multi-day passports, good for either four or five days. With the three theme parks on a multi-day pass, plus a water park (Typhoon Lagoon), several golf courses, various lakes, and a nighttime entertainment complex, Disney has effectively swallowed up the average family's entire vacation. Break away to Sea World or the Kennedy Space Center for the day? How about a day at the ocean (remember the ocean)? Fat chance.

With the opening of the Walt Disney World Swan Resort, Dolphin Hotel, and Conference Center, Disney has taken a quantum leap toward monopolizing the business and convention traveler as well. With over 250,000 square feet of exhibit space, the Conference Center is the largest in the southeast and one of the largest in the United States. Disney is even talking about constructing a monorail to the airport so that visitors will not have to set a single foot in Orlando.

I regret the passing of an era in Florida tourism. The old attractions were more intimate, more personal, more human. The live alligators were more interesting (if less predictable) than the Disney robotic version, and I found I could stomach the pungent odor of a real cougar. Each modest attraction embodied the realization of some maverick's dream, a dream he longed to share with anyone who passed through the turnstile.

But dreams are only as grand as the men who create them, and only the truly visionary endure. Such was the dream of Walt Disney, come to fruition in Walt Disney World. Is his dream a cancer in the breast of tourism? Far from it. It is a testimony to careful planning, harboring of resources, precise timing, and adherence to a standard of quality unprecedented in the entertainment industry. Walt Disney World represents the delivery of a product that amazes and delights, that exceeds the expectations of almost every visitor.

From an entrepreneurial seed, a beloved cartoon mouse, and a California amusement park years ahead of its time has risen an entertainment giant, a giant that sometimes moves clumsily and sometimes with cold hard determination but always with a commitment to quality. Walt Disney World represents the kind of imagination, industry, and farsighted thinking that might have preserved American leadership in steel, automobiles, and electronics. Sure, we all like to see the little guy succeed, and most of us prefer a competitive marketplace. But if giants we must have, would that they all be like Walt Disney World.

Walt Disney World—An Overview

If you are selecting among the tourist attractions in Florida, the question is not whether to visit Walt Disney World but how to see the best of the various Disney offerings with some economy of time, effort, and finances.

Make no mistake, there is nothing on earth quite like Walt Disney World. Incredible in its scope, genius, beauty, and imagination, it is a joy and wonder for people of all ages. A fantasy, a dream, and a vision all rolled into one, it transcends simple entertainment, making us children and adventurers, freeing us for an hour or a day to live the dreams of our past, present, and future.

Certainly we are critics, but it is the responsibility of critics to credit that which is done well as surely as to reflect negatively on that which is done poorly. The Disney attractions are special, a quantum leap beyond and above any man-made entertainment offering we know of. We cannot understand how anyone could visit Florida and bypass Walt Disney World.

—— What Walt Disney World Encompasses ——

Walt Disney World encompasses forty-three square miles, an area twice the size of Manhattan Island. Situated strategically in this vast expanse are two major theme parks, a filmmaking studio and tour, the world's largest swimming theme park, a smaller swimming attraction, a botanical and zoological exhibit, a nightlife entertainment area, several golf courses, hotels, four large interconnected lakes, a shopping complex, a convention center, a permanent nature preserve, and a complete transportation system consisting of four-lane highways, an elevated monorail, and a system of canals.

Most tourists refer to the entire Florida Disney facility as Walt Disney World, or more simply, as Disney World. The Magic Kingdom, EPCOT Center, and Disney-MGM Studios are thought of as being "in" Disney World. Other visitors refer to the Magic Kingdom as Disney World and EPCOT Center as EPCOT, and are not sure exactly how to label the entity as a whole. In our description we will refer to the total Disney facility as Walt Disney World according to popular tradition, and will consider the Magic Kingdom, EPCOT Center, and everything else that sits on that 43-square-mile chunk of real estate to be included in the overall designation.

—— *The Major Theme Parks* ——

The Magic Kingdom

The Magic Kingdom is what most people think of when they think of Walt Disney World. It is the collection of adventures, rides, and shows symbolized by the Disney cartoon characters and Cinderella Castle. Although the Magic Kingdom is only one element of the Disney attraction complex, it remains the heart of Disney World. The Magic Kingdom is divided into seven subareas or "lands," six of which are arranged around a central hub. First encountered is Main Street, U.S.A., which connects the Magic Kingdom entrance with the central hub. Moving clockwise around the hub, other lands are Adventureland, Frontierland, Liberty Square, Fantasyland, and Tomorrowland. Mickey's Starland, the first new land in the Magic Kingdom since the park opened, is situated along the Walt Disney Railroad on three acres between Fantasyland and Tomorrowland. Access is through Fantasyland or via the railroad. Main Street and the other six lands will be described in detail later. Three hotel complexes (Contemporary Resort Hotel, Polynesian Village Resort, and the Grand Floridian Beach Resort) are located close to the Magic Kingdom and are directly connected to it by monorail and by boat.

EPCOT Center

EPCOT (Experimental Prototype Community of Tomorrow) Center opened in October of 1982. Divided into two major areas, Future World and World Showcase, the park is twice the size of and is comparable in scope to the Magic Kingdom. Future World consists of a number of futuristic pavilions, each relating to a different theme concerning man's creativity and technological advancement. World

Showcase, arranged around a 41-acre lagoon, presents the architectural, social, and cultural heritages of almost a dozen nations, with each country represented by famous landmarks and local settings familiar to world travelers. EPCOT Center is generally more educationally oriented than the Magic Kingdom and has been repeatedly characterized as a sort of permanent world's fair. Unlike the Magic Kingdom, which Disney spokesmen represent as being essentially complete, EPCOT Center is pictured as a continually changing and growing entity. EPCOT Center is connected to the Magic Kingdom and resort hotels by monorail.

The Disney-MGM Studios

This $300 million, 100-plus-acre attraction, which opened in 1989, is divided into two areas. The first is a theme park relating to the past, present, and future of the motion picture industry. This section contains movie-theme rides and shows and covers about a third of the Disney-MGM complex. Highlights here include a re-creation of Hollywood Boulevard from the 20s and 30s, audience participation shows on TV production and sound effects, movie stunt demonstrations, the Star Tours ride, and the Great Movie Ride, which takes guests for a journey through the movies' greatest moments.

The second area, encompassing the remaining two-thirds, is a working motion picture and television production facility comprised of three sound stages, a backlot of streets and sets, and creative support services. Access to this area is limited to the public except through studio tours which take visitors behind the scenes for a crash-course on movie making, including the opportunity to witness the actual shooting of feature films and television shows.

The Disney-MGM Studios are connected to other Walt Disney World areas by highway and canal, but not by monorail. Guests can park in the Studios' own pay parking lot or commute by bus from EPCOT Center, the Transportation and Ticket Center, or from any Walt Disney World lodging.

—— The Water Theme Parks ——

There are two major swimming theme parks in Walt Disney World, Typhoon Lagoon and the older River Country. Typhoon Lagoon is the world's largest park of its kind and is distinguished by a wave pool capable of making six-foot waves. River Country, a pioneer among water theme parks, is much smaller but very well done. Since Typhoon Lagoon's opening in 1989, River Country has catered primarily to Walt Disney World campground and resort hotel guests. Both parks are beautifully arranged and landscaped, with great attention paid to atmosphere and aesthetics. Either park can be reached via private vehicle or the Walt Disney World bus system.

—— *The Minor Theme Parks* ——

Pleasure Island

Part of the Walt Disney World Village, Pleasure Island is a six-acre nighttime entertainment center where one cover charge will get a visitor into any of six nightclubs. The clubs are themed and feature a variety of shows and activities. Music ranges from pop-rock to country and western. For the more sedentary (or exhausted) there is a ten-screen movie complex, or for the hungry, several restaurants.

Discovery Island

Situated in Bay Lake close to the Magic Kingdom, Discovery Island is a tropically landscaped, small zoological park primarily featuring birdlife. Small intimate trails wind through the exotic foliage, contrasting with the broad thoroughfares of the major theme parks. Plants and trees are marked for easy identification and the island features an absolutely enormous walk-through aviary, so cleverly engineered that you are essentially unaware of the confining netting. On the negative side, a trip to Discovery Island is fairly pricey (about $8) for a few birds and animals and a short stroll through the woods. As for children, they enjoy Discovery Island if allowed to explore on their own, but become bored and restless touring under the thumb of their elders. One deal for seeing Discovery Island is to buy a River Country/Discovery Island combination ticket (about $15). But of course it's only a good deal if you plan to go to both minor parks anyway. Probably the best deal for those spending four days or more at Walt Disney World is the 5-Day PLUS Super Pass that in addition to providing admission to the three major parks also provides unlimited admission to Typhoon Lagoon, River Country, Pleasure Island, Discovery Island,

and Disney's Boardwalk. Do not spring for the Super Pass, however, unless you intend to take advantage of its features.

There are no lodging accommodations on Discovery Island, but snacks are available. Access is exclusively by boat from the main Bay Lake docks (Magic Kingdom Dock, Fort Wilderness Landing, Resort Hotels' docks).

Disney's Boardwalk (Opens fall 1991)

Located along a walkway connecting the Swan Resort with EPCOT Center's International Gateway, Disney's Boardwalk is an amusement park in the style of Atlantic City and Coney Island. Game arcades, rides, music, food, and bright lights bring back a Disney-clean version of America's traditional amusement park. Guests at the Swan or Dolphin Hotels, or at Disney's Yacht Club or Beach Club Resorts, can walk to Disney's Boardwalk. EPCOT Center guests can access Disney's Boardwalk on foot via the International Gateway between France and the United Kingdom in the World Showcase. Others can reach the boardwalk by private automobile or Disney bus service.

— *Should I Go to Walt Disney World If I've Been to Disneyland in California?* —

Walt Disney World is a much larger and more varied entertainment complex than is Disneyland. There is no EPCOT Center, Disney-MGM Studios, or Typhoon Lagoon at Disneyland. To be specific, Disneyland is roughly comparable to the Magic Kingdom theme park at Walt Disney World in Florida. Both the Magic Kingdom and Disneyland are arranged by "lands" accessible from a central hub and connected to the entrance by a Main Street. Both parks feature many rides and attractions of the same name: Space Mountain, Jungle Cruise, Pirates of the Caribbean, It's a Small World, and Dumbo, the Flying Elephant, to name a few. Interestingly, however, the same name does not necessarily connote the same experience. Pirates of the Caribbean at Disneyland is much longer and more elaborate than its Walt Disney World counterpart. Space Mountain is far wilder in Florida, and Dumbo is about the same in both places.

Disneyland is more intimate than the Magic Kingdom since it doesn't have the room for expansion enjoyed by the Florida park. Pedestrian thoroughfares are more narrow, and everything from Big Thunder Mountain to the Castle is scaled down somewhat. Large crowds are less taxing at the Magic Kingdom since there is more room for them to disperse.

At Disneyland, however, there are dozens of little surprises: small unheralded attractions tucked away in crooks and corners of the park, which give Disneyland a special charm and variety that the Magic Kingdom lacks. And, of course, Disneyland has more of the stamp of Walt Disney's personal touch.

For additional information on Disneyland, see *The Unofficial Guide to Disneyland*, by Bob Sehlinger, Prentice Hall Press.

To allow for a meaningful comparison, we provide a summary of those features found only at one of the parks, followed by a critical look at the attractions found at both.

Attractions Found Only at the Magic Kingdom

Liberty Square:	*Hall Of Presidents*
Tomorrowland:	Dreamflight
	Carousel Of Progress
Mickey's Starland:	All attractions

Attractions Found Only at Disneyland

Main Street:	*Great Moments With Mr. Lincoln*
Frontierland:	Sailing Ship Columbia
	Big Thunder Ranch
Fantasyland:	The Story of Sleeping Beauty
	Pinocchio's Daring Journey
	Casey Jr. Circus Train
	Storybook Land Canal Boats
	Alice In Wonderland
	Matterhorn Bobsleds
	Motor Boat Cruise
	Videopolis
Tomorrowland:	Star Tours (also at Disney-MGM Studios)
Critter Country:	Splash Mountain

Critical Comparison of Attractions Found at Both Parks

Main Street

WDW/Disneyland Railroad	The Disneyland Railroad is far more entertaining by virtue of the Grand Canyon Diorama and the Primeval World components not found at the Magic Kingdom.
Walt Disney Story	More comprehensive film at the Magic Kingdom. More interesting static displays and memorabilia at Disneyland.

Adventureland

Jungle Cruise	More realistic AudioAnimatronic (robotic) animals at Walt Disney World, otherwise about the same.
Enchanted Tiki Birds	About the same at both parks.
Swiss Family Treehouse	Larger at the Magic Kingdom.

New Orleans Square

Pirates of the Caribbean	Far superior at Disneyland.
Haunted Mansion	Slight edge to the Magic Kingdom version.

Critter Country

Country Bear Jamboree	Same production with much less of a wait at Disneyland.

Frontierland

Various river cruises (Canoes, steamboats, keelboats, etc.)	Slight edge to the Magic Kingdom in terms of the sights.
Tom Sawyer Island	Comparable, but a little more elaborate with better food service at the Magic Kingdom.
Big Thunder Mountain Railroad	Ride about the same. Sights and special effects better at the Magic Kingdom.
Golden Horseshoe Jamboree/Diamond Horseshoe Jamboree	Similar at both parks.

Fantasyland

Snow White's Scary Adventures	About the same at both parks.
Peter Pan's Flight	Better at Disneyland.
Mr. Toad's Wild Ride	Better at Disneyland.
Dumbo, the Flying Elephant	The same at both parks.
Carousels	About the same at both parks.
Castles	Far larger and more beautiful at the Magic Kingdom.
Mad Tea Party	The same at both parks.
It's a Small World	About the same at both parks.
Skyway	About the same at both parks.

Tomorrowland

Autopia/Grand Prix Raceway	About the same at both parks.
Mission to Mars	The same at both parks.
Rocket Jets/Starjets	The same at both parks.
PeopleMover	Edge to Disneyland.
World Premier Circle-Vision	The same at both parks.
Space Mountain	Vastly superior in terms of both ride and special effects at the Magic Kingdom.
Submarine Voyage/ 20,000 Leagues Under the Sea	About the same at both parks.

Walt Disney World Summary

P.O. Box 1000, Lake Buena Vista, FL 32830-1000
Call ahead for opening/closing times   Phone: (407) 824-4321

Admissions

Ticket options	Discounts	
One-Park/One-Day Ticket	Children (3–9)	**yes**
4-Day All-Three Parks Passport	Children under 3	**free**
5-Day World Passport	Students	**varies**
Annual Passport	Military	**varies**
	Senior citizens	**varies**
	Group rates	**yes**

Credit cards accepted for admission: **MasterCard, American Express** and **VISA**.
Features included: **All except Frontierland Shootin' Gallery**

Overall Appeal*

By age groups	Preschool	Grade School	Teens	Young Adults	Over 30	Senior Citizens
	★★★★★	★★★★★	★★★★★	★★★★★	★★★★★	★★★★★

Touring Tips

Touring time
  Average: **Full day**
  Minimum: **Full day**
Touring strategy: **See narrative**
Rainy day touring: **Recommended**

Periods of lightest attendance
  Time of day: **Early morning**
  Days: **Friday, Sunday**
  Times of year: **After Thanksgiving until 18th of December**

What the Critics Say

Rating of major features:
(begins on p. 92)

Rating of functional and operational areas	
Parking	★★★★★
Rest rooms	★★★★★
Resting places	★★★★★
Crowd management	★★★★★
Aesthetic appeal of grounds	★★★★★
Cleanliness/maintenance	★★★★★

Services and Facilities

Restaurant/snack bar **Yes**
Vending machines (food/pop) **No**
Handicapped access **Yes**
Wheelchairs **Rental**
Baby strollers **Rental**

Lockers **Yes**
Pet kennels **Yes**
Gift shops **Yes**
Film sales **Yes**
Rain check **No**
Private guided group tours **Yes**

*Critical ratings are based on a scale of zero to five stars with five stars being the best possible rating.

PART ONE—Planning
Before You Leave Home

── *Gathering Information* ──

In addition to this guide, information concerning Walt Disney World can be obtained at the public library and at travel agencies, or by calling or writing any of the following:

Important Walt Disney World Telephone Numbers

General Information	(407) 824-4321
Accommodations/Reservations	(407) 934-7639
	or (407) 824-8000
Dining Reservations for	
WDW Lodging Guests	(407) 828-4000
Resort Dining and	
Recreational Information	(407) 824-3737
Educational Programs	(407) 345-5860
Merchandise Mail Order	(407) 824-4718
Disney Car Care Center	(407) 824-4813
Fort Wilderness Campground	(407) 824-2900
Contemporary Resort Hotel	(407) 824-1000
Polynesian Village Resort	(407) 824-2000
Grand Floridian Beach Resort	(407) 824-3000
Caribbean Beach Resort	(407) 934-3400
Tee Times & Golf Studio	(407) 824-2270
Lost & Found	
Magic Kingdom	(407) 824-4245
EPCOT Center	(407) 560-6105
Disney-MGM Studios	(407) 560-4668
Telecommunication for Deaf	(407) 827-5141

Important Walt Disney World Addresses

Walt Disney World Information
P.O. Box 10040
Lake Buena Vista, FL 32830-0040

Walt Disney World Central Reservations
P.O. Box 10100
Lake Buena Vista, FL 32830-0100

Convention and Banquet Information
P.O. Box 10000
Lake Buena Vista, FL 32830-1000

Walt Disney World Educational Programs
Wonders of Walt Disney World (Ages 10–15)
The Disney Learning Adventure (Adults)
P.O. Box 10000
Lake Buena Vista, FL 32830-1000

Merchandise Mail Order
P.O. Box 10070
Lake Buena Vista, FL 32830-0070

Walt Disney World Ticket Mail Order
P.O. Box 10030
3300 Bonnett Creek Road
Lake Buena Vista, FL 32830-0030

Timing Your Visit

—— *Trying to Reason with the Tourist Season* ——

It is one of the objectives of this book to assist the tourist, when possible, in avoiding crowds. It is useful therefore to understand the overall seasonality and traffic flow of Florida tourism.

Peninsular Florida (all of Florida except the Panhandle) has two peak seasons. One begins just before Christmas and ends just after Easter and is referred to as the "Winter Season" or sometimes just "the Season." The other, known as the "Summer Season" or "Family Season," gets into swing about the middle of June and lasts until late August.

Christmas Week, which effectively kicks off the Winter Season, is Florida's busiest week of the year, with facilities throughout the state (including attractions), being pushed to their limit. Many attractions offer special programs beginning several days prior to Christmas and extending through New Year's Day. Crowds, however, are awesome, with many smaller attractions inundated and long waits in line the norm at larger attractions. Because of the crowded conditions, we do not recommend Christmas Week for attraction touring. If, however, your schedule permits arriving the preceding week (say December 15th or thereabouts) crowds are manageable and sometimes even sparse. Get your touring in by the 22nd and then relax and enjoy the beach over Christmas.

Though the mammoth throngs of Christmas Week dissipate following New Year's Day, the Winter Season remains in full session with heavy attraction attendance through Easter. Easter Week is almost as congested as Christmas Week. During the Winter Season a high concentration of tourists is a fact of life.

The period between Easter and the beginning of the Summer Season in early June is usually slow and is a particularly good time for attraction touring. Activity picks up again toward the middle of June with the arrival of the family vacation traffic. This second season runs through late August when the kids return to school.

Attendance at individual attractions varies, with some attractions more popular with the Winter Season tourist and others more popular with the Summer Season tourist. This is attributable in part to the relatively small number of school-age children present during Winter Season.

September through mid-December is very slow throughout Florida except for the Thanksgiving holiday period. Our research team felt that the nicest time to visit Florida in terms of weather, low-stress touring, and crowd avoidance was the first two weeks in December, just prior to the Christmas crunch.

Holiday weekends throughout the year, as well as special events (Florida Derby, spacecraft launchings, auto races, local festivals, etc.) precipitate heavy attraction attendance in and out of season. On days immediately preceding or following the holiday periods, however, attendance is often extremely light.

The best weather in Florida usually occurs between late fall and mid-April, which coincides, of course, with the busy Winter Season. Attraction touring is pleasant throughout the day, though mornings and late afternoons are best for crowd avoidance during this time of the year.

During the warmer months of the Summer Season, comfort as well as crowd avoidance suggest early day touring.

Rainy days in both the Summer and Winter Seasons often afford excellent opportunities for beating the crowd. Many outdoor attractions offer good protection from the elements and are as enjoyable on a rainy day as on a sunny day. Indoor attractions see their heaviest attendance on rainy days. Here we recommend touring on sunny days during the very hot midday hours (11:30 A.M.–2:30 P.M.).

Off season (mid-April through early June and September through mid-December) touring is characterized by smaller crowds and by somewhat rainier weather, and is generally an excellent time to visit the state's premier, large-scale attractions. However, since attendance is lightest at these times it is not uncommon for certain major rides, shows, and exhibits to be closed for maintenance or revision. A phone call to the attraction under consideration will obtain information concerning which, if any, key features will be out of action during your intended visit.

The Florida Panhandle has a somewhat abridged Winter Season centered around Christmas and New Year's Day then followed by somewhat of a lull until March and April. The big season for the Panhandle is the Summer Season.

— *Florida Traffic Patterns* —

Attraction touring takes place both while traveling en route and at the tourist's vacation destination. Southern Florida is a destination area; tourists, upon arrival, visit local attractions as a supplement to their vacation itinerary. The Orlando area is both a vacation destination and an en route center of tourism. Many visitors spend their entire vacation in the Orlando area while others visit en route to or from southern Florida. Ocala by contrast is largely an en route center of tourism with most tourists stopping on their way to or from other destinations.

Since most tourists do their traveling to and from their vacation destination on weekends, it is possible to identify patterns of traffic which are useful in avoiding crowds. As an example, a Tennessee family whose primary destination is Walt Disney World may tour Silver Springs at Ocala en route. Departing Tennessee on Friday evening or Saturday morning places them at Silver Springs on Sunday, arriving in the Orlando area on Sunday evening. Since this is a very common itinerary, executed by thousands of tourists every week, a traffic pattern becomes discernible. Silver Springs will show its heaviest attendance on weekends. Walt Disney World, as a destination, will show large crowds on Monday, Tuesday, and Wednesday. Sea World, and other Orlando area attractions will see heavier attendance from Wednesday through Friday when visitors, such as our Tennessee family, have finished seeing Walt Disney World and begin to explore other attractions nearby.

Because of the extended driving distance, the average length of stay in Florida is greater for most tourists whose ultimate destination is southern Florida. An Ohio couple departing Columbus on Friday evening might typically tour St. Augustine or Marineland on Sunday and then proceed directly to their Fort Lauderdale destination or stop again for a day or two to tour Orlando area attractions. This itinerary places the couple at their Fort Lauderdale destination sometime late Monday, Tuesday, or Wednesday. Thus in southern Florida, attraction attendance is heaviest toward the end of the week and, as noted above, since visitors to southern Florida stay longer on the average, attendance remains heavy on weekends.

Thus, by understanding the more common patterns of arrival, departure, en route touring, and destination touring, it is possible to plan an attraction visitation itinerary which operates counter to the usual traffic

Visitation patterns of specific centers of Florida tourism

Area	Tourism Classification	Heaviest Attendance	When to Go
Panhandle	Destination	Weekends	Weekdays
St. Augustine, Marineland	En route	Weekends	Weekdays
Ocala	En route	Weekends	Weekdays
Weeki Wachee, Homosassa Springs	En route	Weekends	Weekdays
Orlando, Kissimmee, Cape Canaveral	En route, destination	Monday through Thursday	Friday through Sunday
Tampa	En route, day trip from Orlando and from beaches	Thursday through Sunday	Monday through Wednesday
Clearwater, St. Petersburg	Destination	Winter: Sunday through Tuesday	Wednesday through Saturday
		Summer: Friday through Sunday	Monday through Thursday
Sarasota	En route, destination, day trip from beaches to the north	Varies	Varies
Naples, Bonita Springs	Destination	Varies	Varies
Southern Florida, East Coast	Destination	Thursday through Sunday	Monday through Wednesday
Keys, Key West	Destination, day trip from beaches to the north	Weekdays	Weekends

flow and places the tourist at each chosen attraction on a day of lighter attendance.

Displayed here in summary form is a guide to the visitation patterns of specific centers of Florida tourism. Note that light and heavy attendance are relative terms, with light attendance in season possibly exceeding heaviest attendance out of season. Also remember that traffic patterns described are based on the norm, and that a specific day, according to the law of averages, will probably but not necessarily approximate the norm.

—— *When to Go to Walt Disney World* ——

Selecting the Time of Year for Your Visit

Walt Disney World is busiest of all Christmas Day through New Year's Day. Thanksgiving weekend, the week of Washington's Birthday, spring break for colleges, and the two weeks around Easter are also extremely busy. To give you some idea of what busy means at Walt Disney World, up to 92,000 people have toured the Magic Kingdom alone on a single day! While this level of attendance is far from typical, the possibility of its occurrence should forewarn all but the ignorant and the foolish from challenging this mega-attraction at its busiest periods.

The least busy time of all is from after the Thanksgiving weekend until the week before Christmas. The next slowest times are September through the weekend preceding Thanksgiving, January 4th through the first half of February, and the week following Easter through early June. At the risk of being blasphemous, our research team was so impressed with the relative ease of touring in the fall and other "off" periods that we would rather take our children out of school for a week than do battle with the summer crowds.

Selecting the Day of the Week for Your Visit

A typical vacation scenario is for a family to arrive in the Orlando area on Sunday, visit the Magic Kingdom and EPCOT Center on Monday and Tuesday, visit Disney-MGM Studios on Wednesday, and go to Typhoon Lagoon or a non-Disney area attraction on Thursday. Friday is often reserved for heading home or to another Florida destination.

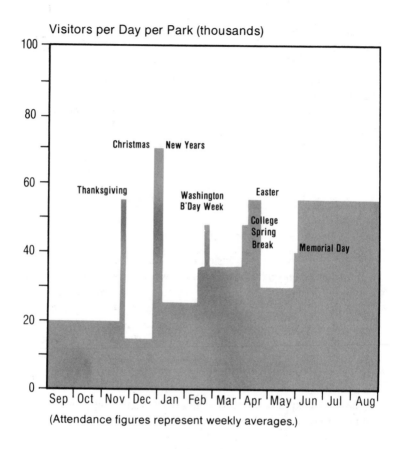

Visitors per Day per Park (thousands)

Thanksgiving
Christmas
New Years
Washington B'Day Week
Easter
College Spring Break
Memorial Day

(Attendance figures represent weekly averages.)

Given this often-repeated pattern, we recommend the following:

		Best Days to Go		Worst Days to Go
Magic Kingdom & EPCOT Center	1	Friday	1	Monday
	2	Sunday	2	Tuesday
	3	Saturday (summer)	3	Wednesday
	4	Thursday		
Disney-MGM Studios	1	Sunday	1	Wednesday
	2	Friday	2	Tuesday
	3	Saturday (summer)	3	Thursday
	4	Monday		

	Best Days to Go		Worst Days to Go	
Typhoon Lagoon	1	Sunday	1	Thursday
	2	Friday	2	Wednesday
	3	Monday	3	Saturday
	4	Tuesday		

—— Operating Hours ——

It cannot be said that the Disney folks are not flexible when it comes to hours of operation for the parks. They run a dozen or more different operating schedules during the year, making it advisable to call (407) 824-4321 for the **exact** hours of operation the day before you arrive.

—— Official Opening Time vs. Real Opening Time ——

The hours of operation that the Disney folks will give you when you call are "official hours." In actuality the park will open earlier. If the official hours of operation are 9 A.M.–9 P.M., for example, the Main Street section of the Magic Kingdom will open at 8 or 8:30 A.M. and the remainder of the park will open at 8:30 or 9 A.M. Many visitors, relying upon the accuracy of the information disseminated by the Disney Guest Relations service, arrive at the stated opening time to find the park fairly thronged with people.

The Disney folks publish their hours of operation well in advance, but allow themselves the flexibility to react to gate conditions on a day-by-day basis. Based on a survey of local hotel reservations, Disney traffic controllers estimate how many visitors to expect on a given day. To avoid bottlenecks at the parking facilities or theme park ticket lines, the theme parks are frequently opened early, absorbing the crowds as they arrive.

We recommend arriving an hour before the official opening time at EPCOT Center, the Disney-MGM Studios, or the Magic Kingdom regardless of the time of year of your visit. If you happen to go on a major holiday, arrive an hour and twenty minutes in advance of the official opening time.

As concerns closing time, the Disney people usually close all rides and attractions at approximately the official stated closing time. Main Street in the Magic Kingdom remains open a half hour to an hour after the rest of the park has closed, as does the World Showcase section of EPCOT Center and Hollywood Boulevard at Disney-MGM Studios.

—— *Packed Park Compensation Plan* ——

The thought of teeming, jostling throngs jockeying for position in endless lines under the baking Fourth of July sun is enough to wilt the will and ears of the most ardent Mouseketeer. Why would anyone go to Walt Disney World during a major holiday period? Indeed, if you have never been to Walt Disney World, and you thought you would just drop in for a few rides and a little look-see on such a day, you might be better off shooting yourself in the foot. The Disney folks, however, being Disney folks, feel kind of bad about those long, long lines and the basically impossible touring conditions on packed days and compensate their patrons with a no-less-than-incredible array of first-rate live entertainment and happenings.

Throughout the day the party goes on with shows, parades, concerts, and pageantry. In the evening, particularly, there is so much going on that you have to make some tough choices. There are concerts, parades, light shows, laser shows, fireworks, and dance occurring almost continually in all parks. No question about it, you can go to Walt Disney World on the Fourth of July (or on any other extended hours, crowded day), never get on a ride, and still get your money's worth five times over. Admittedly, it's not the ideal situation for a first-timer who really wants to see the theme parks, but for anyone else it's one heck of a good party.

If you decide to go on one of the parks' "big" days, we suggest that you arrive an hour and twenty minutes before the stated opening time. Use the Walt Disney World One-Day Touring Plan of your choice until about I P.M. and then take the Monorail to the Walt Disney World resort hotels for lunch and relaxation. Local Floridians visiting Walt Disney World on holidays often chip in and rent a room for the group (make reservations well in advance) in one of the Walt Disney World hotels, thus affording a place to meet, relax, have a drink, or change clothes prior to swimming. A comparable arrangement can be made at other nearby hotels as long as they furnish a shuttle service to and from the parks. After an early dinner, return to the park of your choice for the evening's festivities, which get cranked up about 8 P.M.

A Word About Lodging

While this guide is not about lodging, we have found lodging to be a primary concern of those visiting Walt Disney World. In general, and with one or two exceptions, rooms in hotels served by monorail are the most expensive, while rooms at other Walt Disney World hotel properties run slightly less. Least expensive are motels located outside of Walt Disney World.

In addition to proximity and a certain number of guest privileges, there is special magic and peace of mind associated with staying inside Walt Disney World. "I feel more a part of everything and less like a visitor," is the way one guest described it.

There is no real hardship, however, to staying outside Walt Disney World and driving (or taking the often available hotel shuttle) to the theme parks for your visit. Meals can be had less expensively, too, and there is this indirect benefit: rooming outside "The World" puts you in a more receptive mood towards other Orlando area attractions and eating establishments. Universal Studios Florida, the Kennedy Space Center, Sea World, and Cypress Gardens, among others, are well worth your attention.

Prices for accommodations are subject to change, but our research team lodged in an excellent (though not plush) motel surrounded by beautiful orange groves for one quarter of the cost of staying in Walt Disney World. Our commuting time was 17 minutes one way to the Magic Kingdom or EPCOT Center parking lots.

—— *Staying in the World** ——

The specific privileges and amenities of staying in a Walt Disney World lodging property (listed below) are these:

1. Vastly decreased commuting time made possible by easy access to the Walt Disney World bus, boat, and monorail transportation sys-

* Prices quoted are summer rates, double occupancy, and are subject to change.

tem. This is especially advantageous if you stay in one of the hotels connected by the monorail or by the lake/canal system (boat service). If you stay at the Caribbean Beach Resort Hotel, the Walt Disney World Village, or the Village Hotel Plaza, the most efficient way to get around is to drive your own car.

2. Preferential treatment in making advance reservations to the *Hoop Dee Doo Revue* and other Walt Disney World dinner shows.

3. The privilege of making lunch and dinner reservations over the phone, one to three days in advance, at EPCOT Center, Disney-MGM Studios, and Magic Kingdom full-service restaurants.

4. Various kinds of preferential treatment at the theme parks. Sometimes Walt Disney World lodging guests are allowed into one or another theme park ahead of other guests, and sometimes they are given special admission discounts. These benefits and extras are subject to change without notice and are generally put in effect for a limited time and for a specific purpose, such as promoting a new Walt Disney World theme park or attraction.

5. A number of alternatives for baby-sitting, childcare, and special children's programs. Each of the resort hotels connected by the monorail offers "clubs," or themed childcare centers where potty-trained children, 3 to 12 years, can be left while the adults go out. Also available are the "Fairy Godmother" and Kindercare in-room baby-sitting service.

6. Only Walt Disney World resort guests may leave pets overnight in the kennels.

Expensive, but most convenient, are the hotels situated around the Seven Seas Lagoon or Bay Lake and connected to the Magic Kingdom and EPCOT Center by monorail. These include the giant A-frame Contemporary Resort Hotel, the Polynesian Village Resort, and the new Grand Floridian Beach Resort, modeled after the fabled Florida beach resorts of the nineteenth century. Accommodations in any of these hotels make touring Walt Disney World easier and more relaxing. Commuting to and from the theme parks via monorail is quick and simple, allowing a visitor to return at leisure to his hotel for a nap or a dip. Additionally, the Seven Seas Lagoon and Bay Lake offer a variety of boating, swimming, and other water sports.

Contemporary Resort Hotel

1,050 rooms	lakefront	monorail service	$180–410 per night

Polynesian Village Resort
    863 rooms   lakefront   monorail service $190–245 per night
Grand Floridian Beach Resort
    900 rooms   lakefront   monorail service $215–235 per night

The best lodging deal in Walt Disney World for the economy conscious is the Caribbean Beach Resort. Situated on a 42-acre lake not far from EPCOT Center, the resort offers nightly rates of $74–$99. While it is not serviced by monorail, getting around Walt Disney World is easy via private car or Disney-provided shuttle buses. On the negative side, there are not enough restaurants at the Caribbean Beach Resort. Guests must endure long waits for food or drive to a restaurant elsewhere in or out of the World.

Caribbean Beach Resort
    2,112 rooms   lakefront   shuttle bus service $74–99 per night

Disney Inn (formerly the Golf Resort Hotel) which, in addition to being near the theme parks, offers 72 holes of golf. Walt Disney World transportation is by private car and shuttle bus.

Disney Inn
    288 rooms   golf course   shuttle bus service $175–185 per night

The Walt Disney World Swan Resort, Dolphin Hotel, and Conference Center is the largest convention/resort complex in the southeastern U.S. Built on the shore of a 50-acre lagoon, the complex is connected by canal to the Disney-MGM Studios, and by tram and walkway to EPCOT Center, as well as by bus and highway to other areas of Walt Disney World.

Swan Resort
    760 rooms   lakefront   boat/bus service $210–425 per night
Dolphin Hotel
    1,510 rooms   lakefront   boat/bus service $179–475 per night

Disney's Yacht Club Resort and Disney's Beach Club Resort are located between the Dolphin Hotel and EPCOT Center across a lake from Disney's Boardwalk. EPCOT Center is within walking distance and the Disney-MGM Studios can be reached by boat. Other Walt Disney World destinations are serviced by bus.

Disney's Yacht Club and Beach Club Resorts

1,214 rooms	lakefront	boat/bus service	$175–260 per night

Disney's Port Orleans is a "moderately priced" resort in the style of the Caribbean Beach Resort and is serviced by bus.

Disney's Port Orleans

1,008 rooms	lakefront	bus service	$85–130 per night

Fort Wilderness Campground is a spacious resort campground for both tent and RV camping. Fully equipped, air-conditioned trailers are also available for rent. Aside from economy accommodations, features of Fort Wilderness Campground include full RV hookups, evening entertainment, a group camping area, horseback riding, bike trails, jogging trails, swimming, and a petting farm. River Country is situated near Fort Wilderness Campground. Access to the Magic Kingdom and Discovery Island is via boat from the Fort Wilderness landing on Bay Lake, or to any destination in Walt Disney World via private car or shuttle bus.

Fort Wilderness Campground

827 campsites	boat/bus service	$34–46 per night
363 trailers (sleeps 4–6)	boat/bus service	$165 per night

The Walt Disney World Village is about six minutes from EPCOT Center by car and close to I-4. A huge entertainment/dining/lodging/shopping complex, Walt Disney World Village offers a variety of lodging. The villas in Walt Disney World Village Resort are the only hotel accommodations in Walt Disney World proper which offer kitchen facilities. A not inexpensive grocery is conveniently located in the shopping complex.

Fairway Villas	64 units	bus service	$280–305 per night
Treehouse Villas	60 units	bus service	$270–295 per night
Vacation Villas	119 units	bus service	$200–275 per night
Club Lake Villas	324 units	bus service	$150–175 per night

Village Hotel Plaza. In addition to the Village Resort, seven hotels offering a total of 3,605 rooms are situated in the Village Hotel Plaza. Although commodious, some rooms are more expensive than the Seven Seas Lagoon or Bay Lake hotels; we found few bargains in the Walt Disney World Hotel Plaza, and less of that special excitement you feel when you stay inside "The World." While technically part of Walt Disney World, the feel is different here, like visiting a colony instead of the mother country.

The Hilton	814 rooms	bus service	$135–190 per night
Howard Johnson's Resort Hotel	383 rooms	bus service	$85–145 per night
Hotel Royal Plaza	396 rooms	bus service	$108–150 per night
Guest Quarters Resort	229 rooms	bus service	$115–220 per night
Travelodge Hotel	325 rooms	bus service	$75–110 per night
Grosvenor Resort	614 rooms	bus service	$80–105 per night
Buena Vista Palace	844 rooms	bus service	$125–229 per night

—— *Lodging Outside of Walt Disney World* ——

Lodging costs outside Walt Disney World vary incredibly. If you shop around you can find a nice clean motel with a pool within twenty minutes of Walt Disney World for as low as $25 per night. There are five primary "out-of-the-World" areas to consider:

1. *International Drive area.* This area, about fifteen minutes east of Walt Disney World, parallels I-4 and offers a wide selection of both hotels and restaurants. Accommodations here range from $35–160 per night. Traffic here, however, is very congested.

2. *US 192.* This is the highway to Kissimmee, southeast of Walt Disney World. There are many small, privately owned motels in this area offering good lodging value. Certain motels on US 192 are as close to the Magic Kingdom as the more expensive hotels in the Walt Disney World Village Hotel Plaza. Rooms along US 192 range from $25–140 per night.

3. *US 441, the Orange Blossom Trail.* Especially in the area where US 441 intersects Sand Lake Road, there are nice hotels and restaurants. This is an area where many enjoy staying because of the good local and chain restaurants. Driving time to Walt Disney World is about 15 minutes. Rates go from $30–90 per night.

4. *The I-4 corridor northeast of Walt Disney World.* There are a number of hotels situated on the north side of I-4 between Walt Disney World and Orlando which are convenient and reasonably priced ($40–110 per night).

5. *Downtown Orlando.* While requiring a half-hour commute to Walt Disney World, downtown Orlando offers some good lodging values. Since it markets its rooms more to business travelers than to tourists, you can often get a special deal at a very plush hotel on weekends.

There has been a tremendous amount of new lodging development in and around Walt Disney World. As more and more new rooms become available, the market will become much more competitive, and many of the hotels will have to offer discounted rates to keep their rooms filled. One way to discover these bargains is to check out the brochure racks at the Florida stateline welcome centers and at the service plazas on Florida's Turnpike.

Lodging Discounts in the Walt Disney World Area

A company called EIG (Exit Information Guide) publishes a book of discount coupons for bargain rates at hotels throughout the state of Florida. These books are available free of charge in many restaurants and motels along the main interstate highways leading to the Sunshine State. Since most folks make reservations prior to leaving home, picking up the coupon book en route does not help much. For two dollars ($5 Canadian), however, EIG will mail you a copy before you make your reservations. Write to:

Exit Information Guide
3014 N.E. 21st Way
Gainesville, FL 32609
(904) 371-3948

—— How to Evaluate a Travel Package ——

Dozens of Walt Disney World package vacations are offered to the public each year. Some are created by the Walt Disney Travel Company, others by Certified Vacations in conjunction with Delta Airlines, some by Premier Cruise Lines, and some by independent travel agents and wholesalers. Almost all Walt Disney World packages include lodging at Walt Disney World and a 4-Day All Three Parks Passport. All Certified packages include air transportation on Delta Airlines. Premier Cruise packages mix a three- or four-day cruise with three or four days at Walt Disney World.

Packages should be a win/win proposition for both the buyer and the seller. The buyer only has to make one phone call and deal with a single salesperson to set up the whole vacation: transportation, rental car, admissions, lodging, meals, and even golf and tennis. The seller, likewise, only has to deal with the buyer one time, eliminating the need for separate sales, confirmations, and billing. In addition to streamlining selling, processing, and administration, some packagers also buy air fares in bulk on contract like a broker playing the commodities market. Buying a large number of air fares in advance allows the packager to buy them at a significant savings from posted fares. The same practice is applied also to hotel rooms. Because selling vacation packages is an efficient way of doing business, and because the packager can often buy individual package components (air fare, lodging, etc.) in bulk at discount, savings in operating expenses realized by the seller are sometimes passed on to the buyer so that, in addition to convenience, the package is also an exceptional value. In any event, that is the way it is supposed to work.

All too often, in practice, the seller realizes all of the economies and passes nothing in the way of savings on to the buyer. In some instances, packages are loaded additionally with extras which cost the packager next to nothing, but which run the retail price of the package sky-high. As you might expect, the savings to be passed along to customers are still somewhere in Fantasyland.

When considering a package, choose one that includes features you are sure to use. Whether you use all the features or not, you will most certainly pay for them. Second, if cost is of greater concern than convenience, make a few phone calls and see what the package would cost if you booked its individual components (air fare, rental car, lodging, etc.) on your own. If the package price is less than the a la carte cost, the package is a good deal. If the costs are about the same, the package is probably worth it for the convenience.

An Example   A popular package offered by the Walt Disney Travel Company is the World Adventure Vacation package, which includes:

1. Five nights' accommodation at the Contemporary Resort, the Polynesian Village Resort, Disney Inn, or Disney's Fort Wilderness Campground trailers. A 10% resort tax is included.
2. Six days' use of the Walt Disney World transportation system.
3. Six days' admission to the Magic Kingdom, EPCOT Center, Disney-MGM Studios, and Pleasure Island.

4. Six days' unlimited use of Walt Disney World recreational activities and facilities, including Typhoon Lagoon, River Country, and Discovery Island.
5. Breakfast, lunch, and dinner each day at a wide variety of Walt Disney World restaurants, gratuities included.
6. $5 in Disney Dollars per person.
7. Gratuities for baggage handling and valet parking (twice per party).
8. Steve Birnbaum's *Official Guide to Walt Disney World* (one per party).

This package is interesting because it is one of Walt Disney World's most popular packages and is loaded with benefits and amenities. It is also interesting because you can come out a winner or a loser depending on how you use it. With the package you have a choice of hotels and rooms. If you took the least expensive room at the Contemporary Resort Hotel (wing, parking lot view), the package cost $1,100 per adult, two to a room, in July of 1990 when we did our analysis.

Although the package is set up for six whole days and five nights, most guests either will be traveling on one of those six days or alternatively will have to book an extra night or two at the Contemporary to avoid traveling during their package days.

The six days' use of the transportation system is no big deal. Anyone who parks their car at a Walt Disney World parking lot can ride around all day on the buses, boats, and monorails.

The package provides six days' admission to the Magic Kingdom, EPCOT Center, Disney-MGM Studios, and Pleasure Island, but most guests will not want to go to the theme parks every single day. In the first place it does not take six days to see everything in the major theme parks, and secondly, spending all or part of each day in the parks prevents you from using other package options.

If, instead of getting the package, you buy a four- or five-day pass at the ticket window any unused days are good forever. With the six days' admission on the package, however, it's use 'em or lose 'em. By contrast, if you buy the 5-Day PLUS Super Pass available at the ticket windows, you get five days unlimited use of the three big parks plus unlimited use of Pleasure Island, Typhoon Lagoon, River Country, and Discovery Island. You also have the advantage of redeeming in subsequent visits any unused days on your pass.

The package provides six days' unlimited use of Walt Disney World recreational activities and facilities. This is a big deal if you want to golf, play tennis, boat, fish, and horseback ride. If you golf all morning, for instance, and visit the theme parks in the late afternoon and evening, you will come close to being a winner since you will be using most of the benefits in the package. If you are vacationing at Walt Disney World primarily to enjoy the theme parks, and do not intend to golf, horseback ride, etc., you will be spending extra money on the package for amenities and activities you will not be using. Either way you cannot be in two places at once, and as you are probably beginning to realize, the package is set up in a way that makes it almost impossible not to waste many of its benefits.

If you are a big eater, the inclusion of breakfast, lunch, and dinner each day is a major plus. Not only are these meals included, but you can eat as much as you want, appetizers, desserts, the works. Even tips are included (but not alcoholic beverages). You must eat in a full-service restaurant (no fast-food counter service or room service), but other than these limitations you have your choice. You can even select dinner shows like the *Hoop Dee Doo Revue* (providing space is available) or Disney character breakfasts as part of your meal package. Snacks, room service, counter meals at the parks, and alcoholic beverages are not included.

As far as the rest is concerned, Disney Dollars are just like regular dollars except that they can only be spent at Walt Disney World. Gratuities covered only extend to arrival and departure. If you have a car and use valet parking during your stay the tip is up to you. The *Official Guide to Walt Disney World* by Steve Birnbaum is available at bookstores if you want to buy it exclusive of the package.

In the final analysis, the World Adventure Vacation package is best suited to vacationers who have lots of energy and big appetites, and who like to play golf, tennis, and go boating. It's for vacationers who plan to be on the go from dawn until midnight and visit the theme parks every day.

If you leave out the golf, tennis, boating, and other recreational extras provided by the package (or pay for them a la carte with what you save on the cost of a six-day park admission), here is how the package compares to going it on your own:

Option A: World Adventure Vacation package price for two at Contemporary Resort Hotel (wing room with a parking lot view). $1,100 per person × 2 $2,200

Option B: Creating Your Own Vacation with the Same
Basic Features as the Package

Contemporary Resort Hotel (same room as in package) for five days with 10% resort tax	990
Two 5-Day PLUS Super Passes with sales tax (unlimited admission to Magic Kingdom, EPCOT Center, Disney-MGM Studios, Pleasure Island, Typhoon Lagoon, Discovery Island, and River Country)	286
$47 per person per day meal allowance ($8 for breakfast, $13 for lunch, $20 for dinner, tips included) for two people	564
$5 in Disney Dollars for two people	10
Arrival & departure gratuities	14
Birnbaum's *Official Guide to Walt Disney World*	9
Total for two people	$1,873

Another Example   The simpler the package, the easier to evaluate.
Most of the Certified/Delta packages only involve air fare, lodging, a
4-Day All Three Parks Passport, and a rental car. The cost of a Certified package including round-trip coach air fare from Philadelphia, a
Buick Skylark rental car, a 4-Day All Three Parks Passport, and four
nights lodging in the Contemporary Resort Hotel (wing room with a
parking lot view) was $869 per person or $1,738 per couple in July
of 1990. By making a few phone calls, we determined that you could
book the following components at the prices listed:

Same room at Contemporary Resort Hotel for four nights, including tax	$792
4-Day All Three Parks Passports for two, including sales tax ($110 each)	220
Buick rental car, five days unlimited mileage	125
Total before air fare	$1,137

If you substract the a la carte cost of all components from the total
package price ($1,738 minus $1,137), the remainder amounts to what
you are being charged for your air fare, in this case about $300 per
person ($601 divided by two persons). If you can fly round-trip to

Orlando from Philly for less than $300 a person, the package is not such a great deal. If fares from Philadelphia equal or exceed $300 per person, then the package makes sense.

Disney Reservationists   If you buy a package from Disney, do not expect Disney reservationists to offer suggestions or help you sort out your options. As a rule they will not volunteer information, but will only respond to specific questions you pose, adroitly ducking any query that calls for an opinion. A reader from North Riverside, Illinois, wrote, complaining:

> I have received various pieces of literature from WDW and it is very confusing to try and figure everything out. My wife made two telephone calls and the representatives from WDW were very courteous. However, they only answered the questions posed and were not very eager to give advice on what might be most cost effective. [The] WDW reps would not say if we would be better off doing one thing over the other. I feel a person could spend eight hours on the telephone with WDW reps and not have any more input than you get from reading the literature.

Information Needed for Evaluation   For quick reference and to save phone expense (Walt Disney World does not have an 800 number), write or call Walt Disney World accommodations reservations (see page 23) and ask that you be mailed a Walt Disney World Resort Vacation Guide and a rate sheet for the Walt Disney World lodging properties that shows the various rooms available at each property with their respective rates. The rate sheet also contains a price list for all Walt Disney World theme park admission options, including Pleasure Island, Typhoon Lagoon, Disney's Boardwalk, Discovery Island, and River Country. This in hand, you are ready to evaluate any package that appeals to you. Remember that all packages are quoted per person, double occupancy (two to a room), and that Florida has a 10% room tax and a 6% sales tax (applies to park admissions but not to lodging). Good luck.

Getting There

Directions

If you arrive by automobile you can reach any Walt Disney World attraction or destination via World Drive, off US 192, or via EPCOT Center Drive, off I-4 (see map, page 45).

If you are traveling *south* on the Florida Turnpike: Exit at Clermont, take US 27 south, turn left onto US 192, and then follow the signs to Walt Disney World.

If you are traveling *north* on the Florida Turnpike: Exit westbound onto I-4 and exit I-4 at EPCOT Center Drive.

If you are traveling *west* on I-4: Exit at EPCOT Center Drive and follow the signs.

If you are traveling *east* on I-4: Exit to US 192 northbound and then follow the signs.

Walt Disney World Village has its own entrance separate and distinct from entrances to the theme parks. To reach Walt Disney World Village take FL 535 exit off of I-4 and proceed north, following the signs.

Magic Kingdom and EPCOT Center Parking

The Magic Kingdom and EPCOT Center have their own pay parking lots (each one the size of Vermont), including close-in parking for the handicapped. In the case of the Magic Kingdom, a tram meets you at a loading station near where you parked and transports you to the Transportation and Ticket Center. Here you can buy passes to both the Magic Kingdom and EPCOT Center. If you wish to proceed to the Magic Kingdom you can either ride the ferryboat across Seven Seas Lagoon or catch the monorail. If you wish to go to EPCOT Center, you can board a separate monorail that connects EPCOT Center to the Transportation and Ticket Center. The various sections of the Magic

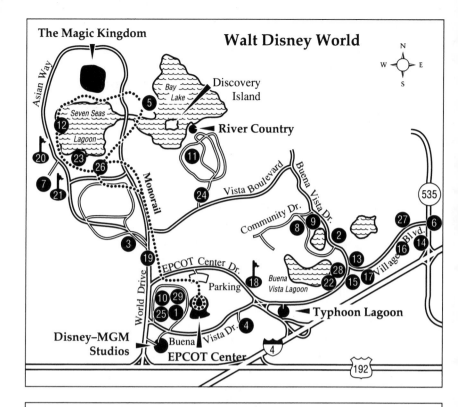

Walt Disney World

The Magic Kingdom

Asian Way

Seven Seas Lagoon

Bay Lake

Discovery Island

River Country

Monorail

Vista Boulevard

Buena Vista Dr.

Community Dr.

535

Village Blvd.

EPCOT Center Dr.

Parking

Buena Vista Lagoon

Typhoon Lagoon

World Drive

Disney–MGM Studios

Buena Vista Dr.

EPCOT Center

4

192

N
W   E
S

Legend

1. Beach Club Resort
2. Buena Vista Palace
3. Car Care Center
4. Caribbean Beach Resort
5. Contemporary Resort Hotel
6. The Crossroads at Lake Buena Vista
7. Disney Inn
8. Disney Village
9. Disney Village Conference Center
10. Dolphin Hotel
11. Fort Wilderness Campground
12. Grand Floridian Beach Resort
13. Grosvenor Resort
14. Guest Quarters Resort
15. The Hilton
16. Hotel Royal Plaza
17. Howard Johnson's Resort Hotel
18. Lake Buena Vista Golf Course
19. Magic Kingdom Toll Plaza
20. Magnolia Golf Course
21. Palm Golf Course
22. Pleasure Island
23. Polynesian Village Resort
24. Reception Outpost
25. Swan Resort
26. Transportation & Ticket Center
27. Travelodge Hotel
28. Village Marketplace
29. Yacht Club Resort

Kingdom (Transportation and Ticket Center) parking lot are named for Disney characters. Guests are given a receipt with the aisle numbers and names of the parking sections listed on the reverse side. Mark where you have parked and jot down the aisle number in the space provided. Put the receipt in your billfold or some other safe place for referral when you return to your car. Failure to take these precautions will often result in a lengthy search for your car at a time when you will be pretty tuckered out.

If you wish to visit EPCOT Center you can park at the Magic Kingdom (Transportation and Ticket Center) parking lot and commute via monorail, or park directly in the EPCOT Center parking lot. Arrangements in the EPCOT Center lot are essentially the same as described above; a tram will shuttle you from where you park to the EPCOT Center entrance, and you will be given a receipt where you can mark your parking place for later reference. At EPCOT Center the sections of the parking lot are named for pavilions in the Future World area of the park. The big difference between parking for the Magic Kingdom and parking for EPCOT Center is that access to the park is direct from the tram at EPCOT Center whereas to reach the Magic Kingdom you must transfer from the tram to the ferryboat or the monorail at the Transportation and Ticket Center. If you park at EPCOT Center and wish to go to the Magic Kingdom you may do so by taking the monorail from EPCOT Center to the Transportation and Ticket Center and then transferring to a Magic Kingdom monorail.

Disney-MGM Studios Parking

The Disney planners seriously underestimated the number of cars the Disney-MGM parking lot would have to accommodate. During the summer of 1990 it was almost routine for the lot to fill by 10:30 or 11 A.M. Monday through Thursday, with thousands of late arriving guests being turned away. If you plan to visit the Studios on a busy day, go early. If you cannot arrive early, are turned away, and are dead set on touring Disney-MGM, park in the EPCOT Center lot and take a Disney bus to the Studios.

Taking a Tram or Shuttle Bus from Your Hotel

Trams and shuttle buses are provided by many hotels and motels in the vicinity of Walt Disney World. They represent a fairly carefree alternative for getting to and from the theme parks, letting you off right at the entrance and saving you the cost of parking. The rub is that they might not get you there as early as you desire (a critical point if you take our touring advice) or be available at the time you wish to return to your lodging. Also, some shuttles go directly to Walt Disney World while others make stops at other motels and hotels in the vicinity. Each shuttle service is a little bit different so check out the particulars when you arrive at your hotel.

Making the Most of
Your Time and Money

Allocating Time

During Walt Disney World's first decade, a family with a week's vacation could enjoy the Magic Kingdom and River Country and still have several days for the beach or other area attractions. Since the opening of EPCOT Center in 1982, however, Walt Disney World has steadily been enlarging to monopolize the same family's entire week. Today, with the additions of Typhoon Lagoon, the Disney-MGM Studios, and Pleasure Island, you had best allocate five days for a whirlwind tour (or seven days if you're old-fashioned and insist on a little relaxation during your vacation). If you do not have five or seven days, or think you might want to venture beyond the edge of "The World," be prepared to make some hard choices.

The theme parks, studios, and swimming attractions are **huge,** require a lot of walking, and sometimes a lot of waiting in lines. Moving in and among typically large crowds all day is exhausting. Oftentimes, the unrelenting central Florida sun zaps the most hearty traveler, making tempers short. In our many visits to Walt Disney World we observed, particularly on hot summer days, a dramatic transition from happy enthusiastic tourists upon arrival to zombies plodding along later in the day. Visitors who began their day enjoying the wonders of Disney imagination lapsed into an exhausted, production-line mentality ("We've got two more rides in Fantasyland, then we can go back to the hotel").

We recommend that you approach Walt Disney World the same way you would approach an eight-course Italian dinner: with plenty of time between courses. The best way not to have fun is to attempt to cram too much into too little time.

Prices Subject to Change Without Notice

Book reviewers who complain that prices quoted in guidebooks are out of date should note that Walt Disney World ticket prices seem to change about as often as the prime rate. If we were publishing a daily newspaper, maybe we could keep up. But since we are covering Walt Disney World in a book, we've decided to throw in the towel; no more listing admission prices. We will tell you this much, however; expect to pay about $33 for an adult 1-Day Ticket, about $111 for a 4-Day All Three Parks Passport, and about $144 for a 5-Day PLUS Super Pass. There are no two- or three-day admission options.

Walt Disney World Admission Options

There are basically four Walt Disney World admission options:

1. One-Park/One-Day Ticket (1-Day Ticket)
2. 4-Day All Three Parks Passport
3. 5-Day PLUS Super Pass
4. Annual Passport

The 1-Day Ticket is good for admission and unlimited use of "attractions and experiences" at the Magic Kingdom *or* EPCOT Center *or* the Disney-MGM Studios, but does *not* provide same day admission to more than one of the three.

The 4-Day All Three Parks Passport "allows you to come and go as you please at the Magic Kingdom, EPCOT Center, and the Disney-MGM Studios, and includes unlimited use of the transportation systems linking the parks."

The 5-Day PLUS Super Pass provides same day admission to all three parks, unlimited use of the transportation systems, plus admission to Pleasure Island, Typhoon Lagoon, River Country, and Discovery Island. Admission to these last is unlimited for a seven-day period beginning the day the pass is first used at one of the three major parks.

With a four- or five-day pass you can tour the Disney-MGM Studios in the morning, stop by the Magic Kingdom for an afternoon parade, and eat dinner at one of EPCOT Center's ethnic restaurants that evening. The four- and five-day passes do not have to be used on consecutive days and are, in fact, good forever. Four-day passes can be upgraded to five-day passes as long as they have at least one day's admission remaining by paying the difference between the four-day and five-day pass price.

Many readers write asking if they can use remaining admissions on partially redeemed four- and five-day passes brought home by relatives. The facts are as follows:

1. The pass is sold to the purchaser on a non-transferable basis. The pass states on the back, "To be valid this Pass must be used by the same person for all days."

2. There is nothing on the pass that in any way identifies the purchaser.

3. Disney admission attendants do not request to see a receipt or any other proof-of-purchase documentation for admission passes.

If you only have one day to spend, select the park that most interests you and buy the 1-Day Ticket. If you have two days and do not plan on returning to Florida for a couple of years, buy two 1-Day Tickets. If you think you might be passing through the area again in the next year or two, go ahead and spring for a four- or five-day pass. Use two days of admission to see as much of all three parks as you can, and save the remaining days for another trip. Remember that with the 5-Day PLUS Super Pass admission to Pleasure Island, Typhoon Lagoon, River Country, and Discovery Island expires within seven days of the first time you use your pass at the Magic Kingdom, EPCOT Center or the Disney-MGM Studios. If you plan to spend three or more days at Walt Disney World, buy the four- or five-day pass. If you live in Florida or plan to spend seven or more days in the major theme parks, the Annual Passport at about $190 is a good buy.

How Much Does It Cost to Go to Walt Disney World for a Day?

Let's say we have a family of four, Mom and Dad, Tim (age 12), and Sandy (age 8), driving their own car and staying outside of Walt Disney World. Since they plan to be in the area for a week they intend to buy 4-Day All Three Parks Passports. Here is how much a typical day would cost, excluding souvenirs, lodging, and transportation:

Breakfast for four at Denny's with tax & tip		$14.25
EPCOT Center parking fee		3.00
One day's admission on a 4-Day All Three Parks Passport		
Dad:	Adult 4-Day with tax = $111 divided by four (days)	27.75
Mom:	Adult 4-Day with tax = $111 divided by four (days)	27.75
Tim:	Adult 4-Day with tax = $111 divided by four (days)	27.75
Sandy:	Child 4-Day with tax = $88 divided by four (days)	22.00

Fast-food lunch (burger, fries, coke), no tip	23.00
Afternoon break (coke and popcorn)	10.50
Dinner at Mexico, with tax & tip	66.95
Souvenirs & extras	?
Total (not including lodging and transportation)	$222.95

Which Park to See First?

This question is less academic than it appears at first glance, especially if there are children or teenagers in your party. Children who see the Magic Kingdom first expect more of the same type of entertainment at EPCOT Center and the Disney-MGM Studios. At EPCOT Center they are often disappointed by the educational orientation and more serious tone (many adults react the same way). Disney-MGM offers some pretty wild action, but here too the general presentation is educational and more adult.

For first-time visitors especially, see EPCOT Center first; you will be able to enjoy it fully without having been preconditioned to think of Disney entertainment as solely in the fantasy/adventure genre. Parties which include children should definitely see EPCOT Center first. Children will be more likely to judge and enjoy EPCOT Center according to its own merits if they see it first, as well as being more relaxed and patient in their touring.

Next, see the Disney-MGM Studios. The Studios help both young and old make a fluid transition from the imposing EPCOT Center to the fanciful Magic Kingdom. Also, because the Studios are smaller, you will not have to walk as much or stay as long. Save the Magic Kingdom for last.

—— *Optimum Touring Situation* ——

An optimum touring situation at Walt Disney World requires a good itinerary, a minimum of five days on site (i.e., not including travel time), and a fair amount of money. It also requires a fairly prodigious appetite for Disney-type entertainment. We will provide the itinerary; the rest is up to you.

The essence of an Optimum Touring Situation is to see the various attractions of Walt Disney World in a series of shorter, less exhausting visits during the cooler, less crowded parts of the day, with plenty of rest and relaxation between visits.

Since an Optimum Touring Situation calls for leaving and returning to the theme parks on most days, it obviously makes for easier logistics if you are staying in one of the Walt Disney World resort hotels connected by the monorail. Also, if you stay in Walt Disney World you are accorded the option of making advance reservations for the *Hoop Dee Doo Revue* and the various dinner shows performed nightly at the resort hotels. In-World guests also have freer use of the bus, boat, and monorail transportation system, and have more alternatives for baby-sitting and children's programs. Sound good? It is, but be prepared to pay.

If you do not plan to stay at a Walt Disney World property, you can still use the day-by-day plan listed below. The plan will not be as efficient owing to increased commuting time, but it will be a whole lot less expensive.

Buy a 5-Day PLUS Super Pass. This will allow you to come and go as you desire at all three theme parks, and it does not have to be used on consecutive days.

If you visit Walt Disney World during a busy period (see page 29), you need to get up early to beat the crowds. Short lines and stress-free touring are basically incompatible with sleeping in. If you want to sleep late *and* enjoy your touring experience, visit Walt Disney World during a time of year when attendance is lighter.

We do not believe that there is one ideal itinerary. Tastes, levels of energy, and basic perspectives on what constitutes entertainment and relaxation vary. This understood, what follows is our personal version of an optimum Walt Disney World vacation week. It is the itinerary we use when asked to host a tour or guide a dignitary.

Before You Go

1. Make reservations as far in advance as possible for the Grand Floridian Hotel. If you cannot afford the Grand Floridian, go for the Contemporary Resort Hotel, the Disney Polynesian Resort, or the Disney Inn in that order (if your party is all adult, make the Disney Inn your second choice). If you end up in the Disney Inn, you will have to drive about one-third of a mile round-trip each day to the Grand Floridian for monorail connections. The other three hotels are situated on the monorail.

2. When you book your accommodations, try to make reservations for the popular *Hoop Dee Doo Revue*, a delightful, rollicking

dinner show performed nightly in Pioneer Hall at the Fort Wilderness Campground. Try to obtain reservations for one of the days on which you do not visit EPCOT Center or the Magic Kingdom.

3. Reserve a rental car if you want to try local (off-World) restaurants or other attractions such as Universal Studios Florida, Sea World, or the Kennedy Space Center.

On Site

Day O—Travel Day

1. Arrive and get settled. Explore the features and amenities of your hotel.

2. If you get checked in by 3 P.M. or earlier, and the Magic Kingdom is open until 9 P.M. or later, go ahead and run the itinerary for Day 4. If you arrive later in the day and are looking for something to do, this would be a perfect night for the *Hoop Dee Doo Revue*.

3. Before 9 P.M. call 828-4000 and make next-day reservations for the EPCOT restaurants of your choice (Walt Disney World resort guests can make one- to three-day advance reservations for any Disney-MGM, EPCOT Center, or Magic Kingdom full-service restaurant). Try for a 1 P.M. lunch seating and a 7 or 8 P.M. dinner seating.

Day 1

1. Tour EPCOT Center using the Touring Plans provided in this guide. Break off the plan after lunch and return to the hotel for a nap and some beach time.

2. Return to EPCOT Center between 4 and 5 P.M., visiting any attractions in the Future World section of the park that you missed during the morning. Tour until dinner time.

3. After dinner, tour the World Showcase section of EPCOT Center until dark. Then find a good vantage point for watching IllumiNations, a fireworks, music, and laser spectacular performed nightly on the World Showcase Lagoon.

Day 2

1. Tour the Disney-MGM Studios according to the Touring Plans in this guide. You should be able to see everything by mid-afternoon.

2. Return to your hotel for rest and rejuvenation.

3. Try a quiet dinner in or out of Walt Disney World and then enjoy a performance of the Electrical Water Pageant at the waterfront of any of the lakeside resort hotels. This is another good night for the *Hoop Dee Doo Revue* or one of the other Walt Disney World or local dinner shows. Early to bed.

Day 3

1. Visit Typhoon Lagoon utilizing the Touring Plan provided in this guide.

2. Return to the hotel sometime after lunch for campers' quiet time.

3. Eat a relatively early dinner in or out of the World and then visit Pleasure Island for a night of Disney family-style nightclubbing. If you have children with you, there are several baby-sitting/children's program alternatives available to choose from (see page 66).

Day 4

1. Sleep late after your big night out. Eat lunch at the hotel and then take the monorail to the Magic Kingdom. If your party includes young children, use the Magic Kingdom Touring Plan for Parents with Small Children, starting at Step 14. If your group consists of adults and children over eight, use Day 2 of the Magic Kingdom Two-Day Touring Plan A.

2. Between 6 and 7 P.M., catch the monorail to one of the resort hotels for dinner. Before or after dinner, call 828-4000 and make next-day dinner reservations for the EPCOT Center restaurant of your choice. Go for a 7 or 8 P.M. seating.

3. Return to the Magic Kingdom after dinner. Continue touring according to the Touring Plan, taking breaks to watch the Main Street Electrical Parade and Fantasy in the Sky fireworks.

Day 5

1. Up early, return to the Magic Kingdom, arriving 45 minutes ahead of the official opening time. If your party includes young children, use the Magic Kingdom One-Day Touring Plan for Parents with Small Children starting with Step 1 and continue until you have seen everything. If your group is made up of adults and children over eight, use Day 1 of the Magic Kingdom Two-Day Touring Plan A.

2. Have a late lunch and get some rest at your hotel. In the late afternoon take the monorail to EPCOT Center. Visit any of the attractions you missed on Day 1 and have dinner.

—— *Seeing Walt Disney World on a Tight Schedule* ——

Many visitors do not have five days to devote to Disney attractions. Some are en route to other destinations or may wish to spend time sampling the attractions of Orlando and central Florida. For these visitors, efficient, time-effective touring is a must. They cannot afford long waits in line for rides, shows, or meals.

Even the most efficient touring plan will not allow the visitor to cover two or more of the major theme parks in one day, so plan on allocating at least an entire day to each park (an exception to this rule is when the theme parks close at different times, allowing the visitor to tour one park until closing time and then proceed to another park). If your schedule permits only one day of touring overall, we recommend concentrating your efforts on only one of the theme parks and saving the others for a subsequent visit.

One-Day Touring

A comprehensive tour of the Magic Kingdom, EPCOT Center, or the Disney-MGM Studios in one day is possible but requires a knowledge of the park, good planning, and no small reserve of energy and endurance. One-day touring does not leave much time for leisurely meals in sit-down restaurants, prolonged browsing in the many shops, or lengthy rest periods. Even so, one-day touring can be a fun, rewarding experience.

Successful one-day touring of either the Magic Kingdom or EPCOT Center, or of the Disney-MGM Studios, hinges on **three cardinal rules**:

1. *Determine in Advance What You Really Want to See*

What are the rides and attractions that appeal to you most? Which additional rides and attractions would you like to experience if you have any time left? What are you willing to forgo?

2. *Arrive Early! Arrive Early! Arrive Early!*

This is the single most important key to efficient touring and avoiding long lines. First thing in the morning there are no lines and relatively few people. The same four rides which you can experience in one hour in the early morning will take more than three hours to see after 11:30 A.M. Have breakfast before you arrive so you will not have to waste your prime touring time sitting in a restaurant.

Always call the park, (407) 824-4321, the day before you visit to inquire at what time the park will open and close.

For the Magic Kingdom: Arrive at the main parking lot an hour before the stated opening time of the park (the parking lot and Transportation and Ticket Center open two hours early), buy your admission pass and take the monorail to the Magic Kingdom. You will find that Main Street, U.S.A. opens a half hour to an hour before the stated opening time of the park. Tour Main Street and be ready to see the other theme areas when they open.

For EPCOT Center: Arrive at the main parking lot 45–50 minutes before the stated opening time. Buy your admission pass and line up at the turnstile to be admitted as soon as the park opens. EPCOT Center sometimes opens a half hour earlier than the stated opening time.

For Disney-MGM Studios: Arrive at the Studios parking lot 65 minutes before the stated opening time. Buy your admission and be ready to go.

Taking our advice about arriving early will work in your favor most of the time, particularly if you are vacationing at Disney World over any holiday period (including American Education Association or spring break), or during the summer. Because Disney opening procedures are flexible, however, you may occasionally suffer a few extra minutes of waiting to be admitted. Rest assured that this investment in time is more than worth it.

The Disney folks vary opening procedures according to the number of visitors they anticipate on a given day. Simply stated, they open up as early as required to avoid crowds overwhelming the parking facilities, ticket sellers, and transportation systems. On busier days this almost always translates into admitting visitors a half hour to an hour before the officially stated opening time.

3. *Avoid Bottlenecks*

Helping you avoid bottlenecks is what this guide is all about. Bottlenecks occur as a result of crowd concentrations and/or less than optimal crowd management. Concentrations of hungry people create bottlenecks at restaurants during the lunch and dinner hours; concentrations of people moving towards the exit near closing time create bottlenecks in the gift shops en route to the gate; concentrations of visitors at new and unusually popular rides create bottlenecks and long waiting lines; rides which are slow in boarding and disembarking passengers create bottlenecks and long waiting lines. Avoiding bottlenecks involves being able to predict where, when, and why they occur. To this end we provide **Touring Plans** for the Magic Kingdom, EPCOT Center, and the Disney-MGM Studios, as well as for Typhoon Lagoon and Pleasure Island, to assist you in avoiding bottlenecks. In addition we provide detailed information on all rides and performances which allows you to estimate how long you may have to wait in line, and which also allows you to compare rides in terms of their capacity to accommodate large crowds. Touring Plans for the Magic Kingdom begin on page 138, Touring Plans for EPCOT Center begin on page 211, and the Touring Plan for Disney-MGM Studios begins on page 257. The Touring Plan for Typhoon Lagoon begins on page 276, and the Pleasure Island Touring Plan may be found on pages 299–302. For your convenience we have also included a One-Day Touring Plan for Universal Studios Florida on pages 270–71.

—— *Touring Plans: What They Are and How They Work* ——

When we interviewed Walt Disney World visitors who toured the theme parks on slow days, say in early December, they invariably waxed eloquent about the sheer delight of their experience. When we questioned visitors who toured on a moderate or busy day, however, they spent much of the interview telling us about the jostling crowds and how much time they stood in line. What a shame, they said, that you should devote so much time and energy to fighting the crowds in a place as special as Walt Disney World.

Given this complaint, we descended on Walt Disney World with a team of researchers to determine whether a touring plan could be devised that would move visitors counter to the flow of traffic and allow them to see any of the theme parks in one day with only minimal waits in line. On some of the busiest days of the year, our team monitored traffic flow into and through the theme parks, noting how the parks filled and how the patrons were distributed among the various attractions. Likewise, we observed which rides and attractions were most popular and where bottlenecks were most likely to form.

After many long days of collecting data, we devised a number of preliminary touring plans which we tested during one of the busiest weeks of the entire year. Each day individual members of our research team would tour the park according to one of the preliminary plans, noting how long it took to walk from place to place and how long the wait in line was for each ride or show. Combining the knowledge gained through these trial runs, we devised a master plan which we retested and fine-tuned. This plan, with very little variance from day to day, allowed us to experience all of the major rides and attractions, and most of the lesser ones, in one day, with an average wait in line at each ride or show of less than five minutes.

From this master plan we developed a number of alternative plans that take into account the varying tastes and personal requirements of different Walt Disney World patrons. Each plan operates with the same efficiency as the master plan but addresses the special needs and preferences of its intended users.

Finally, after all of the plans were tested by our staff, we selected (using convenience sampling) a number of everyday Walt Disney World patrons to test the plans. The only prerequisite for being chosen for the test group (the visitors who would test the touring plans) was that the guest must be visiting a Disney park for the first time. A second group of ordinary patrons was chosen for a "control group," first-time visitors who would tour the park according to their own plans but who would make notes of what they did and how much time they spent waiting in lines.

When the two groups were compared, the results proved no less than amazing. On days when EPCOT Center's and the Magic Kingdom's attendance exceeded 48,000, visitors touring on their own (without the plan) **averaged** 3⅔ hours more waiting in line per day than the patrons touring according to our plan, and they experienced 37 percent fewer rides and attractions.

Will the Plans Continue to Work Once the Secret Is Out?

Yes! First, all of the plans require that a patron be on hand when the theme parks open. Many vacationers simply refuse to make this early-rising sacrifice, but you can see more in the one hour just after the parks open than in several hours once the parks begin to fill. Second, it is anticipated that less than one percent of any given day's attendance will have been exposed to the plans, not enough to bias the results. Last, most groups will interpret the plans somewhat, skipping certain rides or shows as a matter of personal taste.

Variables That Will Affect the Success of the Touring Plans

How quickly you move from one ride to another, when and how many refreshment and restroom breaks you take, when, where, and how you eat meals, and your ability (or lack thereof) to find your way around will all have an impact on the success of the plans. We recommend continuous, expeditious touring until around 11:30 A.M. After that hour, breaks and so on will not affect the plans significantly.

Some variables that can have a profound effect on the touring plans are beyond your control. Chief among these are the manner and timing of bringing a particular ride to full capacity. For example, Big Thunder Mountain, a roller coaster in the Magic Kingdom, has five trains. On a given morning it may begin operation with two of the five, and then add the other three if and when needed. If the waiting line builds rapidly before the Disney operators decide to go to full capacity, you could have a long wait, even early in the morning. This often happens at 20,000 Leagues Under the Sea, also in the Magic Kingdom, causing our team to label the ride as the biggest bottleneck in "the World."

Another variable relates to the time that you arrive for a Disney theater performance. Usually, your wait will be the length of time from your arrival to the end of the presentation then in progress. Thus, if *Country Bear Jamboree* is 15 minutes long, and you arrive one minute after a show has begun, your wait for the next show will be 14 minutes. Conversely, if you happen to arrive just as the ongoing show is wrapping up, your wait will be only a minute or two. It's luck of the draw.

General Overview

The Walt Disney World Touring Plans are step-by-step plans for seeing as much as possible with a minimum of time wasted standing in line. They are designed to assist you in avoiding crowds and bottlenecks on days of moderate to heavy attendance. On days of lighter attendance (see "Selecting the Time of Year for Your Visit," page 29), the plans will still save you time but will not be as critical to successful touring.

—— Letters, Comments, and Questions from Readers ——

Many of those who use *The Unofficial Guide to Walt Disney World* write to us asking questions, making comments, or sharing their own strategies for visiting Walt Disney World. We appreciate all such input, both positive and critical, and encourage our readers to continue writing. Readers' comments and observations are frequently incorporated in revised editions of *The Unofficial Guide* and have contributed immeasurably to its improvement.

How to Write the Author

Bob Sehlinger
The Unofficial Guide to Walt Disney World
P.O. Box 43059
Birmingham, AL 35243

When you write, be sure to put your return address on your letter as well as on the envelope. Sometimes envelopes and letters get separated. And remember, as travel writers we are often out of the office for long periods of time, so forgive us if our response is a little slow.

Questions frequently asked by readers in their letters to the author are listed and answered in an appendix at the end of *The Unofficial Guide*.

Field Research Internship

A small number of qualified graduate students are selected each year to participate in a field research internship held in conjunction with semiannual revision work at the Disney parks and in relation to consulting projects at other American theme parks. The internships focus on theme park planning and design, attraction product design and engineering, vehicular and pedestrian traffic engineering, and the functional areas of marketing and operations. Internships are four days to a week in duration. Applicants must be 21 years of age or older and currently enrolled in an accredited graduate program, preferably in a relevant field of study (business, statistics, engineering, architecture, etc.), and be available at one month's notice for dates in June, July, and August. Those selected will be expected to pay all of their own expenses, to include transportation to the research site, lodging, and meals. To apply, send vitae with cover letter and SASE to:

Field Research Internship
c/o The Unofficial Guide Series
P.O. Box 43059
Birmingham, AL 35243

PART TWO—Tips and Warnings

Credit Cards

- MasterCard, VISA, and American Express are accepted for theme park admission.
- No credit cards are accepted in the theme parks at fast-food restaurants.
- Walt Disney World shops, sit-down restaurants, and theme resort hotels will accept MasterCard, VISA, and American Express credit cards only.

Rain

If it rains, go anyway; the bad weather will serve to diminish the crowds. Additionally, most of the rides and attractions are under cover. Likewise, all but a few of the waiting areas are protected from inclement weather.

Closed for Repairs

It is always a good idea to check in advance with Walt Disney World to see which, if any, rides and attractions may be closed for maintenance or repair during your visit. If you are particularly interested in a certain attraction, this precaution could save you a lot of disappointment.

Small Children

We believe that children should be a fairly mature eight years old to really *appreciate* the Magic Kingdom, though children of almost any age will *enjoy* it.

We believe that much of value at EPCOT Center will be lost on children less than ten years old, although children five years and older will be able to enjoy many specific features.

Small children often become tired and irritable after several hours of standing in line and being jostled among the crowds. If your schedule allows, we recommend small doses at a time of both the Magic Kingdom and EPCOT Center. Go early in the morning to the park of your choice and tour until about lunch time. Go back to your hotel for some food and maybe a nap. Return later in the evening or the morning of the following day.

There is more than enough action and excitement at the Disney-MGM Studios to keep small ones entertained, though they might not understand everything that is going on. Be mindful, however, that the special effects are more real and the monsters "badder" at the Studios. Children who frighten easily may have a few anxious moments.

Strollers.   They are available at a modest fee at all theme parks. For infants and nonwalking toddlers the strollers are a must. We observed several sharp parents renting strollers for somewhat older children (up to four or five years). Having the stroller precluded having to carry children when they ran out of steam, and also afforded a place for children to sit during long waits in line. Strollers can be obtained at the right of the entrance to the Magic Kingdom (at the base of the Main Street Station) and on the left side of the Entrance Plaza of EPCOT Center. At the Disney-MGM Studios, stroller rentals are situated to the right of the entrance at Oscar's Super Service.

NOTE: Sometimes strollers disappear while you are enjoying a ride or a show. Do not be alarmed. You will not have to buy the missing stroller and you will be issued a new stroller for your continued use.

Baby-Sitting.   Each of the three resort hotels connected by the monorail offer a childcare service for potty-trained children between 3 and 12 years of age. Services vary somewhat, but in general children can be left between 4 P.M. and midnight. Milk and cookies are provided at the Grand Floridian (Mouseketeer House) and at the Contemporary Resort (Mouseketeer Clubhouse). A buffet supper is provided at the Disney Polynesian Resort (Neverland Club). Toys, videos, and games are provided. Play is supervised but not organized. Blankets and pillows are also provided. Guests at any Walt Disney World hotel (or campground) may use the childcare service.

Kindercare, Inc., also operates two childcare facilities at Walt Disney World. Intended for the use of Walt Disney World employees, these facilities will care for the children of guests on a space-available basis. Though 48-hours advance notice is requested, space is usually available evenings. Kindercare provides basically the same services as the resort hotel "Clubs" (excepting the buffet).

Also for those staying in the World, in-room baby-sitting is available through Kindercare and through "The Fairy Godmother" service. For rates and vital information concerning childcare or baby-sitting, call (407) 824-3737 (hotels) or (407) 827-5437 (Kindercare). Information can also be obtained at the front desk of your hotel.

Outside of Walt Disney World, childcare services and in-room sitting can be arranged through most of the larger hotels and motels. Inquire when you make your reservations.

Caring for Infants and Toddlers. The Magic Kingdom, EPCOT Center, and Disney-MGM Studios have special centralized facilities for the care of infants and toddlers. Everything necessary for changing diapers, preparing formulas, warming bottles and food, etc., is available in ample quantity. A broad selection of baby supplies is on hand for sale and there are even rockers and special chairs for nursing mothers. In the Magic Kingdom the Baby Center is located next to the Crystal Palace at the end of Main Street. At EPCOT Center, Baby Services is located near the Odyssey Restaurant, situated to the right of the World of Motion in Future World. At Disney-MGM Studios, Baby Care is located in the Guest Services Building to the left of the entrance.

Lost Children. They do not usually pose much of a problem. All Disney employees are schooled to handle the situation should it be encountered. If you lose a child in the Magic Kingdom, report the situation to a Disney employee, and then check in at the Baby Center and at City Hall where lost-children "logs" are maintained. At EPCOT Center the procedure is the same; report the child lost and then check at Baby Services near the Odyssey Restaurant. At Disney-MGM Studios, report the child lost at the Guest Services Building at the entrance end of Hollywood Boulevard. Paging systems are not used in any of the parks, but in an emergency, an "all points bulletin" can be issued throughout the park(s) via internal communications. At all three theme parks, special name tags can be obtained to aid identification should a child become separated from his party.

Disney, Kids, and Scary Stuff. Disney rides and shows are adventures. They focus on the substance and themes of all adventure, and indeed of life itself: good and evil, quest, death, beauty and the grotesque, fellowship and enmity. As you sample the variety of attractions at Walt Disney World, you transcend the mundane spinning and bouncing of midway rides to a more thought-provoking and emotionally powerful entertainment experience. Though the endings are all happy, the impact of the adventures, with Disney's gift for special effects, is often intimidating and occasionally frightening to small children.

There are rides with menacing witches, rides with burning towns, and rides with ghouls popping out of their graves, all done tongue-in-cheek and with a sense of humor, providing you are old enough to understand the joke. And bones, lots of bones: human bones, cattle bones, dinosaur bones, and whole skeletons everywhere you look. There have got to be more bones at Walt Disney World than at the Smithsonian Institution and Tulane Medical School combined. There is a stack of skulls at the headhunter's camp on the Jungle Cruise; a veritable platoon of skeletons sailing ghost ships in Pirates of the Caribbean; a haunting assemblage of skulls and skeletons in the Haunted Mansion; and more skulls, skeletons, and bones punctuating Snow White's Scary Adventures, Peter Pan's Flight, and Big Thunder Mountain Railroad, to name a few.

It should be mentioned that the monsters and special effects at the Disney-MGM Studios are more real and sinister than those of the other theme parks. If your child is having difficulty coping with the witch in Snow White's Scary Adventures, think twice about exposing him to machine-gun battles, earthquakes, and the creature from *Alien* at the Studios.

One reader wrote us the following after taking his preschool children on Star Tours:

> We took a four-year-old and a five-year-old and they had the shit scared out of them at Star Tours. We did this first thing in the morning and it took hours of Tom Sawyer Island and Small World to get back to normal.
>
> Our kids were the youngest by far in Star Tours. I assume that either other adults had more sense or were not such avid readers of your book.
>
> Preschoolers should start with Dumbo and work up to the Jungle Cruise in the late morning, after being revved up and before getting hungry, thirsty, or tired. Pirates of the Caribbean is out for preschoolers. You get the idea.

Most small children take Disney's variety of macabre trappings in stride, and others are quickly comforted by an arm around the shoulder or a little squeeze of the hand. But for those kids whose parents have observed a tendency to become upset when exposed to such sights, we recommend taking it slow and easy, sampling more benign adventures like the Jungle Cruise, gauging reactions, and discussing with children how they felt about the things they saw.

—— Visitors with Special Needs ——

Disabled visitors will find rental wheelchairs available if needed. Most rides, shows, attractions, restrooms, and restaurants at the theme parks are designed to accommodate the disabled. For specific inquiries or problems call (407) 824-4321. If you are in the Magic Kingdom and need some special assistance go to City Hall on Main Street. At EPCOT Center, inquire at the Guest Relations booth in Earth Station at the base of Spaceship Earth. At Disney-MGM Studios, assistance can be obtained at Guest Services to the left of the main entrance on Hollywood Boulevard.

Close-in parking is available for disabled visitors at all Walt Disney World parking complexes. Simply request directions when you pay your parking fee upon entering. All monorails and most rides, shows, restrooms, and restaurants can accommodate wheelchairs. One major exception is the Contemporary Resort Hotel monorail station, where passengers must enter or exit via escalators.

A special information booklet for disabled guests is available at wheelchair rental locations throughout Walt Disney World. Maps of the respective theme parks issued to each guest on admission are symbol-coded to inform nonambulatory guests which attractions accommodate wheelchairs.

Sight- and/or Hearing-Impaired Guests. The Magic Kingdom, EP-COT Center, and the Disney-MGM Studios each provide complimentary tape cassettes and portable tape players to assist sight-impaired guests. They are available at City Hall in the Magic Kingdom, Earth Station at EPCOT Center, and the Guest Services Building at the Disney-MGM Studios. A deposit is required. At the same locations, a Telecommunication Device for the Deaf (TDD) is available for hearing-impaired guests.

Foreign Language Assistance is available throughout Walt Disney World. Inquire by calling (407) 824-4321 or by stopping at City Hall in the Magic Kingdom, Earth Station Guest Relations at EPCOT Center, or at Hollywood Boulevard Guest Services at the Disney-MGM Studios.

Messages can be left at City Hall in the Magic Kingdom, Earth Station Guest Relations at EPCOT Center, or at Hollywood Boulevard Guest Services at the Disney-MGM Studios.

Car Trouble. If your car goes on the fritz, the Disney Car Care Center will come to the rescue. Arrangements can be made for transportation to your Walt Disney World destination and for a lift to the Car Care Center. If the problem is simple, one of the security or tow truck patrols which continually cruise the parking lots might be able to put you back in business.

Lost and Found. If you lose (or find) something in the Magic Kingdom, City Hall (once again) is the place to go. At EPCOT Center the Lost and Found is located in the Entrance Plaza, and at Disney-MGM Studios it is located at Hollywood Boulevard Guest Services. If you do not discover your loss until you have left the park(s), call (407) 824-4245 (for all parks).

—— *Excuse Me, but Where Can I Find . . .* ——

Someplace to Put All These Packages? Lockers are available on the ground floor of the Main Street Railroad Station in the Magic Kingdom, to the right of Earth Station in EPCOT Center, and on both the east and west ends of the Ticket and Transportation Center. At Disney-MGM Studios, lockers are to the right of the entrance on Hollywood Boulevard at Oscar's Super Service.

A Mixed Drink or a Beer? If you are in the Magic Kingdom you are out of luck. You will have to exit the park and proceed to one of the Resort Hotels. In EPCOT Center you can have a drink, but you may need a reservation. Alcoholic beverages are served primarily in full-service eateries, although beer is available at the Cantina de San Angel opposite the Mexican pavilion; at Le Cellier, a cafeteria on the lower right side of the Canadian pavilion; and at the pub section of the Rose & Crown Pub and Dining Room in the United Kingdom complex.

The latter is popular not only because of the availability of beer, but also because of its unparalleled view of the World Showcase Lagoon. Finally, beer is also available at Yakatori House, the fast-food eatery in the Japanese pavilion. At Disney-MGM Studios, beer and wine are available at the Soundstage and Backlot restaurants, at the Catwalk Bar and the Tune In Lounge, and at the full-service Hollywood Brown Derby and 50's Prime Time Cafe.

Some Rain Gear? If you get caught in a central Florida monsoon, here's where you can find something to cover up with:

Magic Kingdom

Main Street:	The Emporium
Tomorrowland:	Mickey's Mart
Fantasyland:	Mad Hatter
	AristoCats
Frontierland:	Frontier Trading Post
Adventureland:	Bwana Bob's

EPCOT Center:	Almost all retail shops

Disney-MGM Studios:	Almost all retail shops

At Disney-MGM Studios and EPCOT Center shops rain gear is available but not always displayed. As the Disney people say, it is sold "under the counter." In other words, if you do not see it, ask for it.

A Cure for This Headache? Aspirin and various other sundries can be purchased on Main Street in the Magic Kingdom at the Emporium (they keep them behind the counter so you have to ask), at most retail outlets in EPCOT Center Future World, and in many of the World Showcase shops. Likewise at the Disney-MGM Studios, aspirin is available at almost all retail shops.

A Prescription Filled? The closest pharmacy is located in the Goodings Supermarket on FL 535 in Lake Buena Vista, (407) 827-1200.

Suntan Lotion? Suntan lotion and various other sundries can be purchased on Main Street in the Magic Kingdom at the Emporium (they keep them behind the counter so you have to ask), at most retail outlets in EPCOT Center Future World, and in many of the World Showcase shops. At the Disney-MGM Studios, suntan lotion is sold at almost all retail shops.

A Smoke? Cigarettes are readily available throughout the Magic Kingdom, EPCOT Center, and the Disney-MGM Studios.

Feminine Hygiene Products? Feminine hygiene products are available in women's restrooms throughout Walt Disney World.

Cash? Branches of the Sun Bank are located respectively on Main Street in the Magic Kingdom, on Hollywood Boulevard at the Disney-MGM Studios, and to the left of the turnstiles as you enter EPCOT Center. Service at the Disney-MGM Studios is limited to an automatic teller machine. At the Magic Kingdom and EPCOT Center the following services are available:

— *Provide cash advances* on MasterCard, VISA, and American Express credit cards ($50 minimum with a maximum equaling the patron's credit limit).

— *Cash personal checks* of $25 and less drawn on U.S. banks upon presentation of a valid driver's license and a major credit card.

— *Cash and sell traveler's checks.* Provide refunds for lost American Express traveler's checks.

— *Facilitate the wiring of money* from the visitor's bank to the Sun Bank.

— *Exchange foreign currency* for dollars.

If you want to use an automatic teller machine in Walt Disney World to obtain cash, your credit card must be compatible with the Cirrus network. All American Express cards will work, but you will need to check the back of other credit cards for the Cirrus logo. If you do not have a Cirrus system card, but are at the Magic Kingdom or EPCOT Center, a bank teller will be able to process your transaction at the teller window. If, however, you are at the Disney-MGM Studios or anyplace else where service is limited to an automatic teller, you will be out of luck.

A Place to Exchange My Foreign Currency? The currency of most countries can be exchanged for dollars before you enter the theme parks, at the Guest Services window of the Ticket and Transportation Center, the Guest Services window in the ticketing area of the Disney-MGM Studios, and at the Guest Services window to the right of the entrance turnstiles at EPCOT Center.

A Place to Leave My Pet?   Cooping up an animal in a hot car while you tour can lead to disastrous results. Additionally, pets are not allowed in the major or minor theme parks. Kennels and holding facilities are provided for the temporary care of your pets, and are located adjacent to the Transportation and Ticket Center, to the left of the EPCOT Center entrance plaza, and to the left of the Disney-MGM Studios entrance plaza. If you are adamant, the folks at the kennels will accept custody of just about any type of animal, though owners of exotic and/or potentially vicious pets must place their charges in the assigned cage. Small pets (mice, hamsters, birds, snakes, turtles, alligators, etc.) must arrive in their own escape-proof quarters.

In addition to the above, there are several other details that you may need to know:

— When traveling with your pet in Florida, bring your certificate of vaccination and immunization.

— It is against the law in the state of Florida to leave a pet in a closed vehicle.

— Advance reservations for animals are not accepted.

— Kennels open one hour before the theme parks open and close one hour after the theme parks close.

— Only Walt Disney World Resort guests may board a pet overnight. Guests who board their pets should be advised that the kennels are not really set up for multi-day boarding. Only the most elementary and essential services are provided; the kennels are not manned overnight, and Disney personnel will not exercise pets.

— Guests leaving exotic pets should supply food for their pet.

Film?   Camera centers are located near the Journey into Imagination pavilion and Spaceship Earth and at other shops throughout EPCOT Center. In the Magic Kingdom, film may be found at the Kodak Camera Center on Main Street, U.S.A., as well as at other shops throughout the park. At Disney-MGM Studios, film is available at most retail shops.

How to Travel Around The World
(or the Real Mr. Toad's Wild Ride)

The multi-day passes allow a guest to visit more than one of the major Walt Disney World theme parks in a day, coming and going at the guest's convenience. A guest can travel to and fro in his car, or take the monorail, the bus, or sometimes even a boat. Unfortunately for the guest, there is precious little convenience.

When considering the much-vaunted monorail, picture three loops. Loop A is an express route which runs counterclockwise connecting the Magic Kingdom with the Transportation and Ticket Center (TTC). A second loop, B, runs clockwise alongside Loop A. Loop B makes all stops, with service to (in this order) the TTC, the Polynesian Village Resort, the Grand Floridian Hotel, the Magic Kingdom, and the Contemporary Resort Hotel (then around again). A third long loop, C, dips like a tail to the southeast connecting the TTC with EPCOT Center. The hub for all three loops is the TTC (where you usually park when visiting the Magic Kingdom).

While your multi-day pass suggests that you can flit from park to park at will, actually getting there is somewhat more complex. You cannot go directly from the Magic Kingdom to EPCOT Center by monorail, for example. You must catch the express monorail (Loop A) to the TTC and there transfer to the Loop C monorail over to EPCOT Center. If you do not have to wait in a long line to board either monorail, you can usually make it over to EPCOT Center in about 25–35 minutes. But should you want to go to EPCOT Center for dinner (as many people do) and you are departing the Magic Kingdom in the late afternoon, you might have to wait a half hour or more just to get on the express Loop A monorail. Adding this wait pops your commuting time up to about 45–55 minutes.

Once, when asking directions to the town of Louisa in the eastern Kentucky mountains, I was told in so many words, "You can't get there from here." Sometimes trying to commute around Walt Disney World gives rise to a similar frustration. "What you can do is this,"

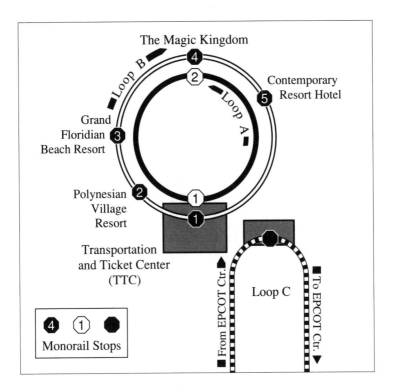

The Magic Kingdom

Loop B

Contemporary
Resort Hotel

Loop A

Grand
Floridian
Beach Resort

Polynesian
Village
Resort

Transportation
and Ticket Center
(TTC)

From EPCOT Ctr.

To EPCOT Ctr.

Loop C

Monorail Stops

a Magic Kingdom street vendor proposed: "You can take the ferry or the monorail to the Transportation and Ticket Center. Then you can get another monorail, or you can catch the bus, or you can take a tram out to your car and drive over there yourself." What the vendor did not say was that any conceivable combination from this transportation smorgasbord would take longer than riding over to EPCOT Center on a mule. This must be what Toffler meant by "future shock."

Now having alerted you that there is no efficient way to travel around Walt Disney World, we will endeavor to help you choose the least inefficient way. Just don't wait until ten minutes before your seating at Alfredo's to get moving.

To go to the Magic Kingdom in the morning from the TTC, you can take a ferry or the monorail. If the line for the monorail extends down the ramp from the loading platform, go with the ferry. Remember, one ferry holds almost as many passengers as three monorail trains. The trip takes the monorail about three-and-a-half to five minutes. Crossing time on the ferry is six-and-a-half minutes. To get to the Magic Kingdom from the TTC any other time of day, the monorail is usually your best bet unless you just happen to catch a ferry loading.

If you close out the day at the Magic Kingdom and need to get back to the TTC, try the ferry first. If the ferry is mobbed (which usually happens only at closing), take the monorail to the Polynesian Resort. Having disembarked, there is a short walkway connecting the hotel to the TTC.

Concerning this last tactic, be forewarned that monorail attendants sometimes demand hotel guest identification before allowing you to board the resort Loop B train. We think this is heavy-handed and totally out of line. Guests lodging outside the World are encouraged to shop, eat, and patronize dinner theaters in the resort hotels, but if it is the end of the day (i.e., not much opportunity remaining to spend more money), then it's "Sorry Charlie, go stand in another line."

Obviously, Disney's intent is to make things easier for its resort lodging guests, but there is a basic inconsistency in the policy. As long as the resort hotels are open to all, be it for a room, a banquet, a business meeting, or just a meal, access to the hotels—by whatever means—should likewise be open. In point of fact, the essence of the problem has nothing to do with whether a visitor is lodging at a resort hotel or what special privileges should accrue to that guest. The bottom line is that Disney cannot handle the traffic to the TTC at closing time and that it chooses to visit the inconvenience of this shortcoming on those not staying at the monorail-connected hotels. A guest at the Magic Kingdom pays for the use of the monorail as part of his admission. We believe a sensible and consistent policy would be to allow a Magic Kingdom guest to board either the express (Loop A) or the resort local (Loop B) at his discretion. Differentiating trains as express versus local has presented riders on every mass transit system in the country with clear and fair commuting alternatives. Why not then at Walt Disney World?

The best way to get to EPCOT Center at any time of day is to drive your own car. If you do not have a car and are staying in one of the hotels connected by the monorail, take the monorail to the TTC and transfer to EPCOT Center. If you are staying at the Swan or Dolphin, or the Yacht Club or Beach Club, take a tram or walk. Take the bus if you are staying at any other Disney hotel or campground.

If you are trying to get to EPCOT Center from the Magic Kingdom in the morning, take the monorail to the TTC and transfer to the EPCOT Center monorail. If you are commuting in the afternoon, take the ferry to the TTC. If you plan to spend the remainder of the day at EPCOT Center and your car is in the TTC lot, go ahead and drive your car over. But if you plan to return to the Magic Kingdom or you do not have a car at the TTC, catch the EPCOT Center monorail.

To go from EPCOT Center to the Magic Kingdom, take the monorail to the TTC and then transfer to the Magic Kingdom express monorail. If you do not plan to return to EPCOT Center and you have a car in the EPCOT Center lot, drive to the TTC and then take the ferry or monorail as crowd conditions suggest.

Coming and going to the Disney-MGM Studios is pretty cut and dried: your car or a bus. Take your car if you have a choice. If you want to leave the Studios for one of the other parks, once again, drive your own car. If you are staying at the Swan or Dolphin, the Yacht Club, or the Beach Club, you can take a boat to the Studios.

Finally, if you are staying at Walt Disney World and there are teens in your party, familiarize yourself with the Walt Disney World bus system. Safe, clean, and operating until I A.M. on most nights, the buses are a great way for the young folks to get around the World. Buses from all over Walt Disney World stop at the TTC, from whence passengers can transfer to such destinations as Fort Wilderness/River Country, Disney-MGM Studios, Typhoon Lagoon, Pleasure Island, Walt Disney World Village, EPCOT Center, and the golf courses.

Walt Disney World Attractions

The primary appeal of Walt Disney World is in its attractions, rides and shows. Understanding how these rides and shows are engineered, and how they are designed to accommodate guests, provides some information which, aside from being interesting, is quite valuable in developing an efficient itinerary.

All the attractions at Walt Disney World, regardless of the theme park in which they are located, are affected by two overriding elements: capacity and popularity. Capacity is simply how many guests the attraction can serve at one time, in an hour, or in a day. Popularity is a comparative term describing how well visitors like a particular attraction.

Capacity can be adjusted for some attractions. It is possible, for instance, to add additional trams at the Disney-MGM Backstage Studios Tour, or to put a couple of extra boats on the water at the Jungle Cruise in the Magic Kingdom. Theoretically, it is possible (though not convenient) to enlarge the theater for EPCOT Center's *Captain EO,* or to add a balcony at the *Country Bear Jamboree.* For the most part, however, capacity remains relatively fixed.

From a designer's perspective, the idea is to match capacity and popularity as closely as possible. A big high-capacity ride which is not very popular is a failure of sorts. Lots of money, space, and equipment have been poured into the attraction, yet there are always empty seats. Dreamflight, a newer ride in the Magic Kingdom, comes closest to fitting this profile.

While it is extremely unusual for a new Disney attraction such as Dreamflight not to measure up, it is fairly common for an older ride to lose its appeal. Many, if not most of the original rides at Disneyland, California, have been replaced. At Walt Disney World, the Magic Kingdom's *Mission to Mars* plays to half-full audiences, as often do the *Walt Disney Story* and the *Tropical Serenade.*

In general Disney attractions are immensely popular when they are new. Some, like Space Mountain (Magic Kingdom), have sustained great appeal years beyond their debut while others, like EPCOT Center's The Living Seas, have declined markedly in popularity after just a year or two of operation. Most attractions, however, work through the honeymoon and then settle down to handle the level of demand for which they were designed. When this happens, there are enough interested guests during peak hours to fill almost every seat, but not so many as to develop a prohibitively long line.

Sometimes Disney properly estimates an attraction's popularity but then fouls up the equation by mixing in a third variable such as location. Spaceship Earth, the ride inside the huge geosphere at EPCOT Center, is a good example. Placing the ride squarely in the path of every tourist entering the park assures that it will be inundated and overwhelmed during the morning hours when the park is filling up. On the other side of the coin, *The American Adventure,* located at the extreme opposite end of EPCOT Center, has a huge capacity but plays to a partially filled theater until about noon, when guests finally work their way into that part of the park.

If demand is high and capacity is low, large lines will materialize. Dumbo, the Flying Elephant in the Magic Kingdom has the smallest capacity of almost any Walt Disney World attraction, yet it is probably the most popular ride among young children. The result of this mismatch is that children and parents must often suffer long, long waits for a one-and-a-half-minute ride. Dumbo is a simple yet visually appealing midway ride. Its capacity (and that of many other attractions, including Space Mountain) is limited by the very characteristics which contribute to its popularity.

Capacity design is always predicated on averages: the average number of people in the park, the normal distribution of traffic to specific areas within the park, and the average number of staff required to operate the ride. On a holiday weekend when all the averages are exceeded, all but a few attractions operate at maximum capacity, and even then are overwhelmed by the huge crowds. On low-attendance fall days full capacity is often not even approximated and guests can literally walk onto most rides without any wait whatsoever.

The Magic Kingdom offers the greatest variety in both capacity and popularity, offering rides and shows of vastly differing sorts. Only the Magic Kingdom offers low-capacity midway rides, spook house genre rides, and roller coasters. Technologically, its product mix ranges from state of the art to the antiquated. This diversity makes efficient touring of the Magic Kingdom much more challenging. If guests do not understand the capacity/popularity relationship and plan accordingly, they might spend most of the day waiting in line.

While EPCOT Center and the Disney-MGM Studios have fewer attractions overall than the Magic Kingdom, almost all of their attractions are major features and rank on a par with the Magic Kingdom's Pirates of the Caribbean and the Jungle Cruise in terms of scope, detail, imagination, and spectacle. All but one or two of the EPCOT Center and Disney-MGM rides are fast-loading, and most have large overall carrying capacities. Thus, EPCOT Center and Disney-MGM attractions are on average well-engineered and very efficient. Lines at EPCOT Center and Disney-MGM are often somewhat longer than in the Magic Kingdom, but usually move more quickly. There are no amusement park rides at EPCOT Center or the Disney-MGM Studios and no attractions which are specifically intended for children.

In the Magic Kingdom, crowded conditions are more a function of the popularity and engineering of individual attractions. At EPCOT Center, traffic flow and crowding is much more affected by the park layout. In terms of touring efficiency, it is important to understand how the Magic Kingdom rides and shows operate. At EPCOT Center this knowledge is decidedly less important.

The Disney-MGM Studios have hosted crowds much larger than anticipated since it opened in 1989. Greater-than-expected attendance coupled with a relatively small overall number of attractions has resulted in long lines, long waits, and frustrated guests. Disney plans to double the size of the theme park by 1992, but in the meantime a well-considered touring plan is essential.

To develop an efficient touring plan it is necessary to understand how the attractions are designed and how they function. At Walt Disney World, attractions essentially fall into two categories: rides and shows. We will examine both.

—— Cutting Down Your Time in Line by Understanding the Rides ——

There are many different types of rides at Walt Disney World. Some rides, like the Great Movie Ride at the Disney-MGM Studios, are engineered to carry more than 3,000 people every hour. At the other extreme, such rides as Dumbo, the Flying Elephant can only accommodate around 300 persons in an hour. Most rides fall somewhere in between. Lots of factors figure into how long you will have to wait to experience a particular ride: the popularity of the ride; how it loads and unloads; how many persons can ride at one time; how many units (cars, rockets, boats, flying elephants, Skyway gondolas, etc.) are in service at a given time; and how many staff personnel are available to operate the ride. Let's take them one by one:

1. *How popular is the ride?*

Newer rides like Star Tours at Disney-MGM Studios attract a lot of people, as do longtime favorites such as the Jungle Cruise in the Magic Kingdom. If you know a ride is popular, you need to learn a little more about how it operates to determine when might be the best time to ride. But a ride need not be especially popular to form long lines; the lines can be the result of less than desirable traffic engineering (i.e., it takes so long to load and unload that a line builds up anyway). This is the situaton at the Mad Tea Party and Cinderella's Golden Carrousel in Fantasyland. Since mostly children ride the Mad Tea Party, it only serves a small percentage of any day's attendance at the Magic Kingdom. Yet, because it takes so long to load and unload this comparatively less popular ride, long waiting lines form.

2. *How does the ride load and unload?*

Some rides never stop. They are like a circular conveyor belt that goes around and around. We call these "continuous loaders." The Haunted Mansion in the Magic Kingdom is a continuous loader, as is Spaceship Earth at EPCOT Center and Peter Pan's Flight in Fantasyland. The number of people that can be moved through in an hour depends on how many cars, pirate ships, or whatever are on the conveyor. The Haunted Mansion and Spaceship Earth have lots of cars on the conveyor belt and consequently can move more than 2,000 people an hour. Peter Pan's Flight has fewer cars (or pirate ships in this case) and can handle only about 1,100 people each hour.

Still other rides are "interval loaders." This means that cars are unloaded, loaded, and dispatched at certain set intervals (sometimes controlled manually and sometimes by a computer). Space Mountain in Tomorrowland is an interval loader. It has two separate tracks (in other words the ride has been duplicated in the same facility). Each track can run up to 14 space capsules, released at 36-second, 26-second, or 21-second intervals. (The bigger the crowd, the shorter the interval.)

In one kind of interval loader, like Space Mountain, empty cars (space capsules) are returned to the starting point where they line up for reloading. In a second type of interval loader, one group of riders enters the vehicle while the last group of riders departs. We call these "in-and-out" interval loaders. It's a Small World is a good example of an in-and-out interval loader. As a boat pulls up to the dock, those who have just completed their ride exit to the left. At almost the same time, those waiting to ride enter the boat from the right. The boat is released to the dispatch point a few yards down the line where it is launched according to whatever time interval is being used.

Interval loaders of both types can be very efficient at moving people if (1) the dispatch (launch) interval is relatively short and (2) the ride can accommodate a large number of vehicles in the system at one time. Since many boats can be floating through Pirates of the Caribbean at a given time, and since the dispatch interval is short, almost 3,000 people an hour can see this attraction. 20,000 Leagues Under the Sea is an in-and-out interval loader which can only run a maximum of nine submarines at a time with a fairly long dispatch interval. Thus 20,000 Leagues can only handle up to 1,600 people an hour.

A third group of rides are "cycle rides." Another name for these rides is "stop-and-go" rides. Here those waiting to ride exchange places with those who have just ridden. The main difference between in-and-out interval rides and cycle rides is that with a cycle ride the whole system shuts down when loading and unloading is in progress. While one boat is loading and unloading in It's a Small World, many other boats are advancing through the ride. But when Dumbo, the Flying Elephant touches down, the whole ride is at a standstill until the next flight is launched. Likewise, with Cinderella's Golden Carrousel, all riders dismount and the Carrousel stands stationary until the next group is mounted and ready to ride. In discussing a cycle ride, the amount of time the ride is in motion is called "ride time." The amount of time that the ride is idle while loading and unloading is called "load time." Load time added to ride time equals "cycle time," or the time expended from the start of one run of the ride until the start of the succeeding run. Cycle rides are the least efficient of all rides in terms of traffic engineering. The only cycle rides at Walt Disney World are in the Magic Kingdom.

3. *How many persons can ride at one time?*

This figure is defined in terms of "per ride capacity" or "system capacity." Either way the figures allude to the number of people who can be riding at the same time. Our discussion above illustrates that the greater the carrying capacity of a ride (all other things being equal) the more visitors it can accommodate in an hour. Also, as mentioned previously, some rides can add extra units (cars, boats, etc.) as crowds build to increase carrying capacity, while others like the Star-Jets in Tomorrowland have a fixed capacity (it being impossible to add additional rockets).

4. *How many "units" are in service at a given time?*

A "unit" is simply our term for the vehicle you sit in during your ride. At the Mad Tea Party the unit is a teacup, at 20,000 Leagues it's a submarine, and at the Grand Prix Raceway it's a race car. On some rides (mostly cycle rides), the number of units in operation at a given time is fixed. Thus, there are always 10 flying elephant units operating on the Dumbo ride, 90 horses on Cinderella's Golden Carrousel, and so on. What this fixed number of units means to you is that there is no way to increase the carrying capacity of the ride by adding more units. On a busy day, therefore, the only way to carry more people each hour on a fixed-unit cycle ride is to shorten the loading time (which, as we will discuss next, is sometimes impossible) or by decreasing the riding time, the actual time the ride is in motion. The bottom line on a busy day for a cycle ride is that you will wait longer and be rewarded for your wait with a shorter ride. This is why we try to steer you clear of the cycle rides unless you are willing to ride them early in the morning or late at night. The following are cycle rides, all located in the Magic Kingdom:

Fantasyland:	Dumbo, the Flying Elephant
	Cinderella's Golden Carrousel
	Mad Tea Party
Tomorrowland:	StarJets

Many other rides throughout Walt Disney World can increase their carrying capacity by adding additional units to the system as the crowds build. Big Thunder Mountain Railroad in Frontierland is a good example. If attendance is very light, Big Thunder can start the day by running one of their five available mine trains on one out of two available feeder tracks. If lines start to build, the other track can be opened and more mine trains placed into operation. At full capacity a total of five trains on two tracks can carry about 2,400 persons an hour. Likewise Star Tours at Disney-MGM Studios can increase its capacity by adding more simulators, and the Maelstrom boat ride at EPCOT Center can add more Viking ships. Sometimes a long line will disappear almost instantly when new units are brought on line. When an interval-loading ride places more units into operation, it usually shortens the dispatch intervals, so more units are being dispatched more often.

5. *How many staff personnel are available to operate the ride?*

Allocation of additional staff to a given ride can allow extra units to be placed in operation, or additional loading areas or holding areas to be opened. In the Magic Kingdom, Pirates of the Caribbean and It's a Small World can run two separate waiting lines and loading zones. The Haunted Mansion has a one-and-a-half-minute pre-show which is staged in a "stretch room." On busy days a second stretch room can be activated, thus permitting a more continuous flow of visitors to the actual loading area.

Additional staff make a world of difference in some cycle rides. Often, one attendant will operate the Mad Tea Party. This single person must clear visitors from the ride just completed, admit and seat visitors for the upcoming ride, check that all teacups are properly secured (which entails an inspection of each teacup), return to the control panel, issue instructions to the riders, and finally activate the ride (whew!). A second attendant allows for the division of these responsibilities and has the effect of cutting loading time by 25 to 50 percent.

By knowing the way a ride loads, its approximate hourly capacity, and its relative popularity, we can anticipate which rides are likely to develop long lines, and more importantly how long we will have to wait to ride at most any given time of day.

—— *Cutting Down Your Time in Line by Understanding the Shows* ——

Many of the featured attractions at Walt Disney World are theater presentations. While not as complex as rides from a traffic engineering viewpoint, a little enlightenment concerning their operation may save some touring time.

Most of the theater attractions at Walt Disney World operate in three distinct phases:

1. There are the guests who are in the theater viewing the presentation.

2. There are the guests who have passed through the turnstile into a holding area or waiting lobby. These people will be admitted to the theater as soon as the presentation in progress is concluded. Several attractions offer a pre-show in their waiting lobby to entertain guests until they are admitted to the main show. Among these are the *Tropical Serenade* (*Enchanted Tiki Birds*) and the *Mission to Mars* in the Magic Kingdom, *Captain EO* and the Universe of Energy at EPCOT Center, and the *Monster Sound Show* at the Disney-MGM Studios.

3. There is the outside line. Those waiting here will enter the waiting lobby when there is room, and will ultimately move from the waiting lobby to the theater.

The theater capacity and the popularity of the presentation, along with the level of attendance in the park, determine how long the lines will be at a given theater attraction. Except for holidays and other days of especially heavy attendance, the longest wait for a show usually does not exceed the length of one complete performance.

Since almost all Walt Disney World theater attractions run continuously, only stopping long enough for the previous audience to leave and the waiting audience to enter, a performance will be in progress when you arrive. If a showing of *Impressions de France* in the French pavilion at EPCOT Center is 18 minutes in duration, the longest wait under normal circumstances should be about 18 minutes if you were to arrive just after the show had begun.

All Walt Disney World theaters (except the Main Street Cinema in the Magic Kingdom and various amphitheater productions) are very strict when it comes to controlling access. Unlike a movie theater at home, you cannot just walk in during the middle of a performance. This being the case, you will always have at least a short wait.

Most of the theaters at Walt Disney World hold a lot of people. Thus when a new audience is admitted, the outside line (if there is one) will usually disappear. Exceptions to this are the *Country Bear Jamboree* in the Magic Kingdom, *The Making of Me* in the Wonders of Life pavilion at EPCOT Center, and the *Monster Sound Show* at the Disney-MGM Studios, where, owing to the shows' popularity and relatively small seating capacities, you may have to wait through two or more shows before you are admitted (unless you go early in the morning).

—— *How to Deal with Obnoxious People* ——

At every theater presentation at Walt Disney World, visitors in the pre-show area elbow, nudge, and crowd one another in order to make sure that they are admitted to the performance. Not necessary— if you are admitted through the turnstile into the pre-show area a seat has automatically been allocated for you in the theater. When it is time to proceed into the theater don't rush; just relax and let other people jam the doorways. When the congestion has been relieved simply stroll in and take a seat.

Attendants at many theaters will instruct you to enter a row of seats and move completely to the far side, filling every seat so that each row can be completely filled. And invariably some inconsiderate, thick-skulled yahoo will plop down right in the middle of the row, stopping traffic or forcing other visitors to climb over him. Take our word for it—there is no such thing as a bad seat. All of the Disney theaters have been designed to provide a near-perfect view from every seat in the house. Our recommendation is to follow instructions and move to the far end of the row, and if you encounter some dummy blocking the middle of the row, have every person in your party step very hard on his toes as you move past him.

The Disney people also ask that visitors not use flash photography in the theaters (the theaters are too dark for the pictures to turn out, *plus* the flash is disruptive to other viewers). Needless to say, this admonition is routinely ignored. Flashers are more difficult to deal with than row-blockers. You can threaten to turn the offenders over to Disney Security, or better yet, simply hold your hand over the lens (you have to be quick) when they raise their cameras.

PART THREE—
The Magic Kingdom

Arriving and Getting Oriented

Both the ferryboat and the monorail discharge passengers at the entrance to the Magic Kingdom—the Train Station at the foot of Main Street. Stroller and wheelchair rentals are to the right, lockers for your use are on the ground floor of the Train Station. Entering Main Street, City Hall is to your left, serving as the center for information, lost and found, some reservations, and entertainment.

If you haven't been given a guide to the Magic Kingdom by now, City Hall is the place to pick one up. The guide contains maps, gives tips for good photos, lists all the attractions, shops, and eating places, and provides helpful information about first aid, baby care, assistance for the handicapped, and more.

While at City Hall inquire about special events, live entertainment, Disney character parades, concerts, and other activities scheduled for that day. Usually City Hall will have a printed schedule of the day's events.

Notice from your map that Main Street ends at a central hub, from which branch the entrances to five other sections of the Magic Kingdom: Adventureland, Frontierland, Liberty Square, Fantasyland, and Tomorrowland. Mickey's Starland is wedged like a dimple between the cheeks of Fantasyland and Tomorrowland, and does not connect to the central hub.

Cinderella Castle serves as the entrance to Fantasyland and is the focal landmark and visual center of the Magic Kingdom. If you start in Adventureland and go clockwise around the Magic Kingdom, the castle spires will always be roughly on your right; if you start in Tomorrowland and go counterclockwise through the park, the spires will always be roughly on your left. Cinderella Castle is a great place to meet if your group decides to split up for any reason during the day, or as an emergency meeting place if you are accidentally separated.

Starting the Tour

Everyone will soon find his own favorite and not-so-favorite attractions in the Magic Kingdom. Be open-minded and adventuresome. Don't dismiss a particular ride or show as being not for you until **after** you have tried it. Our personal experience as well as our research indicates that each visitor is different in terms of which Disney offerings he most enjoys. So don't miss seeing an attraction because a friend from home didn't like it; that attraction may turn out to be your favorite.

We do recommend that you take advantage of what Disney does best—the fantasy adventures like the Jungle Cruise and the Haunted Mansion, and the AudioAnimatronics (talking robots, so to speak) attractions such as the *Hall of Presidents* and Pirates of the Caribbean. Unless you have almost unlimited time, don't burn a lot of daylight browsing through the shops. Except for some special Disney souvenirs, you can find most of the same merchandise elsewhere. Try to minimize the time you spend on carnival-type rides; you've probably got an amusement park, carnival, or state fair closer to your hometown. (Don't, however, mistake rides like Space Mountain and the Big Thunder Mountain Railroad as being amusement park rides. They may be of the roller coaster genre, but they represent pure Disney genius.) Similarly, do not devote a lot of time to waiting in lines for meals. Food at most Magic Kingdom eateries is mediocre and uninspiring at best. Eat a good early breakfast before you come and snack on vendor-sold foods during the touring day.

Main Street, U.S.A.

Main Street opens a half hour to an hour before, and closes a half hour to an hour after, the rest of the park. This section of the Magic Kingdom is where you'll begin and end your visit. We have already mentioned that assistance and information are available at City Hall. The Walt Disney World Railroad stops at the Main Street Station: you can board here for a grand-circle tour of the Magic Kingdom, or you can get off the train in Frontierland or Mickey's Starland.

Main Street is a replication of a turn-of-the-century American small town street. Many visitors are surprised to discover that all the buildings are real as opposed to being elaborate props. Attention to detail here is exceptional with interiors, furnishings, and fixtures conforming to the period. As with any real Main Street the Disney version is essentially a collection of shops and eating places, with a city hall, a fire station, an old-time cinema, and an attraction detailing the life of Walt Disney, *Walt Disney Story*, thrown in for good measure. Horsedrawn trolleys, double-decker buses, fire engines, and horseless carriages offer rides along Main Street and transport visitors to the central hub.

—— Main Street Services ——

Most of the park's service facilities are centered in the Main Street section, including the following:

Wheelchair & Stroller Rental	To the right of the main entrance before passing under the Railroad Station
Banking Services/ Currency Exchange	To the left of City Hall at the Railroad Station end of Main Street
Storage Lockers	On the ground floor of the Railroad Station at the end of Main Street
Lost & Found	City Hall Building at the Railroad Station end of Main Street

Live Entertainment and Parade Information	City Hall Building at the Railroad Station end of Main Street
Lost Persons	City Hall Building
Diamond Horseshoe Jamboree Reservations	Hospitality House, next to *Walt Disney Story*
Walt Disney World & Local Attraction Information	City Hall Building
First Aid	Next to the Crystal Palace around the central hub to the left (toward Adventureland)
Baby Center/Baby Care Needs	Next to the Crystal Palace around the central hub to the left (toward Adventureland)

—— *Main Street Attractions* ——

Walt Disney World Railroad

Type of Attraction: Scenic railroad ride around perimeter of the Magic Kingdom; also transportation to Frontierland and Mickey's Starland.

When to Go: After 11 A.M. or when you need transportation

Special Comments: Main Street usually the least congested station

Author's Rating: Plenty to see; ★★★½ [Critical ratings are based on a scale of zero to five stars. Five stars is the best possible rating.]

Overall Appeal by Age Group:

Pre-school	Grade School	Teens	Young Adults	Over 30	Senior Citizens
★★★★	★★★★	★★½	★★★	★★★½	★★★½

Duration of Ride: About 19 minutes for a complete circuit

Average Wait in Line per 100 People Ahead of You: 8 minutes

Assumes: 2 or more trains operating

Loading Speed: Fast

DESCRIPTION AND COMMENTS   A transportation ride that blends an unusual variety of sights and experiences with an energy-saving way of getting around the park. The train provides a glimpse of all the lands except Adventureland.

TOURING TIPS   Save the train ride until after you have seen the featured attractions, or use when you need transportation. On busy days, lines form at the Frontierland Station, but rarely at the Main Street and Mickey's Starland Stations.

Walt Disney Story

Type of Attraction: Nostalgic look at the Disney success story
When to Go: During the hot, crowded period of the day
Author's Rating: A happy remembrance; ★★★★
Overall Appeal by Age Group:

Pre-school	Grade School	Teens	Young Adults	Over 30	Senior Citizens
★★½	★★★	★★★	★★★½	★★★★½	★★★★½

Duration of Presentation: 23 minutes
Pre-Show Entertainment: Disney exhibits
Probable Waiting Time: Less than 10 minutes

DESCRIPTION AND COMMENTS   A warm and well-produced remembrance of the man who started it all. Well worth seeing, especially touching for those old enough to remember Walt Disney.

TOURING TIPS   You usually do not have to wait long for this show, so see it during the busy times of the day when lines are long elsewhere or as you are leaving the park.

Main Street Cinema

Type of Attraction: Old-time movies and vintage Disney cartoons
When to Go: Whenever you want
Author's Rating: Wonderful selection of hilarious flicks; ★★★½
Overall Appeal by Age Group:

Pre-school	Grade School	Teens	Young Adults	Over 30	Senior Citizens
★★½	★★★	★★★	★★★½	★★★½	★★★½

Duration of Presentation: Runs continuously
Pre-Show Entertainment: None
Probable Waiting Time: No waiting

DESCRIPTION AND COMMENTS   Excellent old-time movies including some vintage Disney cartoons. Since the movies are silent, six are shown simultaneously. No seats; viewers stand.

TOURING TIPS   Good place to get out of the sun or rain, or to kill time while others in your group shop on Main Street. Not something you can't afford to miss.

— *Main Street Minor Attractions* —

Transportation Rides

DESCRIPTION AND COMMENTS   Trolleys, buses, etc., which add color to Main Street.

TOURING TIPS   Will save you a walk to the central hub. Not worth waiting in line.

Penny Arcade

DESCRIPTION AND COMMENTS   The Penny Arcade features some vintage arcade machines which can actually be played for a penny or a nickel. Located toward the central hub end of Main Street on the left as you face the Castle.

TOURING TIPS   If you arrive early when Main Street is the only part of the park open, you might want to spend a few minutes here.

Main Street Eateries and Shops

DESCRIPTION AND COMMENTS   Some of the Magic Kingdom's better food and specialty/souvenir shopping in a nostalgic, happy setting. The Emporium offers the best selection of Disney trademark souvenir items in the Magic Kingdom.

TOURING TIPS   The shops are fun but the merchandise can be had elsewhere (except for certain Disney trademark souvenirs). If seeing the park attractions is your objective, save the Main Street eateries and shops until the end of the day. If shopping is your objective, you will find the shops most crowded during the noon hour and near closing time. Remember, Main Street opens at least a half hour earlier, and closes a half hour to an hour later than the rest of the Magic Kingdom.

The Crystal Palace, at the central hub end of Main Street (towards Adventureland) provides good cafeteria service and is often overlooked by the lunch-hour (but not dinner-hour) masses. Give it a try if you are nearby at the noon hour.

Adventureland

Adventureland is the first land to the left of Main Street and combines a safari/African motif with an old New Orleans/Caribbean motif.

Swiss Family Treehouse

Type of Attraction: Walk-through exhibit
When to Go: Before 11:30 A.M. and after 5 P.M.
Special Comments: Requires climbing a lot of stairs
Author's Rating: A very creative exhibit; ★★★★
Overall Appeal by Age Group:

Pre-school	Grade School	Teens	Young Adults	Over 30	Senior Citizens
★★★★	★★★★	★★★★	★★★★	★★★★	★★★★

Duration of Tour: 10–15 minutes
Average Wait in Line per 100 People Ahead of You: 7 minutes
Assumes: Normal staffing
Loading Speed: Does not apply

DESCRIPTION AND COMMENTS   A fantastic replication of the ship-wrecked family's home will fire the imagination of the inventive and the adventurous.

TOURING TIPS   A self-guided walk-through tour which involves a lot of climbing up and down stairs, but no ropes or ladders or anything fancy. People stopping during the walk-through to look extra long or to rest sometimes create bottlenecks which slow crowd flow. We recommend visiting this attraction in the late afternoon or early evening if you are on a one-day tour schedule, or first thing in the morning of your second day.

Jungle Cruise

Type of Ride: A Disney boat ride adventure
When to Go: Before 11 A.M. or two hours before closing
Author's Rating: A long-enduring Disney masterpiece; ★★★★½
Overall Appeal by Age Group:

Pre-school	Grade School	Teens	Young Adults	Over 30	Senior Citizens
★★★★★	★★★★★	★★★★	★★★★½	★★★★½	★★★★½

Duration of Ride: 8–9 minutes
Average Wait in Line per 100 People Ahead of You: 3½ minutes
Assumes: 10 boats operating
Loading Speed: Moderate to fast

DESCRIPTION AND COMMENTS   A boat ride through jungle waterways. Passengers encounter elephants, lions, hostile natives, and a menacing hippo. A long-enduring Disney favorite, with the boatman's spiel adding measurably to the fun.

TOURING TIPS   One of the park's "not to be missed" attractions. Good staffing and an improved management plan have speeded up the lines for this ride.

Pirates of the Caribbean

Type of Ride: A Disney adventure boat ride
When to Go: Before 10:30 A.M. or after 3:30 P.M.
Special Comments: Frightens some small children
Author's Rating: Our pick as the best attraction at Walt Disney World; ★★★★★
Overall Appeal by Age Group:

Pre-school	Grade School	Teens	Young Adults	Over 30	Senior Citizens
★★★	★★★★★	★★★★★	★★★★★	★★★★★	★★★★★

Duration of Ride: Approximately 7½ minutes
Average Wait in Line per 100 People Ahead of You: 1½ minutes
Assumes: Both waiting lines operating
Loading Speed: Fast

DESCRIPTION AND COMMENTS   Another boat ride, this time indoors, through a series of sets depicting a pirate raid on an island settlement, from the bombardment of the fortress to the debauchery that follows the victory. All in good, clean fun.

TOURING TIPS   Another "not to be missed" attraction. Undoubtedly one of the most elaborate and imaginative attractions in the Magic Kingdom. Engineered to move large crowds in a hurry, Pirates is a good attraction to see during the later part of the afternoon. It has two waiting lines, both under cover.

Tropical Serenade (Enchanted Tiki Birds)

Type of Attraction: AudioAnimatronic Pacific Island musical show
When to Go: Before 11 A.M. and after 3:30 P.M.
Author's Rating: Very, very unusual; ★★★½
Overall Appeal by Age Group:

Pre-school	Grade School	Teens	Young Adults	Over 30	Senior Citizens
★★½	★★★	★★	★★★½	★★★½	★★★½

Duration of Presentation: 15½ minutes
Pre-Show Entertainment: Talking birds
Probable Waiting Time: 15 minutes

DESCRIPTION AND COMMENTS   An unusual sit-down theater performance where more than two hundred birds, flowers, and Tiki-god statues sing and whistle through a musical program.

TOURING TIPS   One of the more bizarre of the Magic Kingdom's entertainments, but usually not too crowded. We like it in the late afternoon when we can especially appreciate sitting for a bit in an air-conditioned theater.

Adventureland Eateries and Shops

DESCRIPTION AND COMMENTS   More specialty shopping a la Banana Republic; and several restaurants, which tend to be less crowded during lunch.

TOURING TIPS   The Adventureland Veranda Restaurant is a good bet for less congestion and speedier service between 11:30 A.M. and 1:30 P.M. Give it a try if you are in the area during lunchtime.

Frontierland

Frontierland adjoins Adventureland as you move clockwise around the Magic Kingdom. The focus here is on the Old West with stockade-type structures and pioneer trappings.

Big Thunder Mountain Railroad

Type of Ride: Tame roller coaster with exciting special effects
When to Go: Before 11 A.M. or after 5:30 P.M.
Special Comments: Children must be 3'4" tall to ride. Those under 7 years must ride with an adult.
Author's Rating: Great effects/relatively tame ride; ★★★★
Overall Appeal by Age Group:

Pre-school	Grade School	Teens	Young Adults	Over 30	Senior Citizens
★★★	★★★★	★★★★	★★★★	★★★★	★★★★

Duration of Ride: Almost 3½ minutes
Average Wait in Line per 100 People Ahead of You: 2½ minutes
Assumes: Both tracks and 5 trains operating
Loading Speed: Moderate to fast

DESCRIPTION AND COMMENTS   A roller coaster ride through and around a Disney "mountain." The time is Gold Rush days, and the idea is that you are on a runaway mine train. Along with the usual thrills of a roller coaster ride (about a 5 on a "scary scale" of 10), the ride showcases some first-rate examples of Disney creativity; lifelike scenes depicting a mining town, falling rocks, and an earthquake, all humorously animated.

TOURING TIPS   A superb Disney experience, but not too wild of a roller coaster. The emphasis here is much more on the sights than on the thrill of the ride itself. Regardless, it's a "not to be missed" attraction. The best bet for riding Big Thunder without a long wait in line is to ride early in the morning or between 10:00–11:00 when the ride has been brought up to peak carrying capacity.

As an example of how differently guests experience Disney attractions, consider this letter we received from a lady in Brookline, Massachusetts:

> Being in the senior citizens' category and having limited time, my friend and I confined our activities to those attractions rated as four or five stars for seniors.
>
> Because of your recommendation and because you listed it as "not to be missed," we waited for one hour to board the Big Thunder Mountain Railroad, (which you) rated a "5" on a scary scale of "10." After living through three-and-a-half minutes of pure terror, I will rate that attraction a "15" on a scary scale of "10." We were so busy holding on and screaming and even praying for our safety that we did not see any falling rocks, a mining town, or an earthquake. In our opinion the Big Thunder Mountain Railroad should not be recommended for seniors or preschool children.

Diamond Horseshoe Jamboree

Type of Attraction: Live song/dance/comedy stage show

When to Go: As per your reservations

Special Comments: Seating by reservation only, made on the day of the show, at the Hospitality House on Main Street. No reservations taken at the Saloon itself. Lunch is available.

Author's Rating: Absolutely superb, not to be missed; ★★★★★

Overall Appeal by Age Group:

Pre-school	Grade School	Teens	Young Adults	Over 30	Senior Citizens
★★★½	★★★★	★★★★	★★★★★	★★★★★	★★★★★

Duration of Presentation: About 30 minutes

Pre-Show Entertainment: None

Probable Waiting Time: See Touring Tips

DESCRIPTION AND COMMENTS A half-hour, G-rated re-creation of an Old West dance hall show, with dancing, singing, and lots of corny comedy. Visitors are seated at tables where sandwiches and beverages (nonalcoholic) can be ordered before the show. This is a clever, wonderfully cast, uproariously funny show that you should try to work into your schedule.

TOURING TIPS Though an excellent show (ranked as "not to be missed"), it is a real hassle to see, particularly if you have only one day at the Magic Kingdom. Here's why: Seating is by reservation only, made in person on the day you want to see the show. To obtain a reservation you have to go to the Hospitality House on Main Street. Reservation lines move very slowly because every visitor needs to ask questions and receive instructions. If you are able to obtain a reservation for one of the several shows you will be required to appear for seating one half hour before showtime when you will wait in line again (this time to be admitted to the theater). Once allowed inside you will wait for another fifteen minutes for food orders to be taken and processed before the show finally begins. By observation and experimentation we have determined that a Magic Kingdom visitor spends an average of 15 minutes making his reservation, and 45 minutes waiting for the show to begin, plus changing his other touring plans to get back to Frontierland in time to be seated. Thus, counting the show itself: a 1½-hour investment of valuable time to see a 30-minute song-and-dance show. We recommend that you see the Jamboree on your second day, if you have one. For those with only one day, we have incorporated the Diamond Horseshoe into our One-Day Touring Plans as an option that combines the show with lunch and eliminates as much wasted time as possible. See "Magic Kingdom Touring Plans," pages 138–61.

Country Bear Jamboree

Type of Attraction: AudioAnimatronic country hoedown stage show
When to Go: Before noon and during the two hours before closing
Special Comments: Changes shows at Christmas and during the summer
Author's Rating: A Disney classic, not to be missed; ★★★★½
Overall Appeal by Age Group:

Pre-school	Grade School	Teens	Young Adults	Over 30	Senior Citizens
★★★★	★★★★	★★★★	★★★★½	★★★★½	★★★★½

Duration of Presentation: 15 minutes
Pre-Show Entertainment: None

Probable Waiting Time: This is a very popular attraction with a comparatively small seating capacity. An average waiting time on a busy day between the hours of noon and 5:30 P.M. would be from 30 to 50 minutes.

DESCRIPTION AND COMMENTS   A cast of charming AudioAnimatronic (robotic) bears sing and stomp their way through a Western-style hoedown. One of the Magic Kingdom's most humorous and upbeat shows.

TOURING TIPS   Yet another "not to be missed" attraction, the Jamboree is extremely popular and draws large crowds even early in the day. We recommend seeing this one before 11:30 A.M.

Tom Sawyer Island and Fort Sam Clemens

Type of Attraction: Walk-through exhibit/rustic playground
When to Go: Mid-morning through late afternoon
Special Comments: Closes at dusk
Author's Rating: The place for rambunctious kids; ★★★★
Overall Appeal by Age Group:

Pre-school	Grade School	Teens	Young Adults	Over 30	Senior Citizens
★★★★★	★★★★★	★★★½	★★★	★★★	★★★

DESCRIPTION AND COMMENTS   Tom Sawyer Island manages to impart something of a sense of isolation from the rest of the park. It has hills to climb, a cave and a windmill to explore, a tipsy barrel bridge to cross, and paths to follow. It's a delight for adults and a godsend for children who have been in tow all day. They love the freedom of the exploration and the excitement of firing air guns from the walls of Ft. Sam Clemens. There's even a "secret" escape tunnel.

TOURING TIPS   Tom Sawyer Island is not one of the Magic Kingdom's more celebrated attractions, but it's certainly one of the better done. Attention to detail is excellent and kids particularly revel in its adventuresome frontier atmosphere. We think it's a must for families with children five through fifteen. If your party is adult, visit the island on your second day or stop by on your first day if you have seen the attractions you most wanted to see.

We like Tom Sawyer Island from about noon until the island closes at dusk. Access is by raft from Frontierland and you will have to stand in line to board both coming and going. Two rafts operate simultaneously, however, and the round trip is usually pretty efficient. Tom Sawyer Island takes about 45 minutes or so to see; many children could spend a whole day visiting.

Davy Crockett's Explorer Canoes

Type of Ride: Scenic canoe ride

When to Go: Before noon or after 5 P.M.

Special Comments: Skip if the lines are long; closes at dusk

Author's Rating: The most fun way of seeing the Rivers of America; ★★★★

Overall Appeal by Age Group:

Pre-school	Grade School	Teens	Young Adults	Over 30	Senior Citizens
★★★★	★★★★	★★★★	★★★★	★★★★	★★★★

Duration of Ride: 9–15 minutes depending how fast you paddle

Average Wait in Line per 100 People Ahead of You: 28 minutes

Assumes: 3 canoes operating

Loading Speed: Slow

DESCRIPTION AND COMMENTS   Paddle-powered ride (your power) around Tom Sawyer Island and Ft. Sam Clemens. Runs the same route with the same sights as the Liberty Square Riverboat and the Mike Fink Keelboats. The canoes only operate during the busy times of the year. The sights are fun and the ride is a little different in that the tourists paddle the canoe.

TOURING TIPS   The canoes represent one of three ways to see the same territory. Since the canoes and keelboats are slower loading, we usually opt for the large riverboat. If you are not up for a boat ride, a different view of the same sights can be had hoofing around Tom Sawyer Island and Ft. Sam Clemens.

Frontierland Shootin' Gallery

Type of Attraction: Electronic shooting gallery

When to Go: Whenever convenient

Special Comments: Costs 25 cents per play

Author's Rating: A very nifty shooting gallery; ★★★½

Overall Appeal by Age Group:

Pre-school	Grade School	Teens	Young Adults	Over 30	Senior Citizens
★★★½	★★★½	★★★½	★★★½	★★★½	★★★½

DESCRIPTION AND COMMENTS   A very elaborate shooting gallery, this is one of the few attractions not included in the Magic Kingdom admission.

TOURING TIPS   Good fun for them "what likes to shoot," but definitely not a place to be blowing your time if you are on a tight schedule. Try it on your second day if time allows.

Walt Disney World Railroad

DESCRIPTION AND COMMENTS   The Walt Disney World Railroad stops in Frontierland on its circle-tour around the park. See the description of the Walt Disney World Railroad under Main Street for additional detail regarding the sights enroute.

TOURING TIPS   A pleasant and feet-saving way to commute to Main Street and Mickey's Starland. Be advised, however, that the Frontierland Station is usually more congested than its two counterparts.

Frontierland Eateries and Shops

DESCRIPTION AND COMMENTS   Coonskin caps and western-theme specialty shopping, along with fast-food eateries that are usually very crowded between 11:30 A.M. and 2 P.M.

TOURING TIPS   Don't waste time browsing shops or standing in line for food unless you have a very relaxed schedule or came specifically to shop.

Liberty Square

Liberty Square recreates the atmosphere of Colonial America at the time of the American Revolution. Architecture is Federal or Colonial, with a real 130-year-old live oak (dubbed the "Liberty Tree") lending dignity and grace to the setting.

Hall of Presidents

Type of Show: AudioAnimatronic historical presentation
When to Go: Anytime
Author's Rating: Impressive and moving; ★★★★
Overall Appeal by Age Group:

Pre- school	Grade School	Teens	Young Adults	Over 30	Senior Citizens
★	★★★	★★★	★★★½	★★★★	★★★★

Duration of Presentation: Almost 23 minutes
Pre-Show Entertainment: None
Probable Waiting Time: Lines for this attraction LOOK awesome but are usually swallowed up as the theater turns over. If you go during the times suggested above, your wait will probably be the remaining time of the show that's in progress when you arrive. Even during the busiest times of the day, however, waits rarely exceed 40 minutes.

DESCRIPTION AND COMMENTS   A 20-minute strongly inspirational and patriotic program highlighting milestones in American history. The performance climaxes with a roll call of presidents from Washington through the present, with a few words of encouragement from President Lincoln. A very moving show coupled with one of Disney's best and most ambitious AudioAnimatronics (robotic) efforts.

TOURING TIPS   Definitely a "not to be missed" attraction. The detail and costume of the chief executives is incredible, and if your children tend to fidget during the show, take notice of the fact that the Presidents do, too. This attraction is one of the most popular, particularly among older visitors, and draws large crowds from 11 A.M. through about 5 P.M. Do not be dismayed by the lines, however. The theater holds more than 700 people, thus swallowing up large lines at a single gulp when visitors are admitted. One show is always in progress while the lobby is being filled for the next show. At less than busy times you will probably be admitted directly to the lobby without waiting in line. When the waiting lobby fills, those remaining in line outside are held in place until those in the lobby move into the theater just prior to the next show, at which time another 700 people from the outside line are admitted to the lobby.

Liberty Square Riverboat

Type of Ride: Scenic boat ride

When to Go: Anytime

Author's Rating: Provides an excellent vantage point; ★★★

Overall Appeal by Age Group:

Pre-school	Grade School	Teens	Young Adults	Over 30	Senior Citizens
★★★	★★★	★★½	★★★	★★★	★★★

Duration of Ride: About 16 minutes

Average Wait to Board: 10–14 minutes

Assumes: Normal operations

DESCRIPTION AND COMMENTS   Large-capacity paddle wheel riverboat that navigates the waters around Tom Sawyer Island and Ft. Sam Clemens. A beautiful craft, the riverboat provides a lofty perspective of Frontierland and Liberty Square.

TOURING TIPS   One of three boat rides that survey the same real estate. Since Davy Crockett's Explorer Canoes and the Mike Fink Keelboats are slower loading, we think the riverboat is the best bet. If you are not in the mood for a boat ride, much of the same sights can be seen by hiking around the island.

Haunted Mansion

Type of Ride: A Disney one-of-its-kind

When to Go: Anytime

Special Comments: Frightens some very small children

Author's Rating: Some of Walt Disney World's best special
   effects; ★★★★★

Overall Appeal by Age Group:

Pre-school	Grade School	Teens	Young Adults	Over 30	Senior Citizens
Varies	★★★★★	★★★★½	★★★★½	★★★★½	★★★★½

Duration of Ride: 7-minute ride plus a 1½-minute pre-show

Average Wait in Line per 100 People Ahead of You: 2½ minutes

Assumes: Both "stretch rooms" operating

Loading Speed: Fast

DESCRIPTION AND COMMENTS   A fun attraction more than a scary one
with some of the best special effects in the Magic Kingdom. In their
guidebook the Disney people say, "Come face to face with 999 happy
ghosts, ghouls, and goblins in a 'frightfully funny' adventure." That
pretty well sums it up. Be warned that some youngsters become overly
anxious concerning what they think they will see. The actual attraction
scares almost nobody.

TOURING TIPS   This attraction would be more at home in Fantasyland,
but no matter, it's Disney at its best; another "not to be missed" feature. Lines at the Haunted Mansion ebb and flow more than do the lines
of most other Magic Kingdom high spots. This is due to the Mansion's
proximity to the *Hall of Presidents* and the Liberty Square Riverboat.
These two attractions disgorge 750 and 450 people respectively at one
time every time they turn over. Many of these folks head right over
and hop in line at the Haunted Mansion. Try this attraction before noon
and after 4:30 P.M. and make an effort to slip in between crowds.

Mike Fink Keelboats

Type of Ride: Scenic boat ride

When to Go: Before 11:30 A.M. or after 5 P.M.

Special Comments: Don't ride if the lines are long; closes at dusk

Author's Rating: ★★★

Overall Appeal by Age Group:

Pre-school	Grade School	Teens	Young Adults	Over 30	Senior Citizens
★★★½	★★★	★★★	★★★	★★★	★★★

Duration of Ride: 9½ minutes

Average Wait in Line per 100 People Ahead of You: 15 minutes

Assumes: 2 boats operating

Loading Speed: Slow

DESCRIPTION AND COMMENTS   Small river keelboats which circle Tom Sawyer Island and Ft. Sam Clemens, taking the same route as Davy Crockett's Explorer Canoes and the Liberty Square Riverboat. The top deck of the keelboat is exposed to the elements.

TOURING TIPS   This trip covers the same circle traveled by Davy Crockett's Explorer Canoes and the Liberty Square Riverboat. Since the keelboats and the canoes load slowly we prefer the riverboat. Another way to see much of the area covered by the respective boat tours is to explore Tom Sawyer Island and Ft. Sam Clemens on foot.

Liberty Square Eateries and Shops

DESCRIPTION AND COMMENTS   American crafts and souvenir shopping, along with one restaurant, the Liberty Tree Tavern, which is often overlooked by the crowds at lunch.

TOURING TIPS   Although the Liberty Tree Tavern is sometimes less crowded, it frequently falls short in terms of service and food quality.

Fantasyland

Truly an enchanting place, spread gracefully like a miniature Alpine village beneath the lofty towers of Cinderella Castle, Fantasyland is the heart of the Magic Kingdom.

It's a Small World

Type of Ride: Scenic boat ride
When to Go: Between 11 A.M. and 5 P.M.
Author's Rating: A delightful change of pace; ★★★★
Overall Appeal by Age Group:

Pre-school	Grade School	Teens	Young Adults	Over 30	Senior Citizens
★★★★	★★★½	★★★	★★★★	★★★★	★★★★

Duration of Ride: Approximately 11 minutes
Average Wait in Line per 100 People Ahead of You: 1¾ minutes
Assumes: Busy conditions with 30 or more boats operating
Loading Speed: Fast

DESCRIPTION AND COMMENTS   A happy, upbeat attraction with a world brotherhood theme and a catchy tune that will roll around in your head for weeks. Small boats convey visitors on a tour around the world, with singing and dancing dolls showcasing the dress and culture of each nation. Almost everyone enjoys It's a Small World, but it stands, along with the *Enchanted Tiki Birds*, as an attraction that some could take or leave while others think it is one of the real masterpieces of the Magic Kingdom. We rank it as a "not to be missed" attraction. Try it and form your own opinion.

TOURING TIPS   A "not to be missed" attraction, It's a Small World is a fast-loading ride with two waiting lines. Usually a good bet during the busier times of the day.

Skyway to Tomorrowland

Type of Ride: Scenic transportation to Tomorrowland

When to Go: Before noon or during special events

Special Comments: If there's a line, it will probably be quicker to walk

Author's Rating: Nice view; ★★★½

Overall Appeal by Age Group:

Pre-school	Grade School	Teens	Young Adults	Over 30	Senior Citizens
★★★★	★★★★	★★★½	★★★½	★★★½	★★★½

Duration of Ride: Approximately 5 minutes one way

Average Wait in Line per 100 People Ahead of You: 10 minutes

Assumes: 45 or more cars operating

Loading Speed: Moderate to slow

DESCRIPTION AND COMMENTS   Part of the Magic Kingdom internal transportation system, the Skyway is a chairlift that conveys tourists high above the park to Tomorrowland. The view is great, and sometimes the Skyway can even save a little shoe leather. Usually, however, you could arrive in Tomorrowland much faster by walking.

TOURING TIPS   We enjoy this scenic trip in the morning, during the afternoon Character Parade, during an evening Electrical Parade, or just before closing (this ride opens later and closes earlier than other rides in Fantasyland). In short, before the crowds fill the park, when they are otherwise occupied or when they are on the decline. These times also provide the most dramatic and beautiful vistas.

Peter Pan's Flight

Type of Ride: A Disney fantasy adventure

When to Go: Before 11 A.M. or after 6 P.M.

Author's Rating: Happy, mellow and well done; ★★★★★

Overall Appeal by Age Group:

Pre-school	Grade School	Teens	Young Adults	Over 30	Senior Citizens
★★★★	★★★★	★★★½	★★★★	★★★★	★★★★

Duration of Ride: A little over 3 minutes

Average Wait in Line per 100 People Ahead of You: 5½ minutes

Assumes: Normal operation

Loading Speed: Moderate to slow

DESCRIPTION AND COMMENTS   Though not considered to be one of the major attractions, Peter Pan's Flight is superbly designed and absolutely delightful with a happy theme, a reunion with some unforgettable Disney characters, beautiful effects, and charming music.

TOURING TIPS   Though not a major feature of the Magic Kingdom, we nevertheless classify it as "not to be missed." Try to ride before 11 A.M. or after 6 P.M., or during the afternoon Character Parade.

Magic Journeys

Type of Show: 3-D fantasy film

When to Go: Between noon and 4 P.M.

Special Comments: Some small children frightened by the film

Author's Rating: Solid production; ★★★★

Overall Appeal by Age Group:

Pre-school	Grade School	Teens	Young Adults	Over 30	Senior Citizens
★★★★	★★★★	★★★½	★★★★	★★★★	★★★★

Duration of Presentation: Approximately 17 minutes

Pre-Show Entertainment: 3-D cartoons

Probable Waiting Time: 12 minutes

DESCRIPTION AND COMMENTS   This delightful film was exported to Fantasyland from EPCOT Center when *Captain EO* arrived. A long-time favorite, *Magic Journeys* appeals to all ages. The production is solid, the theme happy and upbeat, and the 3-D effects incredible. All over the theater, children (and many adults) reach out involuntarily to grab objects which seem to be floating out from the screen. The story is about a group of children and their flights of imagination.

TOURING TIPS   We recommend seeing this film during the heat of the day when 20 minutes of relaxing in an air-conditioned theater might improve your attitude. There is almost never a line for this fine attraction.

Cinderella's Golden Carrousel

Type of Ride: Merry-go-round

When to Go: Before 11 A.M. or after 6 P.M.

Special Comments: Adults enjoy beauty and nostalgia of this ride

Author's Rating: A beautiful children's ride; ★★★

Overall Appeal by Age Group:

Pre-school	Grade School	Teens	Young Adults	Over 30	Senior Citizens
★★★★	★★½	★	★★½	★★★	★★★

Duration of Ride: Approximately 2 minutes

Average Wait in Line per 100 People Ahead of You: 5 minutes

Assumes: Normal staffing

Loading Speed: Slow

DESCRIPTION AND COMMENTS   A merry-go-round to be sure, but certainly one of the most elaborate and beautiful you will ever see, especially when the lights are on.

TOURING TIPS   Unless there are small children in your party we suggest you appreciate this ride from the sidelines. If your children insist on riding, try to get on before 11 A.M. or after 6 P.M. While nice to look at, the Carrousel loads and unloads very slowly.

Mr. Toad's Wild Ride

Type of Ride: Disney version of a spook house track ride

When to Go: Before 11 A.M. or after 6 P.M.

Author's Rating: Just O.K.; ★★½

Overall Appeal by Age Group:

Pre-school	Grade School	Teens	Young Adults	Over 30	Senior Citizens
★★★½	★★★½	★★★	★★½	★★½	★★½

Duration of Ride: About 2¼ minutes

Average Wait in Line per 100 People Ahead of You: 5½ minutes

Assumes: Both tracks operating

Loading Speed: Slow

DESCRIPTION AND COMMENTS   This is an amusement park spook house that does not live up to most visitors' expectations or to the Disney reputation for high quality. The facade is intriguing; the size of the building which houses the attraction suggests an elaborate ride. As it happens, the building is cut in half with similar, though not exactly identical, versions of the same ride in both halves. There is, of course, a separate line for each half.

TOURING TIPS   We receive a lot of mail disagreeing with our critical appraisal of this ride. Clearly, Mr. Toad has his advocates. If you are on a tight schedule, we do not suggest waiting very long for Mr. Toad. If you have two days allotted for the Magic Kingdom, or just want to add your opinion to the controversy, go ahead and ride. If you want to be a supertoad, be sure to try both sides.

Snow White's Scary Adventures

Type of Ride: Disney version of a spook house track ride
When to Go: Before 11 A.M. and after 6 P.M.
Special Comments: Not really very scary
Author's Rating: Worth seeing if the wait is not long; ★★★
Overall Appeal by Age Group:

Pre-school	Grade School	Teens	Young Adults	Over 30	Senior Citizens
★★★	★★★	★★½	★★★	★★★	★★★

Duration of Ride: Almost 2½ minutes
Average Wait in Line per 100 People Ahead of You: 6¼ minutes
Assumes: Normal operation
Loading Speed: Moderate to slow

DESCRIPTION AND COMMENTS   Here you ride in a mining car through a spook house featuring Snow White as she narrowly escapes harm at the hands of the wicked witch. The action and effects are a cut above Mr. Toad's Wild Ride but not as good as Peter Pan's Flight.

TOURING TIPS   This ride is not great, but it is good. Experience it if the lines are not too long or on a second day visit. Ride before 11 A.M. or after 6 P.M. if possible. Also, don't take the "Scary" part too seriously. The witch looks mean but most kids take her in stride.

20,000 Leagues Under the Sea

Type of Ride: Adventure/scenic boat ride
When to Go: Before 10 A.M. or during the hour before the park closes
Author's Rating: Interesting and fun; ★★★

Overall Appeal by Age Group:

Pre-school	Grade School	Teens	Young Adults	Over 30	Senior Citizens
★★★★	★★★★	★★★	★★★	★★★	★★★½

Duration of Ride: Approximately 8½ minutes

Average Wait in Line per 100 People Ahead of You: 8 minutes

Assumes: 9 submarines operating

Loading Speed: Slow

DESCRIPTION AND COMMENTS   This attraction is based on the Disney movie of the same title. One of several rides that have been successful at both Disneyland (California) and the Magic Kingdom, the ride consists of a submarine voyage which encounters ocean-floor farming, various marine life (robotic), sunken ships, giant squid attacks, and other sights and adventures. An older ride, it struggles to maintain its image along with such marvels as Pirates of the Caribbean or Space Mountain. A reader from Hawthorne Woods, Illinois, writes:

> The only ride that I would not rate as highly as you was 20,000 Leagues Under the Sea. The lines were really slow moving and the ride was not nearly as imaginative as some of the others. I almost felt like we were riding through a concrete ditch with plastic fish on strings and coral stuck around the ditch for effect.

Another reader from Pittsburgh made this comment:

> At 20,000 Leagues Under the Sea, lines were long all day, and Grandma (who loves Disney World) said it was stupid.

TOURING TIPS   This ride could be renamed "20,000 Bottlenecks Under the Sun." It is the traffic engineering nightmare of the Magic Kingdom. Even 15 minutes after opening, there are long lines and 20- to 30-minute waits. The problem is mainly due to the fact that this slow-loading boat ride is brought up to maximum carrying capacity (nine subs) very tardily. Ride operators fall behind almost as soon as the park opens and never seem to clear the backlog. If you are a Space Mountain fan, make 20,000 Leagues your second stop. If you do not want to ride Space Mountain, ride 20,000 Leagues first thing when the park opens.

Dumbo, the Flying Elephant

Type of Ride: Disneyfied midway ride
When to Go: Before 10 A.M. and after 5 P.M.
Author's Rating: An attractive children's ride; ★★★½
Overall Appeal by Age Group:

Pre-school	Grade School	Teens	Young Adults	Over 30	Senior Citizens
★★★★★	★★★★	★★	★½	★½	★½

Duration of Ride: 1½ minutes
Average Wait in Line per 100 People Ahead of You: 20 minutes
Assumes: Normal staffing
Loading Speed: Slow

DESCRIPTION AND COMMENTS   A nice, tame, happy children's ride based on the lovable Disney flying elephant, Dumbo. An upgraded rendition of a ride that can be found at state fairs and amusement parks across the country. This notwithstanding, Dumbo is the favorite Magic Kingdom attraction of many younger children.

TOURING TIPS   This is a slow-loading ride that we recommend you bypass unless you are on a very relaxed touring schedule. If your kids are excited about Dumbo, try to get them on the ride before 10 A.M. or just before the park closes.

Mad Tea Party

Type of Ride: Midway-type spinning ride
When to Go: Before 11:30 A.M. and after 5 P.M.
Special Comments: You can make the tea cups spin faster by turning the wheel in the center of the cup.
Author's Rating: Fun, but not worth the wait; ★★
Overall Appeal by Age Group:

Pre-school	Grade School	Teens	Young Adults	Over 30	Senior Citizens
★★★★	★★★★	★★★★	★★½	★★	★★

Duration of Ride: 1½ minutes
Average Wait in Line per 100 People Ahead of You: 7½ minutes
Assumes: Normal staffing

Loading Speed: Slow

DESCRIPTION AND COMMENTS   Well done in the Disney style, but still just an amusement-park ride. The Alice in Wonderland Mad Hatter provides the theme and riders whirl around feverishly in big tea cups. A rendition of this ride, sans Disney characters, can be found at every local carnival and fair.

TOURING TIPS   This ride, aside from not being particularly unique, is notoriously slow loading. Skip it on a busy schedule if the kids will let you. Ride in the morning of your second day if your schedule is more relaxed.

Fantasyland Eateries and Shops

DESCRIPTION AND COMMENTS   If you prefer atmosphere with your dining, you can (with reservations) eat in Cinderella Castle at King Stefan's Banquet Hall. Many of the Magic Kingdom visitors we surveyed wanted to know "What is in the castle?" or "Can we go up into the castle?" Well, Virginia, you can't see the whole thing, but if you eat at King Stefan's you can inspect a fair-sized chunk.

Shops here present more specialty and souvenir shopping opportunities.

TOURING TIPS   To eat at King Stefan's in the castle you must have reservations. If you are lodging in Walt Disney World you can call (407) 828-4000 one to three days in advance to make reservations. If not, make reservations first thing in the morning at the door of the restaurant. We do not recommend a meal at King Stefan's if you are on a tight schedule or if you are sensitive about paying fancy prices for ho-hum food. If you plan to spend two days in the Magic Kingdom and you are curious about the inside of the castle, you might give it a try on your second day. Don't waste time in the shops unless you have a relaxed schedule or unless shopping is a big priority.

Mickey's Starland

Mickey's Starland is the first new "land" to be added to the Magic Kingdom since its opening, and the only land that does not connect to the central hub. Attractions include a live musical stage show featuring the Disney characters, a chance to meet Mickey Mouse, Mickey Mouse's house, a town (Duckburg) of miniature buildings, a petting farm, and a young children's play area.

All in all, as Whoopi Goldberg might say, Mickey's Starland is a strange piece of work. To begin with, it is sandwiched between Fantasyland and Tomorrowland, like an afterthought, on about three acres that were formerly part of the Grand Prix Raceway. It is by far the smallest of the "lands" and seems more like an attraction than a section of the park. Though you can wander in on a somewhat obscure path from Fantasyland, Mickey's Starland is basically set up to receive guests arriving via the Walt Disney World Railroad.

Once you arrive at Mickey's Starland (which is located in the town of Duckburg), there is no indication of where or when the character show takes place. What you see as you leave the train station is a children's play area on your left, and a street of miniature buildings on your right. There is one normally sized house (Mickey's) among the little buildings, with a cluster of what looks like circus tents puffing up colorfully behind. To see the show, go through Mickey's house and watch cartoons in the holding area until showtime.

Mickey's Magical T.V. World

Type of Show: Live musical comedy featuring the Disney characters

When to Go: Between 11 A.M. and 5 P.M.

Special Comments: After the show, guests can meet Mickey backstage at Mickey's Hollywood Theater

Author's Rating: Warm, happy, funny and all Disney; ★★★★

Overall Appeal by Age Group:

Pre-school	Grade School	Teens	Young Adults	Over 30	Senior Citizens
★★★★★	★★★★★	★★★½	★★★★	★★★★	★★★★

Duration of Presentation: Approximately 14 minutes
Pre-Show Entertainment: Mickey Mouse cartoons
Probable Waiting Time: About 10 minutes

DESCRIPTION AND COMMENTS *Mickey's Magical T.V. World*, the feature attraction of Mickey's Starland, is reached by walking through Mickey's House (which is full of Mickey Mouse and Walt Disney memorabilia), through Mickey's backyard, and into an air-conditioned, pre-show tent where Mickey Mouse cartoons are viewed on TV monitors. During the summer of 1990, most patrons who found their way this far had no idea that there was anything more to see. They watched cartoons for a few minutes and then turned around and walked out. Had they stayed, they would have been treated to a funny, happy, and energetic live stage show featuring the Disney characters.

After the show, guests pass through a gift shop and photo opportunity area. As you exit outside, Mickey's Hollywood Theater is on the right. Here Mickey receives visitors in his dressing room to pose for photographs. This is a nice touch, but as with the party, this business of meeting Mickey in person backstage is never made very clear. For the most part, folks just walk into Mickey's Hollywood Theater and line up, not knowing what the line is for.

TOURING TIPS There is no problem catching a performance of *Mickey's Magical T.V. World* once you know it's there and how to get to it. We recommend seeing the show during the hot, early afternoon hours when a few minutes in a nice, air-conditioned theater is relaxing. If you want to meet Mickey backstage without a lot of waiting, try one of the following:

1. In the waiting area for the character show (a tentlike structure with Mickey Mouse cartoons on T.V.), position yourself in front of the farthest left of several doors leading to the theater. When admitted you will proceed down a long passageway to another set of doors. Again try to be in front and on the left. When finally admitted to the actual theater, you will enter a row of seats and move all the way to the far end. At this point you should be positioned perfectly to duck out of the theater as soon as the curtain

falls. When the time comes, hustle out the door to your immediate left, pass quickly through the post-show area, and go outside. Mickey's Hollywood Theater will be on your right and several hundred other guests will be 30 steps behind you and headed for the same place. Or;

2. Enjoy the petting farm or walk around Duckburg for about 15 minutes after exiting the show. Line up to see Mickey just before the show following yours concludes; this is when the line will be shortest. A lady from Pittsburgh wrote suggesting:

You might want to mention that only a few people are let into Mickey's dressing room at a time—maybe four small family groups. When they are done, the next batch comes in. So it's more intimate than, say, seeing Santa at the mall. By the way, Mickey autographed our *Unofficial Guide*, shaking his head sadly, and underlining "unofficial" several times, both on the cover and on the frontispiece.

—— *Other Mickey's Starland Attractions* ——

Grandma Duck's Petting Farm

Type of Attraction: Walk-through petting farm
When to Go: Anytime
Special Comments: Animals are real
Author's Rating: Could use more animals; ★½
Overall Appeal by Age Group:

Pre-school	Grade School	Teens	Young Adults	Over 30	Senior Citizens
★★★	★★★	★½	★½	★½	★½

DESCRIPTION AND COMMENTS   A modest barn and farm with a dozen or so animals. Unlike most petting farms, this one does not let you walk among the animals (goats, pigs, ducks, chickens, calves, etc.). You must pet them when possible through fences. Much of the attraction is along gravel paths, which make walking very difficult.

TOURING TIPS   Visit the animals any time. You will not encounter large crowds here, as a rule.

Small Children's Play Area

DESCRIPTION AND COMMENTS   This area is designed for small children and features slides, tunnels, ladders, and a variety of other creative playground structures. Children enjoy the chance to let off steam while adults enjoy the tour intermission. The big shortcoming is the lack of shade; attending adults must swelter in the hot Florida sun.

TOURING TIPS   If you are on a tight schedule, skip the playground.

Tomorrowland

Tomorrowland is a futuristic mix of rides and experiences that relate to the technological development of man and what life will be like in the years to come. If this sounds a little bit like the EPCOT Center theme, it's because Tomorrowland was very much a breeding ground for the ideas that resulted in EPCOT Center. Yet Tomorrowland and EPCOT Center are very different. Aside from differences in scale, Tomorrowland is more "just for fun." While EPCOT Center educates in its own delightful style, Tomorrowland allows you to hop in and try the future on for size.

Space Mountain

Type of Ride: Roller coaster in the dark

When to Go: First thing when the park opens or during the hour before closing or between 6 and 7 P.M.

Special Comments: Great fun and action, much wilder than Big Thunder Mountain. Children must be 3'8″ tall to ride, and if under seven years old, must be accompanied by an adult.

Author's Rating: A great roller coaster with excellent special effects; ★★★★★

Overall Appeal by Age Group:

Pre-school	Grade School	Teens	Young Adults	Over 30	Senior Citizens
†	★★★★★	★★★★★	★★★★½	★★★★	†

†Some preschoolers loved Space Mountain, others were frightened. The sample size of senior citizens who experienced this ride was too small to develop an accurate rating.

Duration of Ride: Almost 3 minutes

Average Wait in Line per 100 People Ahead of You: 3 minutes

Assumes: Two tracks operating at 21-second dispatch intervals

Loading Speed: Moderate to fast

DESCRIPTION AND COMMENTS   Space Mountain is a roller coaster in the dark. Totally enclosed in a mammoth futuristic structure, the attraction is a marvel of creativity and engineering. The theme of the ride is a spaceflight through the dark recesses of the galaxy. The effects are superb and the ride is the fastest and wildest in the Disney repertoire. As a roller coaster, Space Mountain is a lulu, much zippier than the Big Thunder Mountain ride.

TOURING TIPS   Space Mountain is a "not to be missed" feature (if you can handle a fairly wild roller coaster ride). People who are not timid about going on roller coasters will take Space Mountain in stride. What sets Space Mountain apart is that the cars plummet through the dark with only occasional lighting effects piercing the gloom.

Space Mountain is the favorite attraction of many Magic Kingdom visitors between seven and fifty years of age. Each morning prior to opening, particularly during the summer and holiday periods, several hundred S.M. "junkies" crowd the rope barriers at the central hub awaiting the signal to sprint (literally) the 250 yards to the ride's entrance. As our research team called it, the "Space Mountain Morning Mini Marathon" pits tubby, out-of-shape dads and moms against their svelte, speedy offspring, brother against sister, blossoming co-eds against truck drivers, nuns against beauticians. If you want to ride Space Mountain without a long wait you had better do well in the "Mini Marathon," because at five minutes after opening, Space Mountain has more guests in line waiting to ride than any five other Magic Kingdom attractions combined.

There was a time when Disney personnel tried to keep guests from running (they still tell you not to run) to Space Mountain, but even in the Magic Kingdom reality is a force to be reckoned with. The reality in this case is that a dozen Disney security personnel cannot control several hundred stampeding, flipped-out, early-morning space cadets. So here you are, a nice normal dental hygienist from Toledo, and you are thinking you'd like to ride Space Mountain. Well Virginia, you're in the big league now; tie up them Reeboks and get ready to run.

But first, a word from the coach. There are a couple of things you can do to get a leg up on the competition. First, arrive early; be one of the first in the park. Proceed to the end of Main Street and cut right past the Plaza Restaurant, and stop under an archway that says:

"The Plaza Pavilion Terrace Dining"

where a Disney worker will be standing behind a rope barrier. From this point, you are approximately 100 yards closer to Space Mountain, on a route through the Plaza Pavilion, than your competition waiting to take off from the central hub. From this point of departure, middle-aged folks walking fast can beat most of the teens sprinting from the central hub. And if you are up to some modest jogging, well . . . . Another advantage of starting from the Plaza Pavilion entrance is that your wait until opening will be cool, comfortable, and in the shade.

Couples touring with children too small to ride Space Mountain can both ride without waiting in line twice by taking advantage of a procedure called "switching off." Here is how it works. When you enter the Space Mountain line alert the first Disney attendant (known as Greeter One) that you want to switch off. The attendant will allow you, your spouse, and your small child (or children) to continue together, phoning ahead to Greeter Two to expect you. When you reach Greeter Two (at the turnstile near the boarding area), you will be given specific directions. One of you will go ahead and ride while the other stays with the kids. Whoever rides will be admitted by the unloading attendant to stairs leading back up to the boarding area. Here you switch off; the second parent rides, and the first parent takes the kids down the stairs to the unloading area where everybody joins up and exits. Switching off is also allowed on the Big Thunder Mountain Railroad.

If you do not catch Space Mountain early in the morning, try again during the hour before closing. Often at this time of day, Space Mountain visitors are held in line outside the entrance until all those previously in line have ridden, thus emptying the attraction inside. The appearance from the outside is that the waiting line is enormous when, in reality, the only people waiting are those visible in front of the entrance. This crowd-control technique, known as "stacking," has the effect of discouraging visitors from riding because they perceive the wait to be too long. Stacking is used in several Walt Disney World rides and attractions during the hour before closing to insure that the ride will be able to close on schedule. For those who do not let the long-appearing line run them off, the waiting period is usually short.

Grand Prix Raceway

Type of Ride: Drive-'em-yourself miniature cars
When to Go: Before 11 A.M. and after 5 P.M.
Special Comments: Must be 4'4" tall to drive
Author's Rating: Boring; ★
Overall Appeal by Age Group:

Pre-school	Grade School	Teens	Young Adults	Over 30	Senior Citizens
★★★½	★★★	★	½	½	½

Duration of Ride: Approximately 4¼ minutes

Average Wait in Line per 100 People Ahead of You: 4½ minutes

Assumes: 285-car turnover every 20 minutes

Loading Speed: Slow

DESCRIPTION AND COMMENTS   An elaborate miniature raceway with gasoline-powered cars that will travel at speeds of up to seven miles an hour. The raceway design with its sleek cars, racing noises, and Grand Prix billboards is quite alluring. Unfortunately, however, the cars poke along on a track leaving the driver with little to do. Pretty ho-hum for most adults and teenagers. Of those children who would enjoy the ride, many are excluded by the requirement that drivers be 4′4″ tall.

TOURING TIPS   This ride is appealing to the eye but definitely expendable to the schedule. Try it your second day if the kids are reluctant to omit it. Ride before 11 A.M. or after 5 P.M.

Skyway to Fantasyland

Type of Ride: Scenic transportation to Fantasyland

When to Go: Before noon and during special events

Special Comments: If a line, probably quicker to walk

Author's Rating: Nice view; ★★★½

Overall Appeal by Age Group:

Pre-school	Grade School	Teens	Young Adults	Over 30	Senior Citizens
★★★★	★★★★	★★★½	★★★½	★★★½	★★★½

Duration of Ride: Approximately 5 minutes one way

Average Wait in Line per 100 People Ahead of You: 10 minutes

Assumes: 45 or more cars operating

Loading Speed: Moderate

DESCRIPTION AND COMMENTS   A skylift that will transport you from Tomorrowland to the far corner of Fantasyland near the border it shares with Liberty Square. The view is one of the best in the Magic Kingdom, but walking is usually faster if you just want to get there.

TOURING TIPS   Unless the lines are short, the Skyway will not save you any time as a mode of transportation. As a ride, however, it affords some incredible views. Ride in the morning, during the two hours before the park closes, or during one of the daily parades (this ride sometimes opens later and closes earlier than other rides in Tomorrowland).

StarJets

Type of Ride: Very mild midway-type thrill ride

When to Go: Before 11 A.M. or after 5 P.M.

Author's Rating: Not worth the wait; ★

Overall Appeal by Age Group:

Pre-school	Grade School	Teens	Young Adults	Over 30	Senior Citizens
★★★★	★★★	★★½	★½	★	★

Duration of Ride: 1½ minutes

Average Wait in Line per 100 People Ahead of You: 13½ minutes

Assumes: Normal staffing

Loading Speed: Slow

DESCRIPTION AND COMMENTS   A carnival-type ride involving small rockets which rotate on arms around a central axis.

TOURING TIPS   Slow loading and expendable on any schedule.

WEDway PeopleMover

Type of Ride: Scenic

When to Go: During the hot, crowded period of the day (11:30 A.M.–4:30 P.M.)

Special Comments: A good way to check out the crowd at Space Mountain

Author's Rating: Scenic, relaxing, informative; ★★★½

Overall Appeal by Age Group:

Pre-school	Grade School	Teens	Young Adults	Over 30	Senior Citizens
★★★	★★★	★★½	★★★	★★★½	★★★½

Duration of Ride: 10 minutes

Average Wait in Line per 100 People Ahead of You: 1½ minutes
Assumes: 39 trains operating
Loading Speed: Fast

DESCRIPTION AND COMMENTS   A unique prototype of a linear induction powered system of mass transportation. Tram-like cars take you on a leisurely tour of Tomorrowland, including a peek at the inside of Space Mountain.

TOURING TIPS   A nice, pleasant, relaxing ride where the lines move quickly and are seldom long. A good ride to take during the busier times of the day.

Carousel of Progress

Type of Show: AudioAnimatronic theater production
When to Go: Between 11:30 A.M. and 4 P.M.
Author's Rating: Nostalgic, warm and happy; ★★★★½
Overall Appeal by Age Group:

Pre-school	Grade School	Teens	Young Adults	Over 30	Senior Citizens
★★★	★★★½	★★★½	★★★½	★★★★½	★★★★½

Duration of Presentation: 18 minutes
Pre-Show Entertainment: None
Probable Waiting Time: Less than 10 minutes

DESCRIPTION AND COMMENTS   This is a warm and nostalgic look at the way technology and electricity have changed the lives of an Audio-Animatronics family over several generations. Though not rating a "not to be missed" review, General Electric's *Carousel of Progress* is thoroughly delightful. The family depicted is easy to identify with, and a happy, sentimental tune (which you will find yourself humming all day) serves to bridge the gap between generations.

TOURING TIPS   While not on our "not to be missed" list, this attraction is a great favorite of Magic Kingdom repeat visitors. A great favorite of ours as well, it is included on all of our One-Day Touring Plans. *Carousel of Progress* handles big crowds effectively and is a good choice for touring during the busier times of the day.

Dreamflight

Type of Ride: Special-effects travel ride
When to go: Between 11:30 A.M. and 4:30 P.M.
Author's Rating: Pleasant; ★★★
Projected Overall Appeal by Age Group:

Pre-school	Grade School	Teens	Young Adults	Over 30	Senior Citizens
★★★	★★★	★★★	★★★	★★★	★★★

Duration of Ride: About 6 minutes
Average Wait in Line per 100 People Ahead of You: 3 minutes
Assumes: Normal operation

DESCRIPTION AND COMMENTS: Presented by Delta Airlines, Dreamflight is a somewhat fanciful depiction of the history of flight. Pleasant but not particularly compelling, this new addition to the Tomorrowland lineup could have been a lot more interesting. Having a bit of the feel of Peter Pan's Flight mixed with a very EPCOT Center style of presentation, Dreamflight is best characterized as "nice."

TOURING TIPS   Very seldom is there a line at Dreamflight. See it during the heat of the day or whenever the mood strikes.

World Premier Circle-Vision: American Journeys

Type of Show: Patriotic travelog projected onto multiple screens
When to Go: During the hot, crowded period of the day (11:30 A.M.– 4 P.M.
Special Comments: Audience must stand throughout presentation
Author's Rating: Wonderful; not to be missed; ★★★★½
Overall Appeal by Age Group:

Pre-school	Grade School	Teens	Young Adults	Over 30	Senior Citizens
★★	★★★½	★★★★	★★★★½	★★★★★	★★★★★

Duration of Presentation: About 20 minutes
Pre-Show Entertainment: About 10 minutes
Probable Waiting Time: Less than 10 minutes

DESCRIPTION AND COMMENTS   Here the visitor stands in the center of a huge theater where multiple projectors make an encircling 360°

screen come alive. It's another trip around the world, but this time you not only see where you are going, but what's on either side, and what's behind you. The movie, which demonstrates this cinematic marvel, is fast paced, well produced, and very much deserving of your attention. More than a travelog, *American Journeys* takes you down the awesome rapids of the Colorado River, on a surfing expedition in Hawaii, and in close for a space-shuttle blast-off.

TOURING TIPS   An excellent film and an exciting new motion picture technique make this an attraction you will want to see. The theater has the largest single-room capacity of any theater in the Magic Kingdom, making it a perfect show to see during peak attendance hours.

Mission To Mars

Type of Show: Theater-in-the-round simulation of space journey
When to Go: During the hot, crowded period of the day (11 A.M.– 4:30 P.M.)
Special Comments: Special effects sometimes frighten toddlers
Author's Rating: Worthwhile; ★★★
Overall Appeal by Age Group:

Pre-school	Grade School	Teens	Young Adults	Over 30	Senior Citizens
★★	★★½	★★½	★★★	★★★	★★★

Duration of Presentation: About 12 minutes
Pre-Show Entertainment: About 6 minutes
Probable Waiting Time: Less than 10 minutes

DESCRIPTION AND COMMENTS   Here the visitor takes a simulated space shuttle flight from earth to Mars. The voyage is both dramatic and educational, with realistic special effects.

TOURING TIPS   A long-enduring Magic Kingdom favorite (formerly Spaceflight to the Moon), this attraction still demands attention. Try to see *Mission to Mars* during the hot crowded period of the day.

Tomorrowland Eateries and Shops

DESCRIPTION AND COMMENTS   The Tomorrowland Terrace is the largest and most efficient of the Magic Kingdom's numerous fast-food restaurants.

Several shops provide yet additional opportunities for buying souvenirs and curiosities.

TOURING TIPS Forget browsing the shops until your second day unless shopping is your top priority.

Not to Be Missed at the Magic Kingdom

Adventureland	Jungle Cruise
	Pirates of the Caribbean
Frontierland	Big Thunder Mountain Railroad
	Country Bear Jamboree
	Diamond Horseshoe Jamboree
Liberty Square	*Hall of Presidents*
	The Haunted Mansion
Fantasyland	It's a Small World
	Peter Pan's Flight
Tomorrowland	Space Mountain
Special events	Main Street Electrical Parade

Live Entertainment in the Magic Kingdom

Live entertainment in the form of bands, Disney character appearances, parades, singing and dancing, and ceremonies further enliven and add color to the Magic Kingdom on a daily basis. For specific information about what's going on the day you visit, stop by City Hall as you enter the park. Be forewarned, however, that if you are on a tight schedule, it is impossible to see both the Magic Kingdom's featured attractions **and** take in the numerous and varied live performances offered. In our One-Day Touring Plans we exclude the live performances in favor of seeing as much of the park as time permits. This is a considered, tactical decision based on the fact that some of the parades and other performances siphon crowds away from the more popular rides, thus shortening waiting lines.

But the color and pageantry of live happenings around the park are an integral part of the Magic Kingdom entertainment mix and a persuasive argument for second-day touring. The following is an incomplete list and description of those performances and events that are scheduled with some regularity and for which no reservations are required.

Fantasy Faire Stage	Site of various concerts in Fantasyland.
Steel Drum Bands	Steel drum bands perform daily at the Caribbean Plaza in Adventureland.
Frontierland Stuntmen	Stuntmen stage shootouts in Frontierland according to the daily live entertainment schedule.
Kids of the Kingdom	A youthful song and dance group which performs popular music daily in the Castle Forecourt. Disney characters usually join in the fun.
Flag Retreat	Daily at 5 P.M. at Town Square (the railroad station end of Main Street). Sometimes done

with great fanfare and college marching bands, sometimes with a smaller Disney band.

Main Street Parade	A parade down Main Street and around the central hub featuring marching bands, old-time vehicles, floats, and the Disney characters. Check with City Hall for the parade schedule.
The Main Street Electrical Parade	An elaborated version of the Main Street Parade with thirty floats, more than one hundred performers, and "a million twinkling lights," according to Disney spokesmen. The Electrical Parade is performed twice on holidays and on days when the park is open until midnight, usually at 9 P.M. and 11 P.M.
Bay Lake and Seven Seas Lagoon Floating Electrical Pageant	This is one of our favorites of all the Disney extras, but you have to leave the Magic Kingdom to see it. The Floating Electrical Pageant is a stunning electric light show afloat on small barges and set to nifty electronic music. The Pageant is performed at nightfall on the Seven Seas Lagoon and on Bay Lake. Exit the Magic Kingdom and take the monorail to the Contemporary Resort Hotel or to the Polynesian Village. Proceed to get yourself a drink and have a seat at the waterfront; the show will begin shortly.
Fantasy in the Sky	A stellar fireworks display unleashed after dark on those nights the park is open late.
Tomorrowland Terrace Stage & Tomorrowland Theater	These stages in Tomorrowland feature top-40 rock music, rap, and jazz, as well as Disney characters and the Kids of the Kingdom.
Disney Character Shows & Appearances	On busy days, a character *du jour* is on duty for photo posing 9 A.M. until 10 P.M. next to City Hall. Disney character shows run back-to-back at Mickey's Starland from 9:40 A.M. until 9:30 P.M. (when the park is open late). Shows at the Castle Forecourt Stage (front of the castle) feature the Disney characters several times a day according to the daily entertainment schedule, as do shows in the Tomorrow-

	land Theater. Finally, characters roam the park throughout the day, but can almost always be found in Fantasyland and Mickey's Starland.
Magic Kingdom Bands	Various banjo, dixieland, steel drum, marching, and fife and drum bands roam the Magic Kingdom daily.
Tinkerbell's Flight	A nice special effect in the sky above Cinderella Castle at 10 P.M. to herald the beginning of Fantasy in the Sky fireworks (when the park is open late).

Eating in the Magic Kingdom

The Magic Kingdom is a wonder and a marvel, a testimony to the creative genius of man. But for all of the beauty, imagination, and wholesomeness of this incredible place, it is almost impossible to get a really good meal. Simply put, what is available is that same computerized, homogenized fare that languishes beneath the heat lamps of every fast-food chain restaurant in America. Logistically we are sympathetic; it is overwhelming to contemplate preparing and serving 130,000-or-so meals each day. But our understanding, unfortunately, does not make the food any more palatable. Do not misunderstand, the food at the Magic Kingdom is not awful. It is merely mediocre in a place that has set the standard in virtually every other area for quality in tourism and entertainment. Given the challenge of feeding so many people each day, we might be more accepting of the bland fare if (1) we didn't believe the Disney people could do better, and if (2) obtaining food didn't require such an investment of time and effort. The variety found on the numerous menus indicates that somebody once had the right idea.

—— Alternatives and Suggestions for Eating in the Magic Kingdom ——

Remember, this discussion is about the Magic Kingdom. EPCOT Center and the Disney-MGM Studios are treated separately under a similar heading beginning on pages 201 and 253.

1. Eat a good breakfast before arriving at the Magic Kingdom. You do not want to waste touring time eating breakfast at the park. Besides, there are some truly outstanding breakfast specials at restaurants outside of Walt Disney World.

2. Having eaten a good breakfast, keep your tummy happy as you tour by purchasing snacks from the many vendors stationed

throughout the Magic Kingdom. This is especially important if you have a tight schedule; you cannot afford to spend a lot of time waiting in line for food.

3. If you are on a tight schedule and the park closes early, stay until closing and eat dinner outside of Walt Disney World before returning to your hotel. If the Magic Kingdom stays open late, eat an early dinner at about 4 P.M. or 4:30 P.M. in the Magic Kingdom eatery of your choice. You should have missed the last wave of lunch diners and sneaked in just ahead of the dinner crowd.

4. Take the monorail to one of the resort hotels for lunch. The trip over and back takes very little time, and because most guests have left the hotels for the parks, the resort hotels, restaurants are often slack. The food is better than in the Magic Kingdom, the service is faster, the atmosphere more relaxed, and beer, wine, and mixed drinks are available. Of the resort hotels connected directly to the Magic Kingdom by monorail, we prefer the fare at the Contemporary Resort Hotel. The restaurants at the Grand Floridian are good, but pricey.

5. If you decide to eat in the Magic Kingdom during the midday rush (11 A.M.–2 P.M.) or the evening rush (5 P.M.–8 P.M.), try The Crystal Palace towards Adventureland at the central hub end of Main Street, the Adventureland Veranda to the right of the Adventureland entrance bridge, or El Pirata Y el Perico in Adventureland around the corner from Frontierland's Pecos Bill Cafe. All three of these eateries serve decent food and usually are not crowded. As another alternative, a lunch-hour reservation for the *Diamond Horseshoe Jamboree* combines a good show with an easy meal.

6. Many of the Magic Kingdom restaurants serve a cold sandwich of one sort or another. It is possible to buy a cold lunch (except for the drinks) before 11 A.M. and then carry your food until you are ready to eat. We met a family which does this routinely, with Mom always remembering to bring several small plastic bags in which to pack the food. Drinks are purchased at an appropriate time from any convenient drink vendor.

7. Most fast-food eateries in the Magic Kingdom have more than one service window. Regardless of time of day, check out the

lines at *all* of the windows before queuing. Sometimes a manned, but out of the way, window will have a much shorter line or no line at all.

8. Restaurants which accept reservations for lunch and/or dinner fill their respective meal seatings quickly. To obtain reservations you must hot-foot it over to the restaurant in question (King Stefan's Banquet Hall, etc.) as soon as you enter the park or blow your most effective touring time waiting in line to make your meal reservation. Often you are asked to return well in advance of your seating time, and even then, on many occasions, will have to wait well past your scheduled time for a table. Guests staying at one of the Walt Disney World lodging properties can avoid some of this hassle by making reservations by phone up to three days in advance of their visit.

9. For your general information, the Disney people have a park rule against bringing in your own food and drink. We interviewed one woman who, ignoring the rule, brought a huge picnic lunch for her family of five packed into a large diaper/baby paraphernalia bag. Upon entering the park she secured the bag in a locker under the Main Street Station, to be retrieved later when the family was hungry. A Texas family returned to their camper/truck in the parking lot for lunch where they had a cooler, lawn chairs, and plenty of food a la the college football tailgating tradition.

We receive many letters from readers relating how they approached eating at the Magic Kingdom. Here is one from a family in Pennsylvania:

Despite the warning against bringing food into the park, we packed a double picnic lunch in a backpack and a small shoulder bag. Even with a small discount, it cost $195 for the seven of us to tour the park for a day, and I felt that spending another $150 or so on two meals was not in the cards. We froze juice boxes to keep the meat sandwiches cool (it worked fine), and had an extra round of juice boxes and peanut butter sandwiches for a late afternoon snack. We took raisins and a pack of fig bars for sweets, but didn't carry any other cookies or candy to avoid a "sugar-low" during the day. Fruit would have been nice, but it would have been squashed.

Shopping in the Magic Kingdom

Shops in the Magic Kingdom add realism and atmosphere to the various theme settings and make available an extensive inventory of souvenirs, clothing, novelties, decorator items, and more. Much of the merchandise displayed (with the exception of Disney trademark souvenir items) is available back home and elsewhere at a lower price. In our opinion, shopping is not one of the main reasons for visiting the Magic Kingdom. We recommend bypassing the shops on a one-day visit. If you have two or more days to spend in the Magic Kingdom, browse the shops during the early afternoon when many of the attractions are crowded. Remember that Main Street, with its multitude of shops, opens one hour earlier and closes one hour later than the rest of the park. Lockers in the Main Street Train Station allow you to stash your purchases safely as opposed to dragging them around the park with you.

Our recommendations notwithstanding, we realize that for many guests Disney souvenirs and memorabilia are irresistible. If you have decided that you would look good in a Goofy hat with shoulder-length floppy ears, you are in the right place. What's more, you have plenty of company. Writes one of our readers,

> I've discovered that people have a compelling need to buy Disney stuff when they are at WDW. When you get home you wonder why you ever got a cashmere sweater with Mickey Mouse embroidered on the breast, or a tie with tiny Goofys all over it. Maybe it's something they put in the food.

The same reader, obviously well-informed, advises that Disney merchandise is generally cheaper in Walt Disney World than at an independent shop out of the World. She says the airport shops are the most expensive of all.

Magic Kingdom
Touring Plans

The Magic Kingdom Touring Plans are field-tested, step-by-step plans for seeing as much as possible in one day with a minimum of time wasted standing in line. They are designed to assist you in avoiding crowds and bottlenecks on days of moderate to heavy attendance. On days of lighter attendance (see "Selecting the Time of Year for Your Visit," page 29), the plans will still save you time, but will not be as critical to successful touring as on busier days. Do not be concerned that other people will be following the same touring strategy, thus rendering it useless. Fewer than 1 of every 300 people in the park will have been exposed to this information.

On days of moderate to heavy attendance follow the Touring Plan of your choice exactly, deviating only:

1. When you are not interested in an attraction called for on the Touring Plan. For instance, the Touring Plan may indicate that you go next to Tomorrowland and ride Space Mountain, a roller coaster ride. If you do not enjoy roller coasters, simply skip this step of the plan and proceed to the next step.

2. When you encounter a very long line at an attraction called for by the Touring Plan. Crowds ebb and flow at the Magic Kingdom, and by chance an unusually large line may have gathered at an attraction to which you are directed. For example, upon arrival at the Haunted Mansion, you find the waiting lines to be extremely long. It is possible that this is a temporary situation occasioned by several hundred people arriving en masse from a recently concluded performance of the nearby *Hall of Presidents*. If this is the case, simply skip the Haunted Mansion and move to the next step, returning later in the day to try the Haunted Mansion once again.

The Magic Kingdom Touring Plans below follow this section. Choose one that best fits your group and schedule:

- Magic Kingdom One-Day Touring Plan, for Adults
- Author's Selective Magic Kingdom One-Day Touring Plan, for Adults
- Magic Kingdom One-Day Touring Plan, for Parents with Small Children
- Magic Kingdom Two-Day Touring Plan A, for When the Park Is Open Late
- Magic Kingdom Two-Day Touring Plan B, for Morning Touring and When the Park Closes Early

—— *Traffic Patterns in the Magic Kingdom* ——

When we began our research on the Magic Kingdom we were very interested in traffic patterns throughout the park, specifically:

1. *Which sections of the park and what attractions do visitors head for when they first arrive?* When visitors are admitted to the various lands during the summer and holiday periods, traffic to Tomorrowland and Fantasyland is heaviest, followed by Adventureland and Frontierland, and then Liberty Square and Mickey's Starland. During the school year when there are fewer young people in the park, early-morning traffic is more evenly distributed, but is still heaviest in Tomorrowland and Fantasyland. In our research we tested the claim, often heard, that most people turn right into Tomorrowland and tour the Magic Kingdom in an orderly counterclockwise fashion. We found it without basis. As the park fills, visitors seem to head for the top attractions, which they wish to ride before the lines get long. This more than any other factor determines traffic patterns in the morning. Attractions which receive considerable patronage in the early morning are:

Tomorrowland:	Space Mountain
Frontierland:	Big Thunder Mountain Railroad
Fantasyland:	20,000 Leagues Under the Sea
Adventureland:	Jungle Cruise

2. *How long does it take for the park to reach peak capacity for a given day? How are the visitors dispersed throughout the park?* Lines sampled reached their longest lengths between noon and 2 P.M., indicating more arrivals than park departures into the early afternoon.

For general touring purposes, most attractions developed long lines between 10:30 A.M. and 11:30 A.M. Through the early hours of the morning and the early hours of the afternoon attendance was fairly equally distributed through all of the lands. In late afternoon, however, we noted a concentration of visitors in Fantasyland, Liberty Square, and Frontierland, with a slight decrease of visitors in Adventureland, and a marked decrease of visitors in Tomorrowland. This pattern did not occur consistently day to day, but did happen often enough for us to suggest Tomorrowland as the least crowded land for late afternoon touring.

3. *How do most visitors go about touring the park? Is there a difference in the touring behavior of first-time visitors versus repeat visitors?* Many first-time visitors are accompanied by friends or relatives familiar with the Magic Kingdom, who guide their tour. The tours sometimes do and sometimes do not proceed in an orderly touring sequence. First-time visitors without personal touring guides tend to be more orderly in their touring. Many first-time visitors, however, are drawn to Cinderella Castle upon entering the park and thus commence their rotation from Fantasyland. Repeat visitors usually proceed directly to their favorite attractions.

4. *What effect do special events, such as the daily Main Street Parade, have on traffic patterns?* Special events such as the Main Street Parade do pull substantial numbers of visitors from the ride lines, but the key to the length of the lines remains the number of people in the park.

5. *What are the traffic patterns near to and at closing time?* On our sample days, in season and out of season, park departures outnumbered arrivals beginning mid-afternoon. Many visitors left during the late afternoon as the dinner hour approached. When the park closed early, there were steady departures during the two hours before closing time, with a huge exodus of remaining visitors at closing time. When the park closed late, people left throughout the evening. Departures increased as closing time approached, with a huge throng still left at closing time. Mass departures at closing time mainly affect conditions on Main Street and at the monorail and ferry stops, due to the crowds generated when the other six lands close. In the other six lands, touring conditions are normally uncrowded just before closing time.

6. *I have heard that when there are two or more lines, the shortest wait is always the left line. Is this true?* We do not recommend the "left-line strategy" because, with the occasional exception of food lines, it simply does not hold up. The Disney people have a number of techniques for both internal and external crowd control which distribute line traffic nearly equally. Placing research team members at the same time in each available line, we could discern no consistent pattern as to who would be served first. Further, staffers entering the same attraction via different lines would almost always exit the attraction within 30 to 90 seconds of each other.

—— Magic Kingdom One-Day Touring Plan, for Adults ——

FOR: **Adults without small children.**
ASSUMES: Willingness to experience all major rides (including roller coasters) and shows.

Be forewarned that this plan requires a lot of walking and some backtracking; this is necessary to avoid some long waits in line. A little extra walking coupled with some hustle in the morning will save you from two to three hours of standing in line. Note also that you might not complete the tour. How far you get will depend on how quickly you move from ride to ride, how many times you pause for rest or food, how quickly the park fills, and what time the park closes. With a little zip and some luck, it is possible to complete the Touring Plan even on a busy day when the park closes early.

Before You Go

1. Call (407) 824-4321 the day before you go for the official opening time.
2. Purchase admission prior to your arrival. You can either order tickets through the mail before you leave home, buy them at the Walt Disney World Information Center off I-75 near Ocala if you are driving, purchase them at the Disney store in the Orlando airport, or buy them at Walt Disney World lodging properties.

At Walt Disney World

1. Arrive at the Transportation and Ticket Center (TTC) 50 minutes before the park's stated opening time. This will give you time to park and catch the tram to the TTC. Arrive an hour earlier than opening time if it is a holiday period or if you must purchase your admission that morning.
2. If the line for the monorail is short, take the monorail; otherwise catch the ferry.

3. When you arrive at the Magic Kingdom, proceed through the entry turnstiles. Split your party and have one person go to the Hospitality House (across the square from City Hall) to make reservations for the 12:15 P.M. seating of the *Diamond Horseshoe Jamboree* (show and lunch). Have another person stop at City Hall for park maps and a copy of the daily entertainment schedule.

4. The party who stops at City Hall should proceed quickly to the end of Main Street and stake out a position for your group as follows:

    a. If you want to ride Space Mountain, turn right at the end of Main Street (before you reach the central hub) past the Plaza Ice Cream Parlor and the Plaza Restaurant and stake out a place for your group at the entrance of the Plaza Pavilion. When the rope barrier is dropped at opening time, jog through the Plaza Pavilion and on to Space Mountain. Starting at the entrance to the Plaza Pavilion will give you about a hundred-yard head start and a shortcut over anyone proceeding to Space Mountain from the central hub.

    b. If you do not want to ride Space Mountain, turn left at the end of Main Street past Refreshment Corner and position yourself in front of the Crystal Palace facing the walkway bridge to Adventureland. When the rope barrier is dropped, cross the bridge and turn left into Adventureland. Head straight for the Jungle Cruise and ride.

5. If you elected to ride Space Mountain, proceed now across the park via the central hub to Adventureland and ride the Jungle Cruise. If you started your tour with the Jungle Cruise, proceed to Step 6.

6. Leave Adventureland and go to Fantasyland via the central hub. Ride Snow White's Scary Adventure.

7. While in Fantasyland, ride Peter Pan's Flight.

8. Proceed to Frontierland. Ride the Big Thunder Mountain Railroad (you should arrive just after it has been brought up to full operating capacity).

9. While in Frontierland, see the *Country Bear Jamboree*.

10. Keeping the waterfront on your left, proceed to Liberty Square and experience the Haunted Mansion.

    NOTE: This is about as far as you can go on a busy day before the crowds catch up with you, but you will have experienced seven of the more popular rides and shows and cleared almost all of the Magic Kingdom's traffic bottlenecks. Note also that you are doing a considerable amount of walking and some back-tracking. Do not be dismayed; the extra walking will save you as much as two hours of standing in line. Remember, during the morning (through Step 10) keep moving. In the afternoon, adjust the pace to your liking.

11. Unless you ran into some bad luck, you should be within a half hour or so of your 12:15 P.M. seating at the *Diamond Horseshoe Jamboree* in Frontierland. If you have completed the Touring Plan through Step 10 before noon, go ahead and ride It's a Small World in Fantasyland before you head for the *Jamboree*. If you did not make reservations for the *Diamond Horseshoe Jamboree*, go ahead and eat lunch at El Pirate Y el Perico, a decent but often overlooked eatery, situated in Adventureland around the corner from Frontierland's Pecos Bill Cafe.

12. After lunch and the show, go to Liberty Square and see the *Hall of Presidents*.

13. Leave Frontierland via the passage to the right of the *Diamond Horseshoe Jamboree* and enter Adventureland. See the *Tropical Serenade (Enchanted Tiki Birds)*.

14. While in Adventureland, ride Pirates of the Caribbean.

15. Turn left after you exit Pirates of the Caribbean and go to Frontierland. Take the Walt Disney Railroad to Mickey's Starland.

16. In Mickey's Starland, walk through Mickey's House to see a performance of *Mickey's Magical T.V. World*.

17. After the show you can exit outside and go to Mickey's Hollywood Theater to meet and photograph Mickey. If this is something you want to do, read the Touring Tips for *Mickey's Magical T.V. World* to help you avoid a long wait.

18. Exit Mickey's Starland along the path to Fantasyland. In Fantasyland, see *Magic Journeys*.

19. While in Fantasyland, ride It's a Small World if you missed it before lunch. Otherwise proceed to Step 20.

20. Go to Tomorrowland via the Skyway from Fantasyland (if the line is not long) or on foot. In Tomorrowland, ride the WEDway PeopleMover.

21. While in Tomorrowland, see the *Carousel of Progress*.

22. Try Dreamflight, also in Tomorrowland.

23. Proceed toward the central hub entrance to Tomorrowland and experience the *Mission to Mars*.

24. Walk across the street and view *American Journeys*.

25. If you have some time left before closing, backtrack to pick up attractions you may have missed or bypassed because the lines were too long. Check out any parades, fireworks, or live performances which interest you. Grab a bite to eat. Save Main Street until last since it remains open after the rest of the park closes.

26. Continue to tour until everything closes except Main Street. Finish your day by browsing along Main Street and viewing the *Walt Disney Story*.

27. If you leave the park at closing time, the monorail to the TTC will be mobbed. Either take the ferry or board a monorail to the Polynesian Village Resort and from there take the short walkway to the TTC.

NOTE: Sometimes Walt Disney World monorail personnel ask for proof that you are a guest at one of the monorail-connected hotels before allowing you to board. As restaurants, bars, shows, and shops in the hotels are open to the public this request for guest documentation is inconsistent, inappropriate, and in our opinion, totally out of line. Until the hotel shops and restaurants are declared off-limits to all but guests in residence, you have a perfect right to ride the hotel monorail. Stand your ground.

—— Author's Selective Magic Kingdom One-Day Touring Plan, for Adults ——

FOR: **Adults touring without small children.**

ASSUMES: Willingness to experience all major rides (including roller coasters) and shows.

This Touring Plan is selective and includes only those attractions which, in the author's opinion, represent the best the Magic Kingdom has to offer. Be forewarned that this plan requires a lot of walking and some backtracking; this is necessary to avoid some long waits in line. A little extra walking coupled with some hustle in the morning will save you from two to three hours of standing in line. Note also that you might not complete the tour. How far you get will depend on how quickly you move from ride to ride, how many times you pause for rest or food, how quickly the park fills, and what time the park closes. With a little zip and some luck, it is possible to complete the Touring Plan even on a busy day when the park closes early.

Before You Go

1. Call (407) 824-4321 the day before you go for the official opening time.
2. Purchase admission prior to your arrival. You can either order tickets through the mail before you leave home, buy them at the Walt Disney World Information Center off I-75 near Ocala if you are driving, purchase them at the Disney store in the Orlando airport, or buy them at Walt Disney World lodging properties.

At Walt Disney World

1. Arrive at the Transportation and Ticket Center (TTC) 50 minutes before the park's stated opening time. This will give you time to park and catch the tram to the TTC. Arrive an hour earlier than opening time if it is a holiday period or if you must purchase your admission that morning.

2. If the line for the monorail is short, take the monorail; otherwise catch the ferry.

3. When you arrive at the Magic Kingdom, proceed through the entry turnstiles. Split your party and have one person go to the Hospitality House (across the square from City Hall) to make reservations for the 12:15 P.M. seating of the *Diamond Horseshoe Jamboree* (show and lunch). Have another person stop at City Hall for park maps and a copy of the daily entertainment schedule.

4. The party who stops at City Hall should proceed quickly to the end of Main Street and stake out a position for your group as follows:

   a. If you want to ride Space Mountain, turn right at the end of Main Street (before you reach the central hub) past the Plaza Ice Cream Parlor and the Plaza Restaurant and stake out a place for your group at the entrance of the Plaza Pavilion. When the rope barrier is dropped at opening time, jog through the Plaza Pavilion and on to Space Mountain. Starting at the entrance to the Plaza Pavilion will give you about a hundred-yard head start and a shortcut over anyone proceeding to Space Mountain from the central hub.

   b. If you do not want to ride Space Mountain, turn left at the end of Main Street past Refreshment Corner and position yourself in front of the Crystal Palace facing the walkway bridge to Adventureland. When the rope barrier is dropped, cross the bridge and turn left into Adventureland. Head straight for the Jungle Cruise and ride.

5. If you elected to ride Space Mountain, proceed now across the park via the central hub to Adventureland and ride the Jungle Cruise. If you started your tour with the Jungle Cruise, proceed to Step 6.

6. Leave Adventureland and go to Fantasyland via the central hub. Ride Peter Pan's Flight.

7. While in Fantasyland, ride It's a Small World.

8. Proceed to Frontierland. Ride the Big Thunder Mountain Railroad (you should arrive just after it has been brought up to full operating capacity).

9. While in Frontierland, see the *Country Bear Jamboree*.

10. Keeping the waterfront on your left, proceed to Liberty Square and experience the Haunted Mansion.

NOTE: This is about as far as you can go on a busy day before the crowds catch up with you, but you will have experienced seven of the more popular rides and shows and cleared almost all of the Magic Kingdom's traffic bottlenecks. Note also that you are doing a considerable amount of walking and some backtracking. Do not be dismayed; the extra walking will save you as much as two hours of standing in line. Remember, during the morning (through Step 10) keep moving. In the afternoon, adjust the pace to your liking.

11. Unless you ran into some bad luck, you should be within a half hour or so of your 12:15 P.M. seating at the *Diamond Horseshoe Jamboree* in Frontierland. If you had great luck and have some time before your *Diamond Horseshoe Jamboree* seating, go ahead and ride the riverboat (16 minute ride plus time spent waiting to board) or see the *Hall of Presidents* (23 minute show plus any waiting time). Do not risk your *Diamond Horseshoe* reservations by arriving late for your seating; they will be given to other guests.

12. After lunch and the show, go to Liberty Square and ride the Liberty Square Riverboat. If you ride before lunch, skip ahead to Step 13.

13. While in Liberty Square, see the *Hall of Presidents*. If you saw the show before lunch, proceed to Step 14.

14. Return to Frontierland. Take the Walt Disney Railroad to Mickey's Starland.

15. In Mickey's Starland, walk through Mickey's House to see a performance of *Mickey's Magical T.V. World*.

NOTE: Check your daily entertainment schedule to see if there are any parades, live performances, fireworks, or other events which you would like to integrate into your schedule. If so, simply interrupt the Touring Plan at the appropriate time, and pick up where you left off after the event or live performance is concluded.

16. Exit Mickey's Starland along the path to Fantasyland. In Fantasyland, see *Magic Journeys*.

17. Go to Tomorrowland via the Skyway from Fantasyland (if the line is not long) or on foot.

18. While in Tomorrowland, see the *Carousel of Progress*.

19. See *American Journeys*, also in Tomorrowland.
20. Leave Tomorrowland and proceed via the central hub to Adventureland. See *Tropical Serenade (Enchanted Tiki Birds)*.
21. While in Adventureland, ride Pirates of the Caribbean.
22. Turn right after exiting Pirates of the Caribbean; proceed to the Swiss Family Treehouse for a tour.
23. If you have some time left before closing, backtrack to pick up attractions you may have missed or bypassed because the lines were too long. Check out any parades, fireworks, or live performances which interest you. Grab a bite to eat. Save Main Street until last since it remains open after the rest of the park closes.
24. Continue to tour until everything closes except Main Street. Finish your day by browsing along Main Street and viewing the *Walt Disney Story*.
25. If you leave the park at closing time, the monorail to the TTC will be mobbed. Either take the ferry or board a monorail to the Polynesian Village Resort and from there take the short walkway to the TTC. See note on page 145.

—— *Magic Kingdom One-Day Touring Plan, for Parents with Small Children* ——

FOR: **Parents with children between 4 and 8 years of age.**
ASSUMES: Periodic stops for rest, restrooms, and refreshment.

This Touring Plan represents a compromise between the observed tastes of adults and the observed tastes of younger children. Included in this Touring Plan are many amusement park rides which children may have the opportunity to experience (although in less exotic surroundings) at local fairs and amusement parks. Though these rides are included in the Touring Plan, we suggest, nevertheless, that they be omitted if possible. Often requiring long waits in line, these so-called cycle-loading rides consume valuable touring time. Specifically we refer to:

Mad Tea Party	Dumbo, the Flying Elephant
Cinderella's Golden Carrousel	StarJets

This time could be better spent experiencing the many attractions which best demonstrate the Disney creative genius and are only found in the Magic Kingdom.

Be forewarned that this plan requires a lot of walking and some backtracking; this is necessary to avoid long waits in line. A little extra walking will save you from two to three hours of standing in line. Note also that you may not complete the tour. How far you get will depend on how quickly you move from ride to ride, how many times you pause for rest or food, how quickly the park fills, and what time the park closes. With a little hustle and some luck, it is possible to complete the Touring Plan even on a busy day when the park closes early.

Before You Go

1. Call (407) 824-4321 the day before you go for the official opening time.
2. Purchase admission prior to your arrival. You can either order tickets through the mail before you leave home, buy them at the Walt Disney World Information Center off I-75 near Ocala

if you are driving, purchase them at the Disney store in the Orlando airport, or buy them at Walt Disney World lodging properties.

At Walt Disney World

1. Arrive at the main parking lot at least 50 minutes before the stated opening time. Arrive an hour earlier than opening time if it is a holiday period or if you must purchase your admission that morning.
2. Take the monorail to the Magic Kingdom.
3. Enter the park. Have one person in your party pick up a copy of the daily entertainment schedule at City Hall, while another member of your party makes reservations at the Hospitality House for the 12:15 seating of *Diamond Horseshoe Jamboree*. Rejoin your party at the Hospitality House.
4. Move quickly to the end of Main Street and take a position at the rope barrier at the central hub. When the barrier is dropped on opening, move quickly to 20,000 Leagues Under the Sea in Fantasyland.
5. While in Fantasyland, ride Mr. Toad's Wild Ride.
6. While in Fantasyland, ride Snow White's Scary Adventures.
7. While in Fantasyland, ride Peter Pan's Flight.
8. While in Fantasyland, ride Dumbo the Flying Elephant.
9. Exit Fantasyland via the Castle and the central hub. Go to Adventureland and ride the Jungle Cruise.
10. Exit left from the Jungle Cruise and go to Frontierland. Ride Big Thunder Mountain Railroad. Not too scary, but kids need to be 3'4" to ride. Strictly enforced. Skip to Step 11 if your children are too small.
11. While in Frontierland, see *Country Bear Jamboree*.
12. Keeping the waterfront on your left, go to Liberty Square and experience the Haunted Mansion.
13. At this point, you should be within a half hour of your *Diamond Horseshoe Jamboree* seating at 12:15 P.M. If you have more than 15 minutes before your seating time when you leave the Haunted Mansion, bear left into Fantasyland and ride It's a Small World. Go at 12:15 P.M. to the *Jamboree* for the show and lunch. If you did not make reservations at *Diamond Horseshoe*, eat now at El Pirata Y el Perico or before Step 14 at the Adventureland Veranda.

14. Take the passage on the right side of *Diamond Horseshoe* and return to Adventureland. Tour the Swiss Family Treehouse.

15. While in Adventureland, ride Pirates of the Caribbean.

16. Move next door to Frontierland. Take the raft to Tom Sawyer Island. Children will play here all day, so set some limits based on the closing time of the park, your energy level, and how many additional attractions you wish to experience.

17. Return via raft from Tom Sawyer Island and go to the Frontierland Railroad Station. Catch the Walt Disney World Railroad to Mickey's Starland.

18. Get off the train at Mickey's Starland. Go see *Mickey's Magical T.V. World* (enter through Mickey's House). After the show, visit Mickey in his dressing room at Mickey's Hollywood Theater (see page 118 for instructions on avoiding a long wait). Next enjoy the playground and Grandma Duck's Petting Farm.

19. Exit Mickey's Starland via the path to Fantasyland. In Fantasyland, see *Magic Journeys*.

20. While in Fantasyland, ride It's a Small World if you missed it before lunch. Otherwise, proceed to Step 21.

21. Exit Fantasyland via the Skyway (if not too crowded), or on foot via the Castle and the central hub and go to Tomorrowland. Ride Dreamflight.

22. While in Tomorrowland, ride the WEDway PeopleMover.

23. Enjoy *Carousel of Progress*, also in Tomorrowland.

24. Heading back toward the entrance of Tomorrowland, try *Mission to Mars*.

25. Cross the street and see *American Journeys*.

26. If you have any time or energy left, catch a live performance, grab a bite, or try any attractions you might have missed using the Touring Plan.

27. Save touring Main Street until last, since it stays open later than the rest of the park.

28. If you are parked at the Transportation and Ticket Center (TTC), catch the ferry or ride the monorail to the Polynesian Village Resort and then proceed to the TTC via the short connecting walkway (see footnote on page 145).

—— Magic Kingdom Two-Day Touring Plan A, for When the Park Is Open Late ——

FOR: **Parties who want to enjoy the Magic Kingdom at different times of day,** including evenings and early mornings.

ASSUMES: Willingness to experience all major rides (including roller coasters) and shows.

TIMING: This Two-Day Touring Plan is for those visiting the Magic Kingdom on days when the park is open late (after 8 P.M.). The plan offers morning touring on one day and late afternoon and evening touring on the other day. If the park closes early, or if you prefer to do all your touring during the morning and early afternoon, use the Magic Kingdom Two-Day Touring Plan B on page 158.

Before You Go

1. Call (407) 824-4321 the day before you go for the official opening time.
2. Purchase admission prior to your arrival. You can either order tickets through the mail before you leave home, buy them at the Walt Disney World Information Center off I-75 near Ocala if you are driving, purchase them at the Disney store in the Orlando airport, or buy them at Walt Disney World lodging properties.

Day One

1. Arrive at the Transportation and Ticket Center (TTC) 50 minutes before the park's stated opening time. This will give you time to park and catch the tram to the TTC. Arrive an hour earlier than opening time if it is a holiday period or if you must purchase your admission that morning.
2. If the line for the monorail is short, take the monorail; otherwise catch the ferry.
3. When you arrive at the Magic Kingdom, proceed through the entry turnstiles. Split your party and have one person go to the Hospitality House (across the square from City Hall) to make

reservations for the 12:15 P.M. seating of the *Diamond Horse-shoe Jamboree* (show and lunch). Have another person stop at City Hall for park maps and a copy of the daily entertainment schedule.

4. The party who stops at City Hall should proceed quickly to the end of Main Street and stake out a position for your group as follows:

   a. If you want to ride Space Mountain, turn right at the end of Main Street (before you reach the central hub) past the Plaza Ice Cream Parlor and the Plaza Restaurant and stake out a place for your group at the entrance of the Plaza Pavilion. When the rope barrier is dropped at opening time, jog through the Plaza Pavilion and on to Space Mountain. Starting at the entrance to the Plaza Pavilion will give you about a hundred-yard head start and a shortcut over anyone proceeding to Space Mountain from the central hub.

   b. If you do not want to ride Space Mountain, turn left at the end of Main Street past Refreshment Corner and position yourself in front of the Crystal Palace facing the walkway bridge to Adventureland. When the rope barrier is dropped, cross the bridge and turn left into Adventureland. Head straight for the Jungle Cruise and ride.

5. If you elected to ride Space Mountain, proceed now across the park via the central hub to Adventureland and ride the Jungle Cruise. If you started your tour with the Jungle Cruise, proceed to Step 6.

6. Leave Adventureland and go to Fantasyland via the central hub. Ride Snow White's Scary Adventure.

7. While in Fantasyland, ride Peter Pan's Flight.

8. Proceed to Frontierland. Ride the Big Thunder Mountain Railroad.

9. While in Frontierland, see the *Country Bear Jamboree*.

10. Keeping the waterfront on your left, proceed to Liberty Square and ride the Liberty Square Riverboat.

11. Unless you ran into some bad luck, you should be within a half hour or so of your 12:15 P.M. seating at the *Diamond Horseshoe Jamboree* in Frontierland. If you have completed the Touring Plan through Step 10 before noon, go ahead and experience the Haunted Mansion (also in Liberty Square) before you head for the *Diamond Horseshoe Jamboree*. If you did not make reserva-

tions for the *Diamond Horseshoe* and are hungry, eat lunch at El Pirate Y el Perico, a decent but often overlooked eatery, situated in Adventureland around the corner from Frontierland's Pecos Bill Cafe.

12. After lunch experience the Haunted Mansion if you missed it earlier.
13. While in Liberty Square, see the *Hall of Presidents*.
14. Return to the waterfront and catch a raft to Tom Sawyer Island.
15. After exploring Tom Sawyer Island, return to the mainland and proceed to Frontierland's Walt Disney World Railroad Station.
16. Take the Walt Disney World Railroad to Mickey's Starland.
17. In Mickey's Starland, walk through Mickey's House to see a performance of *Mickey's Magical T.V. World*.
18. After the show you can visit Mickey's Hollywood Theater to meet and photograph Mickey. If this is something you want to do, read the Touring Tips for *Mickey's Magical T.V. World* to help you avoid a long wait.
19. Return to the Mickey's Starland Railroad Station and ride the Walt Disney World Railroad to Main Street.
20. Before you leave the Magic Kingdom, see the *Walt Disney Story*, next to the Hospitality House (where you made reservations for the *Diamond Horseshoe Jamboree*).
21. If for some reason (shopping, eating, parades, etc.), you think you might return to the Magic Kingdom that evening or you plan to visit EPCOT Center or the Disney-MGM Studios, it is necessary for you to have your hand stamped as you exit.

Day Two

1. If you want to see the afternoon parade, arrive at the TTC at about 2 P.M. If the afternoon parade does not interest you, arrive at the TTC at about 4:30 P.M. and skip Step 3.
2. Take the ferry to the Magic Kingdom if it is in port, otherwise catch the monorail.
3. Enter the Magic Kingdom and climb the stairs leading to the Walt Disney World Railroad loading platform. Pick a good spot to watch the parade (the earlier you arrive the better the spot will be) and settle in.
4. After the parade head for Fantasyland via Main Street and the bridge to the castle. In Fantasyland, see *Magic Journeys*.

5. Turn left after *Magic Journeys* and ride It's a Small World.
6. Turn right after exiting, proceed to the Skyway, and ride to Tomorrowland. If the wait for the Skyway is too long, walk to Tomorrowland.
7. While in Tomorrowland, ride the WEDway PeopleMover.
8. Try the *Carousel of Progress*, also in Tomorrowland.
9. In Tomorrowland, also ride Dreamflight.
10. Proceed toward the central hub entrance to Tomorrowland and experience the *Mission to Mars*.
11. Walk across the street and view *American Journeys*.
12. If you are hungry, exit Tomorrowland and proceed via the central hub to the Crystal Palace for dinner. If you prefer a more leisurely meal, leave the park (getting your hand stamped for reentry), and take the monorail to one of the Magic Kingdom resort hotels for dinner.

   NOTE: At this point check your daily entertainment schedule to see if there are any parades, fireworks, or live performances which interest you. Make note of the times and alter the Touring Plan accordingly. Since you have already seen all the attractions for *Day Two* that cause bottlenecks and have big lines, an interruption of the Touring Plan here will not cause you any problems. Simply pick up where you left off before the parade or show. The Main Street Electrical Parade and the Fantasy in the Sky fireworks are particularly worthwhile.

13. After dinner (and after returning to the park if necessary), proceed to Adventureland and tour the Swiss Family Treehouse.
14. While in Adventureland, see the *Tropical Serenade (Enchanted Tiki Birds)*.
15. In Adventureland, also ride Pirates of the Caribbean.
16. If you have some time left before closing, backtrack to pick up attractions you may have missed, such as 20,000 Leagues Under the Sea in Fantasyland, or bypassed because the lines were too long. Explore the shops, but save Main Street until last since it remains open after the rest of the park closes.
17. In the hour just before closing, lines range from short to nonexistent for almost all attractions. If you have a favorite ride you would enjoy experiencing one more time, try it now.
18. Continue touring until everything closes except Main Street. Finish your day by browsing along Main Street.

19. If you leave the park at closing time, the monorail to the TTC will be mobbed. Either take the ferry or board a monorail to the Polynesian Village Resort and from there take the short walkway to the TTC. See note on page 145.

—— Magic Kingdom Two-Day Touring Plan B, for Morning Touring and for When the Park Closes Early ——

FOR: **Parties wishing to spread their Magic Kingdom visit over two days and parties preferring to tour in the morning.**

ASSUMES: Willingness to experience all major rides (including roller coasters) and shows.

TIMING: The following Two-Day Touring Plan takes advantage of early morning touring. On each day you should complete the structured part of the plan by about 3 P.M. or so. If you are visiting the Magic Kingdom during a period of the year when the park is open late (after 8 P.M.), you might prefer our alternate Two-Day Touring Plan which offers morning touring on one day and late afternoon/evening touring on the other day.

Before You Go

1. Call (407) 824-4321 the day before you go for the official opening time.
2. Purchase admission prior to your arrival. You can either order tickets through the mail before you leave home, buy them at the Walt Disney World Information Center off I-75 near Ocala if you are driving, purchase them at the Disney store in the Orlando airport, or buy them at Walt Disney World lodging properties.

Day One

1. Arrive at the Transportation and Ticket Center (TTC) 50 minutes before the park's stated opening time. This will give you time to park and catch the tram to the TTC. Arrive an hour earlier than opening time if it is a holiday period or if you must purchase your admission that morning.
2. If the line for the monorail is short, take the monorail; otherwise catch the ferry.
3. When you arrive at the Magic Kingdom, proceed through the entry turnstiles. Split your party and have one person go to the Hospitality House (across the square from City Hall) to make

reservations for the 12:15 P.M. seating of the *Diamond Horseshoe Jamboree* (show and lunch). Have another person stop at City Hall for park maps and a copy of the daily entertainment schedule.

4. The party who stops at City Hall should proceed quickly to the end of Main Street and stake out a position for your group as follows:

   a. If you want to ride Space Mountain, turn right at the end of Main Street (before you reach the central hub) past the Plaza Ice Cream Parlor and the Plaza Restaurant and stake out a place for your group at the entrance of the Plaza Pavilion. When the rope barrier is dropped at opening time, jog through the Plaza Pavilion and on to Space Mountain. Starting at the entrance to the Plaza Pavilion will give you about a hundred-yard head start and a shortcut over anyone proceeding to Space Mountain from the central hub.

   b. If you do not want to ride Space Mountain, go to Fantasyland, keeping the Grand Prix Raceway on your right, and ride 20,000 Leagues Under the Sea.

5. If you elected to ride Space Mountain, now go to Fantasyland, keeping the Grand Prix Raceway on your right, and ride 20,000 Leagues Under the Sea. If you skipped Space Mountain, go to Step 6.

6. While in Fantasyland, ride Mr. Toad's Wild Ride.

7. While in Fantasyland, ride Snow White's Scary Adventure.

8. If you have small children in your party, let them ride Dumbo, the Flying Elephant.

9. While in Fantasyland, ride It's a Small World.

10. Proceed to Liberty Square and experience the Haunted Mansion.

11. While in Liberty Square, visit the *Hall of Presidents*.

12. Your seating time should be approaching for the *Diamond Horseshoe Jamboree*. If you have enough time, go ahead and ride the Liberty Square Riverboat (the ride takes about 16 minutes plus whatever time you must wait to board—ask the attendant).

13. Enjoy the *Diamond Horseshoe Jamboree* and have lunch during the show.

   NOTE: At this point check your daily entertainment schedule to see if there are any parades or live performances which interest you. Make note of the times and alter the Touring Plan accordingly. Since you have already seen all the attractions for *Day One* that cause bottlenecks and have big lines, an interruption of the Touring Plan here will not cause you any problems. Simply pick up where you left off before the parade or show.

14. If you did not have time to ride the Liberty Square Riverboat before lunch and the *Diamond Horseshoe Jamboree*, ride now.
15. In Frontierland, take a raft to Tom Sawyer Island and explore.
16. After you leave Tom Sawyer Island, go to Adventureland and see the *Tropical Serenade (Enchanted Tiki Birds)*.
17. While in Adventureland, walk through the Swiss Family Treehouse.
18. This concludes the Touring Plan except for one attraction. Enjoy the shops and live entertainment offerings or revisit your favorite attractions until you are ready to leave. As your last stop, see the *Walt Disney Story* at the Town Square end of Main Street.
19. If you leave the park at closing time, the monorail to the TTC will be mobbed. Either take the ferry or board a monorail to the Polynesian Village Resort and from there take the short walkway to the TTC. See note on page 145.

Day Two

1. Call (407) 824-4321 the day before you go for the official opening time.
2. Arrive at the (TTC) 50 minutes before the park's stated opening time. This will give you time to park and catch the tram to the TTC. Arrive an hour earlier than opening time if it is a holiday period.
3. If the line for the monorail is short, take the monorail; otherwise catch the ferry.
4. When you arrive at the Magic Kingdom, proceed through the entry turnstiles. Stop at City Hall for park maps and a copy of the daily entertainment schedule.
5. Proceed to the end of Main Street, turn left past Refreshment Corner, and position yourself in front of the Crystal Palace facing the walkway bridge to Adventureland. When the rope barrier is dropped, cross the bridge, and turn left into Adventureland. Head straight for the Jungle Cruise and ride.
6. While in Adventureland, ride Pirates of the Caribbean.

7. Leave Adventureland and go to Frontierland. Ride the Big Thunder Mountain Railroad.

8. While in Frontierland, see the *Country Bear Jamboree*.

9. Catch the Walt Disney World Railroad and get off at Mickey's Starland.

10. Tour Mickey's House and proceed through Mickey's back door to *Mickey's Magical T.V. World*, a live show featuring the Disney characters.

11. After the show, you can exit the theater and visit Mickey in his dressing room where he will pose with your group for photographs. If this interests you, see the Touring Tips for *Mickey's Magical T.V. World* on page 118.

12. Exit Mickey's Starland via the path to Fantasyland. In Fantasyland, see *Magic Journeys*.

NOTE: At this point check your daily entertainment schedule to see if there are any parades or live performances which interest you. Make note of the times and alter the Touring Plan accordingly. Since you have already seen all the attractions that cause bottlenecks and have big lines, an interruption of the Touring Plan here will not cause you any problems. Simply pick up where you left off before the parade or show.

13. Turn left after *Magic Journeys* and proceed to the Skyway. If the line is not too long, take the Skyway to Tomorrowland. If the wait seems prohibitive, walk to Tomorrowland via the Castle entrance and the central hub.

14. In Tomorrowland, if you are hungry, eat lunch at Tomorrowland Terrace or the Plaza Pavilion.

15. While in Tomorrowland, ride the WEDway PeopleMover.

16. Try the *Carousel of Progress*, also in Tomorrowland.

17. In Tomorrowland, also ride Dreamflight.

18. Proceed toward the central hub entrance to Tomorrowland and experience the *Mission to Mars*.

19. Walk across the street and view *American Journeys*.

20. This concludes the Touring Plan. Enjoy the shops and live entertainment offerings or revisit your favorite attractions until you are ready to leave.

21. If you leave the park at closing time, the monorail to the TTC will be mobbed. Either take the ferry or board a monorail to the Polynesian Village Resort and from there take the short walkway to the TTC. See note on page 145.

PART FOUR—EPCOT Center

—— Contrasting EPCOT Center and the Magic Kingdom ——

EPCOT Center is more than twice the physical size of the Magic Kingdom, and it has lines every bit as long as those waiting for the Jungle Cruise or Space Mountain. Obviously, visitors must come prepared to do a considerable amount of walking from attraction to attraction within EPCOT Center and a comparable amount of standing in line.

The size and scope of EPCOT Center also means that one can't really see the whole place in one day without skipping an attraction or two and giving other areas a cursory glance. A major difference between the Magic Kingdom and EPCOT Center, however, is that some of the EPCOT attractions can be either lingered over or skimmed, depending on one's personal interest. A good example is the General Motors' World of Motion pavilion consisting of two sections. The first section is a fifteen-minute ride while the second section is a collection of educational walk-through exhibits and mini-theaters. Nearly all visitors opt to take the ride, but many people, due to time constraints or lack of interest, bypass the exhibits.

Generally speaking, the rides at the Magic Kingdom tend to be designed to create an experience of adventure or fantasy. The experiences created in the EPCOT Center attractions tend to be oriented towards education or inspiration.

Some people will find that the attempts at education are superficial; others will want more entertainment and less education. Most visitors are somewhere in between, finding plenty of entertainment **and** education.

In any event, EPCOT Center is more of an adult place than the Magic Kingdom. What it gains in taking a futuristic, visionary, and technological look at the world, it loses, just a bit, in warmth, happiness, and charm.

As in the Magic Kingdom, we have identified several attractions in EPCOT Center as "not to be missed." But part of the enjoyment of a place like EPCOT Center is that there is something for everyone. If

165

you go in a group, no doubt there will be quite a variety of opinions as to which attraction is "best."

—— *Arriving and Getting Oriented* ——

Arriving at EPCOT Center by private automobile is easy and direct. The park has its own parking lot and, unlike the Magic Kingdom, there is no need to take a monorail or ferryboat to reach the entrance. Trams serve the entire EPCOT Center lot, or if you wish you can walk to the front gate. Monorail service does connect EPCOT Center with the Transportation and Ticket Center, the Magic Kingdom (transfer required), and with the Magic Kingdom resort hotels (transfer also required).

Like the Magic Kingdom, EPCOT Center has theme sections, but only two: Future World and World Showcase. The technological resources of major corporations and the creative talent of Disney combine in Future World, which represents a look at where man has come from and where he is going. World Showcase, featuring the distinctive landmarks, cuisine, and culture of a number of nations, is meant to be a sort of permanent world's fair.

From the standpoint of finding your way around, however, EPCOT Center is not at all like the Magic Kingdom. The Magic Kingdom is designed so that at nearly any location in the park you feel a part of a very specific environment—Liberty Square, let's say, or Main Street, U.S.A. Each of these environments is visually closed off from other parts of the park to preserve the desired atmosphere. It wouldn't do for the Jungle Cruise to pass the roaring blacktop of the Grand Prix Raceway, for example.

EPCOT Center, by contrast, is visually open. And while it seems strange to see Liberty Hall on the same horizon with the Eiffel Tower, in-park navigation is normally simplified. A possible exception is in Future World where the enormous east and west CommuniCore buildings effectively hide everything on their opposite sides.

While Cinderella Castle is the focal landmark of the Magic Kingdom, Spaceship Earth is the architectural symbol of EPCOT Center. This shiny, 180-foot "geosphere" is visible from almost every point. Like Cinderella Castle, it can help you keep track of where you are in the park. But because it's in a high-traffic location, and because it's not centrally located, it does not make a very good meeting place.

Any of the distinctively designed national pavilions make good meeting places, but be more specific than, "Hey, let's meet in Japan!" That may sound fun and catchy but remember that the national pavilions are mini-towns, with buildings, monuments, gardens, and plazas. You could wander around quite awhile "in Japan" without making connections with your group. Pick out a specific place in Japan, the sidewalk side of the pagoda, for example.

More Information and Help Galore— WorldKey Information Service

Whether you need more information or assistance or not, you should know about the innovative WorldKey Information Service. It not only may be useful as you visit EPCOT Center, it will also give you some experience dealing with what may be one of the common video systems of the future.

WorldKey is a network of interactive video display terminals—televisions that react when you touch certain parts of the screen.

The WorldKey system, developed by the Bell System and Walt Disney Productions, will provide you with up to 40 minutes of information about EPCOT Center, showing maps and pictures, and describing attractions, restaurants, entertainment, guest services, and shops.

Be patient with the WorldKey and it will guide you, step by step, through an explanation of how to use the system—in English or in Spanish (French and German are to be added later). Stick with the program through at least a few steps and you can use the WorldKey to contact an attendant. Via two-way television and hands-free two-way speakers, the WorldKey attendant can answer your questions, make hotel or restaurant reservations, and help find lost children, among other things.

Because the WorldKey system is so novel, a lot of visitors "play" with it as though it were just another video game. For most people this play is actually an educational experience. They are using what could become one of the data retrieval systems of tomorrow. They are learning about touch-sensitive screens. (You don't need to press, by the way; sometimes the system reacts even before your finger touches the screen.)

But whether people play with the WorldKey or put it to work, they usually end up walking away from the screen without completing the WorldKey program and setting it up for the next user. If people get frustrated with the WorldKey it's usually because they walked up to it while it was in the middle of showing the last user what he asked to see.

If, as opposed to finding a program in progress left from a previous user, you initiate the program, the WorldKey will quickly show you, step by step, how to use the system.

If you wish to speak to an attendant, work through the program until a prompt for an attendant is displayed on the screen. Touch the screen as indicated and soon one of the WorldKey attendants will come "live" onto the screen, ready to communicate with you.

Future World

Gleaming, futuristic structures of immense proportions leave little in doubt concerning the orientation of this, the first encountered theme area of EPCOT Center. The thoroughfares are broad and punctuated with billowing fountains, reflected in the shining facades of space-age architecture. Everything, including the bountiful landscaping, is clean and sparkling to the point of asepsis and seemingly bigger than life. Pavilions dedicated to man's past, present, and future technological accomplishments form the perimeter of the Future World area with the Spaceship Earth and its flanking CommuniCores East and West standing preeminent front and center.

SPACESHIP EARTH

Type of Ride: Educational journey through past, present, and into the future

When to Go: As soon as the park opens or after 5:30 P.M.

Special Comments: If lines are long when you arrive, try again between 5 and 6 P.M.

Author's Rating: One of EPCOT's best; ★★★★½

Overall Appeal by Age Group:

Pre-school	Grade School	Teens	Young Adults	Over 30	Senior Citizens
★★★★	★★★★½	★★★★½	★★★★½	★★★★½	★★★★½

Duration of Ride: About 16 minutes

Average Wait in Line per 100 People Ahead of You: 3 minutes

Assumes: Normal operation

Loading Speed: Moderate to fast

DESCRIPTION AND COMMENTS   This Bell System ride spirals through the 17-story interior of EPCOT Center's premier landmark, taking visitors past AudioAnimatronics scenes depicting man's developments in communications, from cave painting to printing to television to space communications and computer networks. The ride is compelling and well done as you ascend the geosphere but, to us, a little disappointing on the way back down. Even so, it's a masterpiece and is thus accorded a "not to be missed" rating.

TOURING TIPS   This is one of the toughest attractions in EPCOT Center to see without literally investing hours of your time standing in line. The only way we know to beat the crowd at Spaceship Earth is to be one of the first visitors in the park when it opens. If lines are long when you arrive, try again after 4:30 P.M. Do not miss it, however, even if you have to stand awhile in line; it's one of Disney's prize achievements.

EARTH STATION

DESCRIPTION AND COMMENTS   Not an attraction as such. Earth Station is situated at the base of the geosphere and serves as the exit of Spaceship Earth. It also serves as EPCOT Center's primary guest relations and information center. Attendants staff information booths and a number of WorldKey terminals are available. If you have spent any time in the Magic Kingdom, Earth Station is EPCOT Center's version of City Hall.

TOURING TIPS   If you wish to eat in one of the EPCOT Center sit-down restaurants, you can make your reservations from Earth Station through a WorldKey Information Service attendant (instead of running to the restaurant itself and standing in line for reservations, which is another alternative). See the description of the WorldKey system, page 167, and the section dealing with eating in EPCOT Center, page 201.

COMMUNICORE

Type of Attraction: Multifaceted attraction featuring static and "hands-on" exhibits relating to energy, communications, information processing, and future EPCOT developments

When to Go: On your second day at EPCOT or after you have seen all the major attractions

Special Comments: Most exhibits demand time and participation to be rewarding; not much gained here by a quick walk-through

Author's Rating: Interesting on the whole, though not particularly compelling; *Rollercoaster* (you design your own roller coaster with the assistance of a computer) in EPCOT Computer Central (Communicore East) is our pick of the litter; ★★½

Overall Appeal by Age Group:

Pre-school	Grade School	Teens	Young Adults	Over 30	Senior Citizens
★★½	★★★	★★½	★★★	★★★	★★★

DESCRIPTION AND COMMENTS The name stands for "Community Core," and it consists of two huge, crescent-shaped, glass-walled structures housing industry-sponsored walk-through and "hands-on" exhibits, restaurants, and a gift shop. The Disney people like to describe it as a "twenty-first-century village square where the town crier is an array of computer-fed, interactive video screens and high technology electronics libraries."

TOURING TIPS CommuniCore (two buildings: east and west) provides visitors an opportunity to sample a variety of technology in a fun, "hands-on" manner through the use of various interactive communication devices. Some of the exhibits are quite intriguing while others are a little dry. We observed a wide range of reactions by visitors to the many CommuniCore exhibits and can only suggest that you form your own opinion. In terms of touring strategy, we suggest you spend time in CommuniCore on your second day at EPCOT Center. If you only have one day, visit sometime during the evening if you have time. Be warned, however, that CommuniCore exhibits are almost all technical and educational in nature and may not be compatible with your mood or level of energy toward the end of a long day of touring. Also be advised that you cannot get much of anything out of a quick walk-through of CommuniCore; you have to play with the equipment to understand what is going on.

Attractions in CommuniCore East include:

EPCOT Computer Central

DESCRIPTION AND COMMENTS Touch-sensitive video terminals show users through simple and entertaining games how computers are used in design and control. A robot called SMRT-1 plays guessing games with guests by decoding yes and no answers through a voice recognition box.

TOURING TIPS   See comments in CommuniCore Touring Tips.

Travelport

DESCRIPTION AND COMMENTS   This American Express exhibit in CommuniCore East has "vacation stations" equipped with touch-sensitive video terminals similar to those in the WorldKey system. If you work with a terminal you can see different types of vacations in different geographical areas.

TOURING TIPS   See comments in CommuniCore Touring Tips.

Energy Exchange

DESCRIPTION AND COMMENTS   There are also touch-sensitive video terminals in this Exxon exhibit, permitting users to tap into information about a variety of energy topics. Stationary displays are devoted to specific energy sources—solar, coal, nuclear, oil, and others. Visitors can use some of the devices to demonstrate the generation and expenditure of energy.

TOURING TIPS   See comments in CommuniCore Touring Tips.

Electronic Forum

DESCRIPTION AND COMMENTS   This section of CommuniCore consists of World News Center, which has TV monitors carrying live news broadcasts from around the world. At Future Choice Theater visitors can participate in an on-going opinion poll by pushing buttons built into the armrests of their seats. Responses appear on the theater screen so guests can see how their opinions stack up against those of other visitors.

TOURING TIPS   See comments in CommuniCore Touring Tips.

Backstage Magic

DESCRIPTION AND COMMENTS   This Sperry exhibit gives visitors a look through the windows of the EPCOT Center Computer Control Room.

TOURING TIPS   This exhibit is produced in a small theater, so there is almost always a minimum wait in line of 20 minutes. The show is not particularly compelling or informative; one of EPCOT Center's less appealing offerings in our opinion.

Attractions in CommuniCore West include:

FutureCom

DESCRIPTION AND COMMENTS   A Bell System exhibit with a variety of electronic games demonstrating facets of telecommunications. Another part of the exhibit demonstrates video teleconferencing, putting visitors face-to-face via two-way television with an attendant. Still another section has touch-sensitive video terminals that enable guests to "call up" information on any U.S. state and its current events.

TOURING TIPS   See additional comments in CommuniCore Touring Tips.

Expo Robotics

DESCRIPTION AND COMMENTS   One of the newer and certainly one of the better and more fascinating of all CommuniCore exhibits, Expo Robotics is an active, fast-paced demonstration of advanced robotic applications. On stage, five robots demonstrate juggling and top spinning. Nearby, guests can have their portrait sketched by a robot (no charge).

TOURING TIPS   See additional comments in CommuniCore Touring Tips.

EPCOT Outreach and Teacher's Center

DESCRIPTION AND COMMENTS   EPCOT Outreach consists of static displays illustrating various EPCOT projects and developments, and a library service that provides information on demand concerning any topic presented in either Future World or World Showcase. If you have used these services in the past, note that their location in CommuniCore West has been moved to the FutureCom area.

TOURING TIPS   This is where someone will try to answer that question you have been kicking around all day. If you are an educator with a group, special tour-enhancing handouts can be obtained here.

THE LIVING SEAS

Type of Attraction: Multifaceted attraction consisting of an underwater ride beneath a huge saltwater aquarium and a number of exhibits and displays dealing with oceanography, ocean ecology, and sea life

When to Go: Before 10 A.M. or after 3 P.M.

Special Comments: The ride is only a small component of this attraction. See description and touring tips below for information on the rest of the attraction.

Author's Rating: An excellent marine exhibit; ★★★★

Overall Appeal by Age Group:

Pre-school	Grade School	Teens	Young Adults	Over 30	Senior Citizens
★★★	★★★½	★★★½	★★★★	★★★★	★★★★

Duration of Ride: 3 minutes

Average Wait in Line per 100 People Ahead of You: 3½ minutes

Assumes: All elevators in operation

Loading Speed: Fast

DESCRIPTION AND COMMENTS   The Living Seas is one of the most ambitious Future World offerings. The focus is a huge, 200-foot diameter, 27-foot-deep main tank containing fish, mammals, and crustaceans in a simulation of a real ocean ecosystem. Scientists and divers conduct actual marine experiments underwater in view of EPCOT Center guests. Visitors can view the undersea activity through eight-inch-thick viewing windows below the surface (including viewing windows in the Coral Reef Restaurant), and via a three-part adventure/ride which is the featured attraction of The Living Seas. This last consists of a movie dramatizing the link between the ocean and man's survival followed by an elevator descent to the bottom of the tank. Here guests board gondolas for a three-minute voyage through an underwater viewing tunnel.

The fish population of The Living Seas appears to have increased somewhat, but the underwater ride is over before you have gotten comfortably situated in the gondola. No matter, the strength of this attraction lies in the dozen or so exhibits offered after the ride. Visitors can view aqua culture fish-breeding experiments, watch short films about various forms of sea life, and much more. You can stay as long as you wish in the exhibit area.

The Living Seas is a high-quality marine/aquarium exhibit, but is no substitute for visiting Sea World, an enormous marine life theme park every bit on a par in terms of quality, appeal, educational value, and entertainment with the Magic Kingdom, EPCOT Center, or Disney-MGM Studios.

TOURING TIPS   The exhibits at the end of the ride are the best part of The Living Seas. In the morning, these are often bypassed by guests trying to rush or stay ahead of the crowd. The Living Seas needs to be lingered over at a time when you are not in a hurry. We recommend seeing The Living Seas in the late afternoon or evening, or on your second day at EPCOT Center.

THE LAND

DESCRIPTION AND COMMENTS   The Land is in fact a huge pavilion sponsored by Kraft which contains three attractions (discussed next) and a number of restaurants.

TOURING TIPS   The Land is a good place for a fast-food lunch; if you are there to see the attraction, however, don't go during meal times.

Attractions in The Land include:

Listen to the Land

Type of Ride: A boat ride/adventure through the past, present and
    future of U.S. farming and agriculture
When to Go: Before 10:30 A.M. or after 7:30 P.M.
Special Comments: Take this ride early in the morning but save the
    other Land attractions for later in the day; located on the lower
    level of The Land pavilion
Author's Rating: Interesting and fun; ★★★★★
Overall Appeal by Age Group:

Pre-school	Grade School	Teens	Young Adults	Over 30	Senior Citizens
★★★	★★★★	★★★★	★★★★★	★★★★★	★★★★★

Duration of Ride: About 12 minutes
Average Wait in Line per 100 People Ahead of You: 3 minutes
Assumes: 15 boats operating
Loading Speed: Moderate

DESCRIPTION AND COMMENTS   A boat ride which takes visitors through a simulated giant seed germination, past various inhospitable environments man has faced as a farmer, and through a futuristic, innovative greenhouse where real crops are being grown using the latest agricultural technologies. Inspiring and educational with excellent effects and a good narrative, this attraction should "not be missed."

TOURING TIPS This "not to be missed" attraction should be seen before the lunch crowd hits The Land restaurants, i.e., before 10:30 A.M., or in the evening after 7:30 P.M.

If you really enjoy this ride, or if you have a special interest in the agricultural techniques demonstrated, consider taking the Harvest Tour. Free of charge, this 45-minute guided tour takes guests behind the scenes for an in-depth examination of advanced and experimental growing methods. Reservations for the Harvest Tour are made on a space available basis at the Guided Tour Waiting Area (to the far right of the restaurants on the lower level).

Kitchen Kabaret

Type of Show: AudioAnimatronic variety show about food and nutrition
When to Go: Before 11 A.M. or after 3 P.M.
Special Comments: Located on the lower level of The Land pavilion
Author's Rating: Lively and amusing; ★★★½
Overall Appeal by Age Group:

Pre-school	Grade School	Teens	Young Adults	Over 30	Senior Citizens
★★★★	★★★★	★★★	★★★½	★★★½	★★★★

Duration of Presentation: Approximately 13 minutes
Pre-Show Entertainment: None
Probable Waiting Time: Less than 10 minutes

DESCRIPTION AND COMMENTS Disney AudioAnimatronic (robotic) characters in the forms of various foods and kitchen appliances take the stage in an educational musical revue, which tells the story of the basic food groups (protein, carbohydrates, etc.). It's a cute show with entertainment provided by such characters as Bonnie Appetit, the Cereal Sisters, and the comedy team of Mr. Hamm and Mr. Eggz.

TOURING TIPS One of the few light entertainment offerings at EPCOT Center. Slightly reminiscent of the *Country Bear Jamboree* in the Magic Kingdom (but not quite as humorous or endearing in our opinion). Though the theater is not large, we have never encountered any long waits at the *Kitchen Kabaret* (even during meal times). Nevertheless, we recommend you go before 11 A.M. or after 3 P.M.

Harvest Theater: Symbiosis

Type of Show: Film exploring man's relationship with his environment
When to Go: Before 11 A.M. and after 3 P.M.
Author's Rating: Extremely interesting and enlightening; ★★★★
Overall Appeal by Age Group:

Pre-school	Grade School	Teens	Young Adults	Over 30	Senior Citizens
★★½	★★★	★★★½	★★★½	★★★★	★★★½

Duration of Presentation: Approximately 18½ minutes
Pre-Show Entertainment: None
Probable Waiting Time: 10–15 minutes

DESCRIPTION AND COMMENTS   This attraction features a 70mm Panavision film, *Symbiosis*. The subject is the interrelationship of man and his environment, and demonstrates how easily man can upset the ecological balance. The film is superb in its production and not too heavy-handed in its sobering message. The cinematic technique is "state of the art."

TOURING TIPS   This extremely worthwhile film should be part of every visitor's touring day. Long waits are usually not a problem at the Harvest Theater, but as with *Kitchen Kabaret*, we recommend you go before 11 A.M. or after 3 P.M.

JOURNEY INTO IMAGINATION

DESCRIPTION AND COMMENTS   Another multi-attraction pavilion, located on the west side of CommuniCore West and down the walk from The Land. Outside is an "upside-down waterfall" and one of our favorite Future World landmarks, the so-called "jumping water," a leap-frogging fountain that seems to hop over the heads of unsuspecting passers-by.

TOURING TIPS   We recommend early morning or late evening touring. See the individual attractions for further specifics.

Attractions in Journey into Imagination include:

Journey into Imagination Ride

Type of Ride: Fantasy adventure
When to Go: Before 10:30 A.M. or after 7 P.M.
Author's Rating: Colorful but dull; ★★★
Overall Appeal by Age Group:

Pre-school	Grade School	Teens	Young Adults	Over 30	Senior Citizens
★★★★	★★★★	★★★½	★★★	★★★	★★★

Duration of Ride: Approximately 13 minutes
Average Wait in Line per 100 People Ahead of You: 3 minutes
Assumes: 20 trains operating
Loading Speed: Moderate to fast

DESCRIPTION AND COMMENTS   This ride features two Disney characters—Figment, an impish purple dragon, and Dreamfinder, a red-bearded adventurer who pilots a contraption designed to search out and capture ideas. This ride, with its happy, humorous orientation, is one of the lighter and more fanciful offerings in the park. It is the favorite ride of some, while others find it dull and vacuous.

TOURING TIPS   This ride, combined with *Captain EO* in the same building, draws large crowds beginning about 10:45 A.M. We recommend riding before 10:30 A.M. or after 7 P.M.

The Image Works

Type of Attraction: Hands-on creative playground employing color, music, touch-sensation, and electronic devices
When to Go: Anytime you please
Special Comments: You do not have to wait in the long line for the ride in this pavilion to gain access to The Image Works. Simply go through the open door just to the left of where the line for the ride is entering. You will not have a wait.
Author's Rating: A fun change of pace; be sure to see the Dreamfinder's School of Drama; ★★★
Overall Appeal by Age Group:

Pre-school	Grade School	Teens	Young Adults	Over 30	Senior Citizens
★★★	★★★½	★★★	★★★	★★★	★★★

Probable Waiting Time: No waiting required

DESCRIPTION AND COMMENTS This is a playground for the imagination utilizing light, color, sound, and electronic devices which can be manipulated by visitors. There's the Magic Palette, with a video-screen canvas and an electronic paintbrush. Especially fun is the Electronic Philharmonic, which enables visitors to conduct the brass, woodwind, percussion, and string sections of an orchestra by movements of the hand. (The secret is raising and lowering your hands over the labeled discs on the console. Don't try pressing the discs as if they were buttons. Pretend you're a conductor—raise a hand away from the disc labeled brass, for example, and you will get louder brass. Lower your hand toward the disc labeled woodwinds and you'll get less volume from the woodwinds section.)

TOURING TIPS There are quite a number of interesting things to do and play with here, far more than the representative examples we listed. If you have more than one day at EPCOT Center, save The Image Works for the second day. If you are on a one-day schedule, try to work it in during the evening or late afternoon.

Magic Eye Theater: Captain EO

Type of Show: 3-D rock and roll space fantasy film

When to Go: Before 11 A.M. or after 5 P.M.

Special Comments: Adults should not be put off by the rock music or sci-fi theme; they will enjoy the show as much as the kids

Author's Rating: An absolute hoot! Not to be missed; ★★★★

Overall Appeal by Age Group:

Pre-school	Grade School	Teens	Young Adults	Over 30	Senior Citizens
★★★★★	★★★★★	★★★★★	★★★★½	★★★★½	★★★★

Duration of Presentation: Approximately 17 minutes

Pre-Show Entertainment: 8 minutes

Probable Waiting Time: 12 minutes (at suggested times)

DESCRIPTION AND COMMENTS *Captain EO* is sort of the ultimate rock video. Starring Michael Jackson and directed by Francis Coppola, the 3-D space fantasy is more than a film; it is a happening. Action on the screen is augmented by lasers, fiber-optics, cannons, and a host of other special effects in the theater. There's not much of a story, but there's plenty of music and dancing performed by some of the most unlikely creatures ever to shake a tail feather.

TOURING TIPS *Captain EO* draws large crowds. During the summer and holiday periods when there are large numbers of kids in the park, it's best to see *Captain EO* before 10:30 A.M.

THE WORLD OF MOTION

DESCRIPTION AND COMMENTS Presented by General Motors, this pavilion is to the left of Spaceship Earth when you enter and down toward World Showcase from the Universe of Energy pavilion. The pavilion is home to It's Fun to Be Free, a ride, and to TransCenter, an assembly of stationary exhibits and mini-theater productions on the theme of transportation.

Attractions in The World of Motion include:

It's Fun to Be Free

Type of Ride: AudioAnimatronic survey of the history of transportation
When to Go: Before noon and after 4 P.M.
Author's Rating: Not to be missed; ★★★★★
Overall Appeal by Age Group:

Pre-school	Grade School	Teens	Young Adults	Over 30	Senior Citizens
★★★★	★★★★★	★★★★	★★★★★	★★★★★	★★★★★

Duration of Ride: Approximately 14½ minutes
Average Wait in Line per 100 People Ahead of You: 2¾ minutes
Assumes: Normal operation
Loading Speed: Moderate to fast

DESCRIPTION AND COMMENTS A "not-to-be-missed" attraction, this ride conducts visitors through a continuum of twenty-four Audio-Animatronics scenes depicting where and how man has traveled, and what the future has in store for travel. The detail-work in individual scenes is amazing and the tongue-in-cheek, humorous tone of the ride makes the history lesson more than tolerable.

TOURING TIPS This ride has a large carrying capacity and an efficient loading system, keeping lines generally manageable. Many days you can hop on this ride any time you want. Its largest crowds build between noon and 4 P.M.

TransCenter

Type of Attraction: Exhibits and mini-theater productions concerning the evolution and future of transportation, particularly as relates to the automobile

When to Go: On your second day or after you've seen the major attractions

Special Comments: World of Motion has a separate entrance to the exhibit area, making visitation possible other than when you take the It's Fun to Be Free ride

Author's Rating: Informative with a healthy dose of humor; ★★★

Overall Appeal by Age Group:

Pre-school	Grade School	Teens	Young Adults	Over 30	Senior Citizens
★★½	★★★	★★★	★★★	★★★	★★★

Probable Waiting Time: No waiting required if you enter through the rear entrance

DESCRIPTION AND COMMENTS Most visitors enter TransCenter when they disembark from the ride described above, but there are separate doors on the east side of the pavilion for those who wish to visit the various exhibits without taking the ride. TransCenter is a walk-through attraction of 33,000 square feet, and deals with a wide range of topics relating to transportation. One major display demonstrates the importance of aerodynamics to fuel economy, while others evaluate the prospects of future power systems and explains why the industry is turning to robotic production techniques. Yet another display shows some advanced designs for the possible land, sea, and air conveyances of tomorrow.

TOURING TIPS There's a lot to see here. How much you take in will be determined by your interest in the subject and the flexibility of your schedule. We like TransCenter on the second day of a two-day visit, or during the mid-afternoon if you enjoy this sort of display more than the offerings of World Showcase. Late evening after you have finished your "must list" is also a good time.

HORIZONS

Type of Ride: A look at man's evolving perception of the future

When to Go: Before 10:30 A.M. or after 3:30 P.M.

Special Comments: Periodically inundated when the Universe of Energy discharges an audience

Author's Rating: Not to be missed; ★★★★½

Overall Appeal by Age Group:

Pre-school	Grade School	Teens	Young Adults	Over 30	Senior Citizens
★★★★	★★★★	★★★★	★★★★½	★★★★½	★★★★½

Duration of Ride: Approximately 15 minutes

Average Wait in Line per 100 People Ahead of You: 4 minutes

Assumes: Normal operation

Loading Speed: Moderate to fast

DESCRIPTION AND COMMENTS   The General Electric pavilion takes a look back at yesterday's visions of the future, including Jules Verne's concept of a moon rocket and a 1930s preview of a neon city. Elsewhere guests visit FuturePort and ride through a family habitat of the next century, with scenes depicting apartment, farm, and underwater and space communities.

TOURING TIPS   The entire Horizons pavilion is devoted to a single, continuously loading ride, which has a large carrying capacity. This "not to be missed" attraction can be enjoyed almost any time of day without long waits in line. An exception occurs immediately following the conclusion of a Universe of Energy performance, when up to 580 patrons often troop over and queue up for Horizons en masse. If you chance to encounter this deluge or its aftermath, take a 15-minute break. Chances are when you return to Horizons you will be able to walk right in.

WONDERS OF LIFE

DESCRIPTION AND COMMENTS   Presented by the Metropolitan Life Insurance Company, this newest addition to the Future World family is a multifaceted pavilion dealing with the human body, health, and medicine. Housed in a 100,000-square-foot, gold-domed structure, Wonders of Life houses a variety of attractions focusing on the capabilities of the human body and the importance of keeping it fit.

Attractions in Wonders of Life include:

Body Wars

Type of Ride: Flight simulator ride through the human body

When to Go: As soon as possible after the park opens

Special Comments: Not recommended for pregnant women or those prone to motion sickness

Author's Rating: Absolutely mindblowing, not to be missed; ★★★★★

Overall Appeal by Age Group:

Pre-school	Grade School	Teens	Young Adults	Over 30	Senior Citizens
★★★★★	★★★★★	★★★★★	★★★★★	★★★★★	★★★★★

Duration of Ride: 5 minutes

Average Wait in Line per 100 People Ahead of You: 4 minutes

Assumes: All simulators operating

Loading Speed: Moderate to fast

DESCRIPTION AND COMMENTS   This is a thrill ride through the human body, developed in the image of the Star Tours space simulation ride. The idea is that you are a passenger on a sort of miniature space capsule that is injected into a human body. Once inside the body your mission is to pick up a scientist who has been inspecting a splinter in the patient's finger. Before retrieval, however, the scientist gets sucked into the circulatory system and you end up chasing her all over the body in an attempt to rescue her. The simulator creates a vividly realistic experience as guests seem to hurtle at fantastic speeds through anatomical images as the body fights disease. The sights are as mind-boggling as the ride is breathtaking, in this "not to be missed" attraction.

TOURING TIPS   This is EPCOT Center's first and only thrill ride and is popular with all age groups. Ride first thing after the park opens or just before closing time. Be advised that Body Wars makes a lot of people motion sick and that it is not at all unusual for a simulator to be taken off-line to clean up some previous rider's mess. If you are at all susceptible to motion sickness we suggest you reconsider riding Body Wars. If you are on the ride and begin to get nauseated, close your eyes. Without the visual effects, the ride itself is not rough enough to disturb most guests. If you do get queasy, there are rest rooms to your left on exiting the ride. As an aside, Star Tours, another simulator ride at the Disney-MGM Studios, is just as wild but makes very few people sick. If you successfully rode Star Tours, that does not necessarily mean that Body Wars will not upset you. Conversely, if Body Wars made you ill, you cannot assume that Star Tours will do the same.

Cranium Command

Type of Show: AudioAnimatronic character show about the brain

When to Go: Before 11 A.M. or after 3 P.M.

Author's Rating: Funny, outrageous, and educational. Not to be missed; ★★★★★

Overall Appeal by Age Group:

Pre-school	Grade School	Teens	Young Adults	Over 30	Senior Citizens
★★★★	★★★★★	★★★★★	★★★★★	★★★★★	★★★★★

Duration of Presentation: About 20 minutes

Pre-Show Entertainment: Explanatory lead-in to feature presentation

Probable Waiting Time: Less than 10 minutes at touring times suggested

DESCRIPTION AND COMMENTS *Cranium Command* is EPCOT Center's great sleeper attraction. Stuck on the backside of the Wonders of Life pavilion and far less promoted than Body Wars, many guests elect to bypass this most humorous of all EPCOT Center offerings. Disney characters called "Brain Pilots" are trained to operate human brains. The show consists of a day in the life of one of these Cranium Commanders as he tries to pilot his assigned brain (that of an adolescent boy). We do not know who designed this attraction, but EPCOT Center in particular, and Walt Disney World in general, could use a lot more of this type of humor.

TOURING TIPS   The presentation kicks off with a pre-show cartoon that is essential to understanding the rest of the show. If you arrive in the waiting area while the cartoon is in progress, make sure you see enough to understand the story line before going into the main theater.

The Making of Me

Type of Show: Humorous movie about human conception and birth
When to Go: Early in the morning or after 4:30 P.M.
Author's Rating: Well done; ★★★★
Overall Appeal by Age Group:

Pre-school	Grade School	Teens	Young Adults	Over 30	Senior Citizens
★★★	★★★★	★★★★½	★★★★½	★★★★	★★★★

Duration of Presentation: 14 minutes

Pre-Show Entertainment: None

Probable Waiting Time: About 25 minutes or more unless you go early in the morning or after 4:30 P.M.

DESCRIPTION AND COMMENTS   This funny, lighthearted and very sensitive movie about human conception, gestation, and birth was considered to be a controversial addition to the Wonders of Life pavilion. In point of fact, Disney audiences have received it well, with most guests agreeing that the material is tastefully and creatively presented. The plot is in the *Back to the Future* genre and has the main character going back in time to watch his parents date, fall in love, marry, and, yes, conceive and give birth to him. The sexual material is well handled with loving relationships given much more emphasis than plumbing. Parents of children under seven tell us that the sexual information presented went over their children's heads for the most part. For children a little older, however, the film seems to precipitate quite a few questions. You be the judge.

TOURING TIPS   *The Making of Me* is an excellent film shown in a theater not much larger than a phone booth. It is our fervent hope that the Disney people will soon relocate this show to a larger, more suitable theater. At present, however, the diminutive size of the theater insures that there will be a long wait unless you go just after the park opens or during the very late afternoon and evening.

Fitness Fairgrounds

DESCRIPTION AND COMMENTS   Much of the pavilion's interior is devoted to an assortment of visitor participation exhibits, where guests can test their senses in a fun house, receive computer-generated health analyses of their personal lifestyles, work out on electronically sophisticated exercise equipment, and watch a video presentation called "Goofy About Health" (starring who else?).

TOURING TIPS   We recommend you save the Fitness Fair exhibits for your second day, or the end of your first day at EPCOT Center.

UNIVERSE OF ENERGY

Type of Attraction: Combination ride/theater presentation about energy

When to Go: Before 10:30 A.M. or after 4:30 P.M.

Special Comments: Don't be dismayed by large lines; 580 people disappear into the pavilion each time the theater turns over

Author's Rating: One of EPCOT's premier presentations; ★★★★½

Overall Appeal by Age Group:

Pre-school	Grade School	Teens	Young Adults	Over 30	Senior Citizens
★★★★½	★★★★½	★★★★½	★★★★½	★★★★½	★★★★½

Duration of Presentation: Approximately 26½ minutes

Pre-Show Entertainment: 8 minutes

Probable Waiting Time: 20–40 minutes

DESCRIPTION AND COMMENTS   The AudioAnimatronic dinosaurs and the unique traveling theater make this Exxon pavilion one of the most popular in Future World. Since this is a theater with a ride component, the line does not move at all while the show is in progress. When the theater empties, however, a large chunk of the line will disappear as people are admitted for the next show. At this "not to be missed" attraction, visitors are seated in what appears to be a fairly ordinary theater while they watch an animated film on fossil fuels. Then, the theater seats divide into six 97-passenger traveling cars which glide among the swamps and reptiles of a prehistoric forest. The special effects include the feel of warm, clammy air from the swamp, the smell of sulphur from an erupting volcano, and the sight of red lava hissing and bubbling toward the passengers. The remainder of the performance utilizes some nifty cinematic techniques to bring you back to the leading edge of energy research and development.

TOURING TIPS   This "not to be missed" attraction draws large crowds beginning early in the morning. Either catch the show before 10:30 A.M. or wait until after 4:30 P.M. Waits for the Universe of Energy are normally within tolerable limits, however, since the Universe of Energy can operate more than one presentation at a time.

World Showcase

The second theme area of EPCOT Center is World Showcase. Situated around picturesque World Showcase Lagoon, it is an ongoing world's fair, with the cuisine, culture, history, and architecture of almost a dozen countries permanently on display in individual national pavilions. The so-called pavilions, which generally consist of familiar landmarks and typically representative street scenes from the host country, are spaced along a 1.2-mile promenade which circles the impressive forty-acre Lagoon. Double-decker omnibuses carry visitors to stops around the promenade, and boats ferry guests across the lagoon (the lines at the bus stops tend to be pushy, however, and it's almost always quicker to walk than to use the buses or the boats). Moving clockwise around the promenade, the nations represented are:

Mexico

DESCRIPTION AND COMMENTS   Two pre-Columbian pyramids dominate the architecture of this exhibit. The first makes up the facade of the pavilion and the second overlooks the restaurant and plaza alongside the boat ride, El Rio del Tiempo, inside the pavilion.

El Rio del Tiempo, The River of Time, is a boat trip which winds among AudioAnimatronics and cinematic scenes depicting the history of Mexico from the ancient cultures of the Maya, Toltec, and Aztec civilizations to modern times. Special effects include fiber-optic projections that provide a spectacular fireworks display near the end of the ride.

TOURING TIPS   A romantic and exciting testimony to the charms of Mexico, this pavilion probably contains more authentic and valuable artifacts and objets d'art than any other national pavilion. Many people zip right past these treasures, unfortunately, without even stopping to look. The village scene on the interior of the pavilion is both beautiful and exquisitely detailed. We recommend seeing this pavilion before 11 A.M. or after 6 P.M.

Attractions in Mexico include:

El Rio del Tiempo

Type of Ride: Boat ride
When to Go: Before 11 A.M. or after 7:00 P.M.
Author's Rating: Light and relaxing; ★★★
Overall Appeal by Age Group:

Pre-school	Grade School	Teens	Young Adults	Over 30	Senior Citizens
★★★	★★★	★★★	★★★	★★★	★★★

Duration of Ride: Approximately 7 minutes (plus 1½-minute wait to disembark)
Average Wait in Line per 100 People Ahead of You: 4½ minutes
Assumes: 16 boats in operation
Loading Speed: Moderate

Norway

DESCRIPTION AND COMMENTS   A very different addition to the World Showcase international pavilions, the Norwegian pavilion is complex, beautiful, and architecturally diverse. There is a courtyard surrounded by an assortment of traditional Scandinavian buildings including a replica of the 14th-century Akershus Castle, a wooden stave church, red-tiled cottages, and replicas of historic buildings representing the traditional designs of Bergen, Ålesund, and Oslo. Attractions in Norway include an adventure boat ride in the mold of Pirates of the Caribbean, followed by a movie about Norway, and, in the stave church, a gallery of art and artifacts. Located between China and Mexico, the Norway pavilion houses the Akershus Restaurant, a reservations/sit-down eatery featuring koldtboard (cold buffet) plus a variety of hot Norwegian fare. For those on the run there is an open-air café and a bakery. For shoppers there is an abundance of native handicrafts.

Attractions in Norway include:

Maelstrom

Type of Ride: Disney adventure boat ride
When to Go: Before 10 A.M. or after 3 P.M.

Author's Rating: One of EPCOT Center's most exciting rides, also
one of its shortest; ★★★★

Overall Appeal by Age Group:

Pre-school	Grade School	Teens	Young Adults	Over 30	Senior Citizens
★★★★	★★★★	★★★★	★★★★	★★★★	★★★★

Duration of Ride: About 4½ minutes, followed by a five-minute film
with a short wait in between; about 14 minutes for the whole
show.

Average Wait in Line per 100 People Ahead of You: 4 minutes

Assumes: Twelve or thirteen boats operating

Loading Speed: Fast

DESCRIPTION AND COMMENTS   Guests board dragon-headed ships for
an adventure voyage through the fabled rivers and seas of Viking history and legend. In one of Disney's shorter water rides, guests brave
trolls, rocky gorges, waterfalls, and a storm at sea. A new-generation
Disney water ride, the Viking voyage assembles an impressive array of
special effects, combining visual, tactile, and auditory stimuli in a fast-
paced and often humorous odyssey. After the ride guests are shown a
short (five-minute) film on Norway.

TOURING TIPS   Ride Maelstrom before 11 A.M. or in the late afternoon. Sometimes several hundred guests from a recently concluded
performance of the *Wonders of China* arrive at Maelstrom en masse.
Should you encounter this horde, bypass Maelstrom for the time being.

People's Republic of China

DESCRIPTION AND COMMENTS   A half-sized replica of the Temple of
Heaven in Beijing (Peking) identifies this pavilion. Gardens and reflecting ponds simulate those found in Suzhou, and an art gallery features
a "Lotus Blossom" gate and formal saddle roof line.

Pass through the Hall of Prayer for Good Harvest to see the Circle-
Vision 360 motion picture, *Wonders of China.* Warm and appealing,
the film serves as a brilliant introduction to the people and natural
beauty of this little-known nation. Two restaurants have been added to
the China pavilion since its opening, a fast-food eatery and a lovely,
reservations-only, full-service establishment.

TOURING TIPS   A truly beautiful pavilion, serene yet exciting. The movie, *Wonders of China*, plays in a theater where guests must stand, but can usually be enjoyed at any time during the day without much waiting. If you are touring the World Showcase in a counterclockwise rotation and plan to go next to Norway and ride Maelstrom, take up a viewing position on the far left of the theater (as you face the attendant's podium). After the show, make sure you are one of the first to exit the theater. Hustle over to Maelstrom as fast as you can to arrive ahead of the several hundred other *Wonders of China* patrons who will be right behind you.

We recommend the same visitation times for *Wonders of China*, an excellent film, as for the pavilion in general.

Attractions in People's Republic of China include:

Wonders of China

Type of Show: Film essay on the Chinese people and country
When to Go: Anytime
Special Comments: Audience stands throughout performance
Author's Rating: Charming and enlightening; ★★★★½
Overall Appeal by Age Group:

Pre-school	Grade School	Teens	Young Adults	Over 30	Senior Citizens
★★★	★★★½	★★★½	★★★★½	★★★★½	★★★★

Duration of Presentation: Approximately 19 minutes
Pre-Show Entertainment: None
Probable Waiting Time: 10 minutes

Germany

DESCRIPTION AND COMMENTS   A clocktower adorned with boy and girl figures overlooks the platz, or plaza, which identifies the pavilion of the Federal Republic of Germany. Dominated by a fountain depicting St. George's victory over the dragon, the platz is encircled by buildings reflecting traditional German architecture. The focal attraction is the Biergarten, a full-service (reservations only) restaurant featuring German food and beer. Yodeling, German folk dancing, singing, and oompah band music accompany the fare.

TOURING TIPS   The pavilion is pleasant and festive. Germany is recommended for touring at any time of the day.

Italy

DESCRIPTION AND COMMENTS   The entrance to the Italian pavilion is marked by the 105-foot campanile, or bell tower, said to be a mirror image of the tower that overlooks St. Mark's Square in Venice. To the left of the campanile is a replica of the fourteenth-century Doge's Palace, also a Venetian landmark. Other buildings are composites of architecture found throughout Italy. The style is Florentine, for example, for L'Originale Alfredo di Roma Ristorante. Visitors can watch pasta being made in this popular restaurant which specializes in Fettuccine All'Alfredo. The Italian pavilion even has a small Venetian island with gondolas tied to barber-pole-striped moorings at the edge of the World Showcase Lagoon.

TOURING TIPS   The streets and courtyards in the Italian pavilion are among the most realistic in World Showcase—you really feel as if you have been transplanted to Italy. Since there is no attraction (film, ride, etc.) at the Italian pavilion, touring is recommended for all hours.

United States

DESCRIPTION AND COMMENTS   The United States pavilion, generally referred to as the American Adventure for the historical production performed there, consists of (typically) a fast-food restaurant and a patriotic, AudioAnimatronics show.

The American Adventure is a composite of everything the Disney people do best. Situated in an almost life-size replica of Philadelphia's Liberty Hall, the production is a stirring, 29-minute rendition of American history narrated by the AudioAnimatronic figures of Mark Twain (who carries a smoking cigar) and Ben Franklin (who climbs a set of stairs to visit Thomas Jefferson). Behind a stage that's almost half the size of a football field is a 28 × 155-foot, rear-projection screen (the largest ever used) on which appropriate motion picture images are interwoven with the action occurring on stage. Definitely a "not to be missed" attraction.

TOURING TIPS   Large and patriotic, but not as interesting externally as most of the other pavilions. The Liberty Inn restaurant is one of the few places in the World Showcase to obtain a quick, fast-food meal.

The American Adventure is, in the opinion of our research team, the very best attraction at EPCOT Center. It usually plays to capacity audiences from around noon through 3:30 P.M., so try to see it early or late.

Because of the theater's large capacity, waiting during the busy times of the day would hardly ever approach an hour, and would probably average 25–40 minutes.

Attractions in the United States include:

The American Adventure

Type of Show: Patriotic mixed-media and AudioAnimatronic presentation on U.S. history

When to Go: Before noon and after 3:30 P.M.

Author's Rating: Possibly the best attraction at EPCOT Center; not to be missed; ★★★★★

Overall Appeal by Age Group:

Pre-school	Grade School	Teens	Young Adults	Over 30	Senior Citizens
★★★	★★★★	★★★★	★★★★½	★★★★★	★★★★★

Duration of Presentation: Approximately 29 minutes

Pre-Show Entertainment: Voices of Liberty choral singing

Probable Waiting Time: 16 minutes

Japan

DESCRIPTION AND COMMENTS   The five-story, blue-roofed pagoda, inspired by a shrine built in Nara in the seventh century, sets this pavilion apart from its neighbors. A hill garden rises behind it with arrangements of waterfalls, rocks, flowers, lanterns, paths, and rustic bridges. The building on the right (as one faces the entrance) was inspired by the ceremonial and coronation hall on the Imperial Palace Grounds at Kyoto. It contains restaurants and a large retail store.

TOURING TIPS   A tasteful and elaborate pavilion which creatively blends simplicity, architectural grandeur, and natural beauty, Japan can be toured at any time of day.

Morocco

DESCRIPTION AND COMMENTS   The bustle of the market, narrow, winding streets, lofty minarets, and stuccoed archways recreate the romance and intrigue of Tangiers and Casablanca. Attention to detail makes Morocco one of the most exciting of the World Showcase pavilions. In addition to the bazaar, Morocco also features a museum of Moorish art and the Marrakech Restaurant, which serves some unusual and difficult-to-find North African ethnic specialities.

TOURING TIPS   Since there is no ride or theater attraction in Morocco, it can be toured anytime at your convenience.

France

DESCRIPTION AND COMMENTS   Naturally there is a replica of the Eiffel Tower (and a big one at that), but the rest of the pavilion is meant to reflect a more general ambience of France in the period 1870 to 1910, a period known as La Belle Epoque (the beautiful time). The sidewalk cafe and the restaurant are both very popular here, but so is the pastry shop. You won't be the first visitor to get the idea of buying a croissant to tide you over until you can obtain a decent meal.

Impressions de France is the name of an 18-minute movie which is projected over 200 degrees onto five screens. They let you sit down in France (compared to the standing theaters in China and Canada) to view a well-made film introduction to the people, cities, and natural wonders of France.

TOURING TIPS   This pavilion is rich in atmosphere attributable to its detailed street scenes and bygone era flavor.

The streets of the French pavilion are diminutive and become quite congested when visitors line up for the film. Waits in line can be substantial here, so we recommend viewing before 11 A.M. and after 7 P.M.

Attractions in France include:

Impressions de France

Type of Show: Film essay on the French people and country
When to Go: Before 11 A.M. and after 7 P.M.
Author's Rating: An exceedingly beautiful film; not to be missed; ★★★★★
Overall Appeal by Age Group:

Pre-school	Grade School	Teens	Young Adults	Over 30	Senior Citizens
★★½	★★★½	★★★½	★★★★½	★★★★½	★★★★½

Duration of Presentation: Approximately 18 minutes
Pre-Show Entertainment: None
Probable Waiting Time: 12 minutes (at suggested times)

United Kingdom

DESCRIPTION AND COMMENTS   A variety of periods and facades, with attempts to create city, town, and rural atmospheres, are compressed into this pavilion, which is mostly shops. The Rose & Crown Pub and Dining Room is the only World Showcase full-service restaurant with dining on the water side of the promenade. A city square, with classic formal facade, copies a look found in London and Edinburgh. One street has a 1500s style thatched-roof cottage, a four-story timber and plaster building, a pre-Georgian plaster building, a formal Palladian exterior of dressed stone, and a city square with Hyde Park bandstand (whew!).

TOURING TIPS   There are no attractions here to create congestion, so tour at any time you wish. Reservations are not needed to enjoy the Pub section of the Rose & Crown Pub, making it a nice place to stop for a beer along about mid-afternoon.

Canada

DESCRIPTION AND COMMENTS   The cultural, natural, and architectural diversity of the United States' neighbor to the north is reflected in this large and impressive pavilion. 30-foot totem poles embellish an Indian village situated beneath the gables of a magnificent château-style hotel. Near the hotel is a rugged stone building said to be modeled after a famous landmark near Niagara Falls, reflective of Canada's British influence. Canada also has a fine film extolling its many national, cultural, and natural virtues. Titled *O Canada!* the film is very enlightening, and demonstrates the immense pride Canadians have in their beautiful country. Visitors leave the theater through Victoria Gardens, inspired by the famed Butchart Gardens of British Columbia.

TOURING TIPS   A large-capacity theater attraction (guests must stand) that sees fairly heavy late morning attendance since it is the first pavilion encountered as one travels counterclockwise around World Showcase Lagoon. We recommend late afternoon or early evening as the best time for viewing the film. Le Cellier, a restaurant serving cafeteria-style on the lower level of the Canadian pavilion, is the only non-fast-food restaurant in the World Showcase that does not require reservations.

Attractions in Canada include:

O Canada!

Type of Show: Film essay on the Canadian people and country

When to Go: Late afternoon or early evening

Special Comments: Audience stands during performance

Author's Rating: Makes you want to catch the first plane to Canada! ★★★★½

Overall Appeal by Age Group:

Pre-school	Grade School	Teens	Young Adults	Over 30	Senior Citizens
★★½	★★★	★★★½	★★★★	★★★★½	★★★★½

Duration of Presentation: Approximately 18 minutes

Pre-Show Entertainment: None

Probable Waiting Time: 10 minutes

Not to Be Missed at EPCOT Center

World Showcase	*The American Adventure*
Future World	Spaceship Earth
	Listen to the Land
	Captain EO
	It's Fun to Be Free
	Universe of Energy
	Body Wars
	Cranium Command
	Horizons

Live Entertainment in EPCOT Center

Live entertainment in EPCOT Center is somewhat more diversified, as might be expected, than that of the Magic Kingdom. World Showcase provides almost unlimited potential for representative entertainment from the respective nations, and Future World allows for a new wave of creativity in live entertainment offerings.

Some information concerning the live entertainment on the day of your visit can be obtained from the information desk in the Earth Station lobby. Another source of information is the WorldKey Information Service. WorldKey usually has the answers, but it is not as direct as quizzing an attendant.

Listed below are some of the performers and performances you are likely to encounter.

Future World Brass	A roving brass band that marches and plays according to a more or less extemporaneous schedule near Spaceship Earth and at other Future World locations.
Disney Characters	The Disney characters, once believed to be inconsistent with the image of EPCOT Center, have now been imported in number. The Disney characters appear for breakfast at the Stargate Restaurant in Future World at 9 A.M., and at the Odyssey Restaurant and Showcase Plaza several times each day according to the daily live entertainment schedule available at Earth Station.
American Gardens Stage	The site of EPCOT Center's premier live performances is near the American Adventure, facing World Showcase Lagoon, in a large amphitheater. Top talent imported from all over the world plays the American Gar-

dens Stage on a limited engagement basis. Many shows highlight the music, dance, and costumes of the performer's home country.

IllumiNations

An after-dark show, consisting of music, fireworks, erupting fountains, special lighting, and laser technology performed on the World Showcase Lagoon when the park is open late. Not to be missed.

Around World Showcase

A variety of unscheduled, impromptu performances take place in and around the various pavilions of World Showcase. You may encounter a strolling mariachi group in Mexico, street actors in Italy, a fife-and-drum corps or a singing group (The Voices of Liberty) at the American Adventure, traditional songs and dances in Japan, comical street drama in the United Kingdom, white-faced mimes in France, and bagpipes in Canada. There is a street entertainment performance at most of the World Showcase pavilions about every half hour (though not scheduled *on* the hour or half hour).

Dinner & Lunch Shows

The restaurants in World Showcase serve up healthy portions of live entertainment to accompany the victuals. Examples of restaurant floorshow fare include folk dancing and a baskapelle band in Germany, singing waiters in Italy, and belly dancers in Morocco. Restaurant shows are performed at dinner only in Italy, but at both lunch and dinner in Germany and Morocco. Reservations are required (see "Eating in EPCOT Center," below).

World Showcase Lagoon

The World Showcase Lagoon provides the stage for a number of shows during the course of the day featuring boats, kites, hang gliders, music, and a variety of other unlikely combinations. Check the daily entertainment schedule for times and details.

—— *Where to View IllumiNations and Other World Showcase Lagoon Performances* ——

Probably the best place to be for any World Showcase Lagoon presentation is seated comfortably on the lakeside veranda of the Cantina de San Angel in Mexico. Come early (*at least* 45 minutes for IllumiNations) and relax with a cold drink while you wait for the show. There is also outdoor Lagoonside seating at the Rose & Crown Pub in the United Kingdom, but the view is not as good as at the Cantina.

Because of islands that block the view in the northern (American Adventure) half of the Lagoon, the most popular spectator positions are along the southern half, from Norway and Mexico on around to Canada and the United Kingdom. While the perspective is a little better here, you must stake out your viewing position at least 45 minutes before showtime. If you do not want to invest the time, or if your dinner runs late, try the rail between China and Germany. It is not usually too crowded and you can see around the islands. Furthermore, if you line up just right, you will be able to see the distant, Fantasy in the Sky fireworks show over the Magic Kingdom.

After IllumiNations, chill out somewhere or repeat your favorite attractions. It is a pleasant crowd-free time to tour, and you will stay out of the way of the more than 40,000 guests who all leave the park immediately following the show.

Eating in EPCOT Center

Having reviewed the restaurants of EPCOT Center since the park opened in 1982, we have seen a lot of changes, most of them for the better. There is more variety now than ever before, and more choices for folks who do not want to take the time for a full-service, sit-down meal. The quality of fast food available is quite good, better than in the Magic Kingdom, and the newest addition to the full-service restaurants, the Akershus Restaurant in Norway, is exceptional in every respect.

Where certain World Showcase restaurants were once timid about delivering an honest representation of the host nation's cuisine, we are now seeing bold ethnic menus in Norway, *mole* in Mexico, and finally, sushi in Japan. Restaurants in England and China, however, still sacrifice ethnic authenticity to please the tastes of most Americans, who, more than anyone, need their palates challenged (or need not to be eating in ethnic restaurants).

Many EPCOT Center restaurants are overpriced, most conspicuously Alfredo's (Italy), Mitsukoshi (Japan), Nine Dragons (China), and the Coral Reef at The Living Seas pavilion. Les Chefs and Le Bistro (France), Akershus (Norway), Biergarten (Germany), and San Angel Inn (Mexico) represent good value through a combination of well-prepared food, ambiance, and in the case of Germany, entertainment.

Making reservations for full-service restaurants still involves standing in line in the morning when you would rather be doing something else, and in most cases, abandoning your touring itinerary to hustle (usually from the opposite side of the park) to the restaurant to be seated. The restaurants are such an integral part of EPCOT Center, however, that we think it would be a mistake not to have a meal in at least one of them.

— Getting a Handle on the World Showcase Restaurants —

Getting a reservation for a particular restaurant depends on its popularity and seating capacity, and, of course, the size of the crowd on the day of your visit. Each restaurant has seatings for both lunch and dinner.

Guests staying at a Walt Disney World hotel or campground may make reservations one to three days in advance by calling (407) 828-4000 between 8 A.M. and 9 P.M. (yes, you can call from home before you arrive at Walt Disney World). Reservations can likewise be made for restaurants at the Disney-MGM Studios and at the Magic Kingdom. Those guests who are lodging out of the World must make their reservations at EPCOT Center on the day of the meal.

For those who are making same-day reservations, arrive at the entrance turnstiles, passport in hand, 45 minutes before EPCOT Center opens. Upon admission go quickly to Earth Station (the building at the base of the dome). Both lunch and dinner reservations can be made at the same time. Be prepared with alternatives for both restaurants and seatings in case your first choices are filled. If members of your group are susceptible to motion sickness and have elected to skip Body Wars, they might make the meal reservations while the remainder of the group rides. They can easily rejoin the group at the eastside entrance of Earth Station as you return from Body Wars en route to Spaceship Earth.

If you don't follow this plan, you will have a long wait in line to make reservations with no guarantee that anything will be available. On many days the World Showcase restaurants book solid for preferred seating times within an hour to an hour and a half of the park opening. Even if you get a reservation, you will have spent your most productive/crowd-free touring time in the process.

If you follow one of our touring plans, you will be near the United States pavilion (The American Adventure) at noon. We suggest, therefore, a lunch reservation for 12:30 P.M. or 1 P.M. at nearby Germany. For dinner, we recommend reservations at the San Angel Inn in Mexico or at the Akershus in Norway. If you plan to eat your evening meal at the Coral Reef, you may want to wait until after dinner to see the attraction itself.

If you blow it and arrive late but still want to eat in one of the World Showcase restaurants, here are some strategies that often pay off:

1. Go to a WorldKey Information terminal in or out of Earth Station (there are some located around the bridgeway connecting Future World to World Showcase) and use the system as described on page 167 to call up an attendant. Try to make a reservation.

2. If you can't get a reservation via WorldKey, go to the restaurant of your choice and apply at the door for a reservation. Sometimes only lunch reservations are taken at the door, but lunch and dinner menus are comparable if not the same. Just have your main meal at lunch.

3. If neither of the foregoing work, go to the restaurant of your choice and ask the hostess to call you if she gets a cancellation. A reservation is held about 15–20 minutes before the vacancy is filled with "standby" diners. Very early and very late seatings have more "no-shows."

4. If the options mentioned above do not pan out, you can often get a table just by showing up at the Moroccan Restaurant (reservations often go unfilled owing to American unfamiliarity with the cuisine). If Moroccan is too adventurous for you, try Le Cellier, a cafeteria in the Canadian pavilion, or the Land Grille Room in The Land pavilion, which is often overlooked at dinner time.

—— The Restaurants of EPCOT Center ——

While eating at EPCOT Center can be a consummate hassle, it is likewise true that an afternoon in the World Showcase section of EPCOT Center without a dinner reservation is something like not having a date on the day of the prom. Each pavilion has a beautifully seductive ethnic eatery, offering the hungry tourist the gastronomic delights of the world. To tour one after another of these exotic foreign settings and not partake is almost beyond the limits of willpower.

In all honesty, the food in some of the World Showcase restaurants is not very compelling, but the overall experience is exhilarating. And if you fail to dine in the World Showcase, you will miss out on one of EPCOT Center's more delightful features.

In our opinion there is no logical correlation between price, quality, and popularity of the World Showcase restaurants. Our researchers, for example, found L'Originale Alfredo di Roma Ristorante (Italy) frequently disappointing in spite of the fact that it is almost always one of the first two restaurants to fill its seatings. To help you make your choice, a data summary of each World Showcase restaurant requiring reservations (plus the Canadian Le Cellier) is presented below. All full-service restaurants have children's menus.

Canada

Le Cellier (No Reservations Required)

This is the only cafeteria-style restaurant in the World Showcase and represents a tasty and economical choice for those who want a nicer meal but do not have reservations elsewhere.

Time to go: Lunch—before 11:30 and after 2:00

Dinner—before 5:30 and after 8:00

Entree Prices: Lunch, $7–$15   Dinner, $7–$15

United Kingdom

Rose & Crown Pub & Dining Room (Reservations Required)

Seating Capacity: 152

Popularity: More popular for lunch. About the fifth to book for dinner, owing more to its small size than to its popularity.

Critic's Rating: Hearty, but undistinguished food; great Bass ale, Guinness-Harp beer on tap. Stop and refresh yourself on a hot (or cold) afternoon.

Atmosphere: Excellent, warm pub interior with an unparalleled view of the World Showcase Lagoon.

Entree Prices: Lunch, $7–$10   Dinner, $11–$18

Entertainment: Madrigal music with lute.

Comments: Fish & chips, steak and kidney pie, roast beef and basic pub fare make up the menu here.

France

Les Chefs de France (Reservations Required)

Seating Capacity: 162

Popularity: Usually the third restaurant to fill its reservations.

Critic's Rating: Very good and sometimes excellent.

Atmosphere: Elegant and bright, but not intimate or romantic.

Entree Prices: Lunch, $9–$14   Dinner, $10–$20

Entertainment: None.

Comments: Les Chefs apply their art with great success to fresh Florida seafood.

Le Bistro de Paris (Reservations Required)

Seating Capacity: 150

Popularity: Very popular. Many patrons make reservations here by mistake, thinking they are scheduling for Les Chefs.

Critic's Rating: Good, but lacking the creativity and delicacy of Les Chefs.

Atmosphere: Bright and bustling.

Entree Prices: Lunch, $9–$15   Dinner, $14–$25

Entertainment: None.

Comments: A good choice for picky American "meat and potato" diners. Specializes in continental peasant fare.

Morocco

El Marrakech (Reservations Required)

Seating Capacity: 250

Popularity: Normally the seventh or eighth restaurant to fill its reservations.

Critic's Rating: Different, usually good; portions sometimes skimpy.

Atmosphere: Colorful and exotic.

Entree Prices: Lunch, $8–$14   Dinner, $10–$19

Entertainment: Belly dancing and a Moroccan band.

Comments: Interesting fare almost impossible to find except in the largest of U.S. cities. Because Moroccan food is so unknown to most visitors, El Marrakech sometimes has tables available for walk-ins.

Japan

Mitsukoshi Restaurant (Reservations Required)

Seating Capacity: Teppanyaki Dining, 160; Tempura Kiku, 27

Popularity: Normally the sixth or seventh restaurant to fill its reservations.

Critic's Rating: Nothing to write home about. Eschews the diverse and beautiful traditional Japanese fare for teppan table cooking a la Benihana of Tokyo chain restaurants. In the Matsu No Ma Lounge, however, very nice sushi and sashimi can be had at reasonable prices.

Atmosphere: Enchanting stained wood and paper walls; traditional Japanese surroundings.

Entree Prices: Lunch, $8–$14   Dinner, $13–$26

Entertainment: Provided by the chopping, juggling teppan chefs.

Comments: This restaurant has missed a wonderful opportunity to introduce authentic Japanese cuisine to the American public. If you go, we recommend the Tempura Kiku, a small section of the dining room specializing in tempura. Finally, be aware that diners at the teppan tables (large tables with a flattop grill in the middle) are seated at a common table with other parties.

Italy

L'Originale Alfredo di Roma Ristorante (Reservations Required)

Seating Capacity: 254

Popularity: Usually the first or second restaurant to fill its seating.

Critic's Rating: Overrated and somewhat overpriced. Our guess is that many diners feel more familiar with Italian food than with the other ethnic cuisines available at EPCOT Center, thus making Alfredo's popular beyond its ability to deliver.

Atmosphere: Elegant, bright, with beautiful murals adorning several walls.

Entree Prices: Lunch, $10–$21   Dinner, $12–$21

Entertainment: Wonderfully talented singing waiters and waitresses erupting in a profusion of song, including Italian traditional, classical, and opera.

Comments: If you go, try veal or chicken. If you must have pasta, order an appetizer portion or a side dish.

Germany

Biergarten (Reservations Required)

Seating Capacity: 360

Popularity: Usually the fifth or sixth to book its reservations.

Critic's Rating: Food is good. The dinner show is fun and rousing, and the overall atmosphere is festive.

Atmosphere: The largest of the reservation restaurants. Multiple tiers of diners surround a stage where yodelers, dancers, and a German band perform at each scheduled seating. The beer flows freely and diners join in the singing, making the Biergarten a happy, delightful place to dine.

Entree Prices: Lunch, $8–$10   Dinner, $12–$18

Entertainment: Yodelers, dancers, singers, and a German band.

Comments: Best bets are the wursts and the spitted chicken. Because of the size of the Biergarten, it is an above-average bet for getting in without a reservation as a "standby."

China

Nine Dragons (Reservations Required)

Seating Capacity: 200

Popularity: Usually the sixth or seventh restaurant to fill its reservations.

Critic's Rating: Mediocre Chinese food at outrageous prices. If you want Chinese food try one of Orlando's several fine Chinese restaurants.

Entertainment: None.

Atmosphere: Traditional Chinese.

Entree Prices: Lunch, $8–$14   Dinner, $10–$21

Comments: Menu items, preparations, and serving style make it almost impossible to eat family style as do the Chinese and as do most Americans in traditional Chinese restaurants. Instead, each diner gets a "big ol' platter all to his own self, like at the Ponderosa."

Norway

Akershus Restaurant

Seating Capacity: 200

Popularity: Steadily growing as the word spreads of its quality.

Critic's Rating: The most interesting menu in Walt Disney World.

Atmosphere: Scandinavian, bright and scrubbed, clean and cheery.

Entree Price: Lunch, $10, kids $5   Dinner, $15, kids $7

Entertainment: None.

Comments: A beautiful cold and hot buffet features salmon, herring, various Norwegian salads, and a variety of meats. Hearty, adventurous eating. One of the best of the World Showcase restaurants.

Mexico

San Angel Inn Restaurante (Reservations Required)

Seating Capacity: 158

Popularity: Usually the third or fourth restaurant to fill its reservations.

Critic's Rating: Excellent food and excellent value.

Atmosphere: Superb, truly romantic. You sit beneath the stars in a re-creation of a small village on the banks of the Rio del Tiempo with the jungle and an Aztec pyramid in the background.

Entree Prices: Lunch, $8–$14   Dinner, $10–$21

Entertainment: None.

Comments: Delightful menu goes beyond the normal Mexican fare, offering regional and special dishes that are very difficult to find in the U.S. Try the chicken mole.

Future World Reservation Restaurants

Future World restaurants are primarily fast-food establishments. There are, however, two exceptions, and both are worthy competitors of the World Showcase ethnic restaurants in terms of food quality, atmosphere, and menu creativity. What's more, they are sometimes forgotten in the great morning reservations rush.

The Land Pavilion

The Land Grille Room (Reservations Required)

Seating Capacity: 232

Popularity: Most popular at lunch. Often overlooked for dinner.

Critic's Rating: Good food and creative menu. A good choice for finicky eaters and beef-and-potato lovers.

Atmosphere: Elegant revolving platform which overlooks rain forest, prairie, and farm scenes along the Listen to the Land boat-ride route. Unexpectedly intimate and romantic.

Snack Prices: Lunch, $7–$12   Dinner, $7–$12

Entree Prices: Lunch, $8–$15   Dinner, $12–$24

Entertainment: None.

Comments: A nice change of pace. The only full-service restaurant in EPCOT Center that serves breakfast.

Living Seas Pavilion

Coral Reef Restaurant (Reservations Required)

Seating Capacity: 250

Popularity: Popular because of its novelty and fresh seafood specialty. Often the first to fill its reservations.

Critic's Rating: Does not live up to expectations.

Atmosphere: Diners eat fresh seafood and are surrounded by even fresher (live) seafood. Very interesting.

Entree Prices: Lunch, $10–$35   Dinner, $16–$37

Entertainment: Live fish viewing.

Comments: Great view, but the food is average and way overpriced. Go to the attractions to view fish and to one of Orlando's good local seafood restaurants to eat them.

Alternatives and Suggestions for Eating in EPCOT Center

Listed below are some suggestions for any dauntless, epicurean adventurer who is determined to eat at EPCOT Center:

1. Do not stand in lines at restaurants unless absolutely necessary. Use the WorldKey terminals (calling up an attendant) to make your reservations. If you are staying at a Walt Disney World lodging or campground property make your reservation by phone before you come.

2. For fast-food meals, EPCOT Center is like the Magic Kingdom; eat before 11 A.M. or after 2 P.M. The Odyssey Restaurant and the Liberty Inn at the United States pavilion move people through pretty speedily, and sometimes you can get served in a reasonable time in The Land pavilion (the latter being a bit more iffy). The Land is a cut above the average, as are many of the counter service restaurants in the World Showcase. For special treats, try the incredibly good pastries of Boulangerie Patisserie in France.

3. Review the "Alternatives and Suggestions for Eating in the Magic Kingdom," page 134. Many tips for the Magic Kingdom also apply to EPCOT Center.

Shopping in EPCOT Center

The shops in Future World seem a little out of place, the atmosphere being too visionary and grandiose to accommodate the pettiness of the bargain table. Similarly, it obviously has been difficult to find merchandise consistent with the surroundings. Expressed differently, what is available for purchase in Future World is also available at a lot of other places (EPCOT and Disney trademark souvenirs being the exception).

The World Showcase shops add a lot of realism and atmosphere to the street scenes of which they are part. Much of the merchandise is overpriced and is readily available elsewhere. On the other hand, some of the shops in the World showcase really are special. In the United Kingdom, visit the Queen's Table (fine china); in China, Yong Feng Shangdian (crafts, rugs, carvings, furniture).

EPCOT Center
Touring Plans

The EPCOT Center Touring Plans are field-tested, step-by-step itineraries for seeing all of the major attractions at EPCOT Center with a minimum of waiting in line. They are designed to keep you ahead of the crowds while the park is filling in the morning and to place you at the less crowded attractions during EPCOT Center's busier hours of the day. They assume that you would be happier doing a *little* extra walking as opposed to a lot of extra standing in line.

Touring EPCOT Center is much more strenuous and demanding than touring the Magic Kingdom. To begin with, EPCOT Center is about twice as large as the Magic Kingdom. Secondly, and unlike the Magic Kingdom, EPCOT Center has essentially no effective in-park transportation system; wherever you want to go, it's always quicker and easier to walk. Where visitors arriving at the Magic Kingdom disperse rather evenly, visitors arriving at EPCOT Center tend to cluster. Spaceship Earth forms immense lines ten minutes after opening, while the rest of the park is virtually empty. The Touring Plans will assist you in avoiding crowds and bottlenecks on days of moderate to heavy attendance, but cannot lessen the distance you will have to walk. Wear comfortable shoes and be prepared for a lot of hiking. On days of lighter attendance, when crowd conditions are not a critical factor, the Touring Plans will serve primarily to help you organize your tour.

On days of moderate to heavy attendance follow the Touring Plans exactly; do not deviate from them except:

1. When you do not want to experience an attraction called for on the Touring Plans—if an attraction is listed that does not interest you, simply skip that step and proceed to the next step.

2. When you encounter an extremely long line at an attraction called for by the Touring Plans—the central idea is to avoid crowds, not to join them. Crowds build and dissipate throughout the day for a variety of reasons. The Touring Plans anticipate most normally re-

curring crowd-flow patterns but cannot predict spontaneously arising situations (Spaceship Earth breaking down, for instance, with the hundreds of people standing in line suddenly descending on the nearby Universe of Energy). If the line is ridiculously long, simply skip that step and move on to the next, coming back later for another try.

Touring Plans for EPCOT Center

Touring Plans provided for EPCOT Center include the following:

- EPCOT Center One-Day Touring Plan
- Author's Selective EPCOT Center One-Day Touring Plan
- EPCOT Center Two-Day Touring Plan

EPCOT Center Touring Plans and Small Children

EPCOT Center is educationally oriented and considerably more adult in tone and presentation than the Magic Kingdom. Most younger children enjoy EPCOT Center if their visit is seven hours or less in duration, and if their tour emphasizes the Future World section of the park. Younger children, especially grade-school children, find the international atmosphere of the World Showcase exciting but do not have the patience for much more than a quick walk-through. While we found touring objectives of adults and younger children basically compatible in Future World, we noted that children tired quickly of World Showcase movies and shows, and tried to hurry their adult companions.

If possible, we recommend that adults touring with children eight years old and younger use the Two-Day Touring Plan (page 225) or the Author's Selective One-Day Touring Plan (page 221). The Two-Day Touring Plan is comprehensive but divides the tour into two less arduous visits. The Author's Selective One-Day Touring Plan includes only EPCOT Center's very best attractions (according to the author) and is, therefore, shorter and less physically demanding. Adults with small children following the One-Day Touring Plan should consider bypassing movies in Canada and China where the audience must stand, and also evaluate the advisability of meals in full-service restaurants where children would be confined a minimum of one hour in a relatively formal setting. Finally, Body Wars is frightening to many smaller children and, in addition, causes motion sickness among a number of guests of all ages.

Traffic Patterns in EPCOT Center

After admiring for many years the way traffic is engineered at the Magic Kingdom, we were somewhat amazed at the way EPCOT Center was laid out. At the Magic Kingdom, Main Street, U.S.A., with its many shops and eateries, serves as a huge gathering place when the park opens and subsequently funnels visitors to the central hub; from there, equally accessible entrances branch off to the various lands. Thus the crowds are first welcomed and entertained (on Main Street) and then distributed almost equally to the respective lands.

At EPCOT Center, by contrast, Spaceship Earth, the park's premier architectural landmark and one of its featured attractions, is situated just inside the main entrance. When visitors enter the park they invariably and almost irresistibly head right for it. Hence crowds tend to bottleneck as soon as the park opens less than 75 yards from the admission turnstiles. For those in the know, however, the congestion at Spaceship Earth provides some excellent opportunities for escaping waits at other rides and shows in the Future World section of EPCOT Center. If you are one of the first in the gate do not hesitate to experience Spaceship Earth (you will probably not find a shorter line later).

Early-morning crowds are contained in the Future World half of EPCOT Center for the simple reason that most of the rides and shows are located in Future World. Except for Spaceship Earth, and Body Wars in the Wonders of Life pavilion, distribution of visitors to the various Future World attractions is fairly equal. Before the opening of the Wonders of Life pavilion, attractions on the west side of Future World (The Living Seas, The Land, Journey into Imagination) drew larger crowds. With the addition of Body Wars and the other Wonders of Life attractions, traffic is now more evenly distributed.

Between 9 A.M. and 11 A.M., there are more people entering Future World via the entrance than departing Future World into World Showcase. Attendance continues building in Future World until sometime between noon and 2 P.M. World Showcase attendance builds rapidly with the approach of the midday meal. Exhibits at the far end of World Showcase Lagoon report playing to full-capacity audiences from about noon on through 6:30 P.M.–7:30 P.M.

The central focus of World Showcase in the eyes of most visitors is its atmosphere, featuring international landmarks, romantic street scenes, quaint shops, and ethnic restaurants. Unlike the Magic Kingdom with its premier rides and attractions situated along the far perimeters of its respective lands, World Showcase has only two major entertainment draws (Maelstrom in Norway, and *The American Adventure*). Thus, where the Magic Kingdom uses its super attractions to draw and distribute the crowds rather evenly, EPCOT Center's cluster of premier attractions in Future World serves to hold the greater part of the crowd in the smaller part of the park. There is no compelling reason to rush to the World Showcase. The bottom line in Future World is a crowd that builds all morning and into the early afternoon. The two main sections of EPCOT Center do not approach equality in attendance until the approach of the evening meal. It should be stated, however, that evening crowds in World Showcase do not compare with the size of morning and midday crowds in Future World. Attendance throughout EPCOT Center is normally lighter in the evening.

An interesting observation at EPCOT Center from a crowd-distribution perspective is the indifference of repeat visitors relative to favoring one attraction over another. At the Magic Kingdom repeat visitors make a mad dash for their favorite ride and their preferences are strong and well defined. At EPCOT Center, by contrast, many returning tourists indicate that (with the possible exceptions of Body Wars and *The American Adventure*) they enjoy the major rides and features "about the same." The conclusion suggested here is that touring patterns at EPCOT Center will be more systematic and predictable (i.e., by the numbers, clockwise, counterclockwise, etc.) than at the Magic Kingdom.

While some guests leave EPCOT Center in the early evening, the vast majority troop out en masse following IllumiNations (about one hour before the park closes). Upwards of 40,000 people head at the same time for the parking lot and monorail station. To avoid this rush, just continue to enjoy the park until closing.

Closing time at EPCOT Center does not precipitate congestion similar to that observed when the Magic Kingdom closes. One primary reason for the ease of departure from EPCOT Center is that its parking lot is adjacent to the park as opposed to being separated by a lake as in the Magic Kingdom. At the Magic Kingdom, departing visitors bottleneck at the monorail to the Transportation and Ticket Center and main parking lot. At EPCOT Center you can proceed directly to your car.

—— EPCOT Center One-Day Touring Plan ——

FOR: **All parties.**

ASSUMES: Willingness to experience all major rides and shows.

Be forewarned that this plan requires a lot of walking and some backtracking; this is necessary to avoid long waits in line. A little extra walking and some early morning hustle will save you from two to three hours of standing in line. Note also that you might not complete the tour. How far you get will depend on how quickly you move from attraction to attraction, how many times you pause for rest and food, how quickly the park fills, and what time the park closes.

Before You Go

1. Call (407) 824-4321 the day before you go for the official opening time.
2. Purchase admission prior to your arrival. You can either order tickets through the mail before you leave home, buy them at the Walt Disney World Information Center off I-75 near Ocala if you are driving, purchase them at the Disney store in the Orlando airport, or buy them at Walt Disney World resort hotels.
3. Make lunch and dinner reservations before your arrival if you are lodging in a Walt Disney World property. Call (407) 828-4000 between 8 A.M. and 9 P.M. to make EPCOT Center lunch and dinner reservations from one to three days in advance. You do not have to wait until you check in, but can make your reservations from home.

At EPCOT Center

1. Arrive 45–50 minutes prior to the park's opening time. Wait to be admitted at the *farthest left, manned turnstile*.
2. When admitted to the park, move as quickly as possible (jog if you are up to it—but do not run) around the left side of Spaceship Earth to Earth Station (the round building directly

behind and adjoining the big globe) to make lunch and dinner reservations. If a couple of members of your group are swift and energetic, send them ahead to take care of the reservations while the remainder of the group goes directly to Step 4 or Step 5.

If you do not wish to make lunch or dinner reservations, or have made them already by phone, the entire group should skip ahead to Step 4 or Step 5.

3. When you arrive at Earth Station, an attendant will direct you to one of many two-way television monitors to make your reservations for lunch and dinner. Simply look into the monitor and state your preference, for instance, "I would like reservations for four persons for lunch at 12:30 in Germany." If you want to eat a meal in France, which has more than one restaurant, you will be asked to specify the restaurant of your choice by name. Though France is not on our list of top recommendations, we prefer Chefs de France over Bistro de Paris for most entrees.

Lunch Situation A. If your group is small (four persons or less) and you follow this Touring Plan walking at a moderately fast pace throughout the morning, this is approximately where you will be during the lunch hours:

If You Want to Eat at	*You Will Be Near*
11:00–11:30 A.M.	France, Morocco
11:30–12:00 noon	Morocco, Japan, Italy
12:00–12:30 P.M.	Italy, Germany
12:30– 1:00 P.M.	Germany, China
1:00– 1:30 P.M.	China, Norway
1:30– 2:00 P.M.	Norway, Mexico
2:00– 2:30 P.M.	Mexico, Odyssey (no reservations required)

Lunch Situation B. If your group is large (five persons or more), **or** you follow this Touring Plan walking at a slow and leisurely pace throughout the morning, this is approximately where you will be during the lunch hours:

If You Want to Eat at	*You Will Be Near*
11:00–11:30 A.M.	Canada, United Kingdom
11:30–12:00 noon	United Kingdom, France, Morocco

12:00–12:30 P.M.	France, Morocco, Japan
12:30– 1:00 P.M.	Japan, Italy, Germany
1:00– 1:30 P.M.	Italy, Germany, China
1:30– 2:00 P.M.	China, Norway
2:00– 2:30 P.M.	Norway, Mexico

Author's Recommendation for Lunch: Regardless of whether you are moving fast or slow, we recommend lunch in Germany.

Author's Recommendation for Dinner: You can eat your evening meal in any of EPCOT Center's restaurants without interrupting the sequence and efficiency of the Touring Plan. We recommend a 7 P.M. reservation during periods of the year when it gets dark early and an 8 P.M. reservation during the late spring, summer, and early fall. The timing of the reservation is important if you want to see IllumiNations, EPCOT Center's nightly grand laser and fireworks spectacular, held over the World Showcase Lagoon shortly after dark. Our suggestions for dinner include the premier restaurants in Norway, Mexico, Germany, and Morocco. We also like sashimi at the Matsu No Ma Lounge in Japan followed by dinner in the Tempura Kiku Restaurant.

4. EPCOT Center utilizes two basic opening precedures:

   a. Some days, usually when attendance is expected to be heavy, all of EPCOT Center opens at once. If this is the case, go next to the Wonders of Life pavilion and ride Body Wars. Body Wars, incidentally, has quite a track record for making people sick. Be sure to check our Touring Tips on pages 183–84 before riding.

   b. On other days, when guests are admitted to the park, only Spaceship Earth (the ride in the globe) and Earth Station will be open. If this is the case, ride Spaceship Earth after you make your dining reservations and then line up at the door of CommuniCore East (out to the left of Earth Station as you exit the ride); be ready when the rest of the park opens to move through CommuniCore East and proceed directly to the Wonders of Life pavilion. At the Wonders of Life pavilion, ride Body Wars.

5. If you were able to proceed directly from making your dining reservations to riding Body Wars, save the other attractions at

the Wonders of Life pavilion for later and return posthaste to Spaceship Earth. When you arrive the line may appear long. If the line forms *outside* the curb and runs along rope and pole barriers, go ahead and ride. If, in addition to rope and pole barriers along the curb, the line *also* winds through a maze of permanent chrome barriers situated *inside* the curb, skip Spaceship Earth until later.

6. Go next to The Land pavilion and ride Listen to The Land. Save other attractions in The Land for later and move directly to Step 7.

7. Leave The Land and move to the right. Proceed to the Journey into Imagination pavilion and take the Journey into Imagination ride.

8. Exit the ride, but do not go back outside; follow the corridor to the Magic Eye Theater and see *Captain EO*.

9. After *Captain EO*, leave the Journey into Imagination pavilion and take the first available path to your right. Follow the path out of Future World and into the World Showcase.

10. Bypass Canada and the United Kingdom. (If you need a rest room stop now, the rest rooms on your right as you approach the United Kingdom are most convenient.)

   NOTE: Be aware of the time in respect to your lunch reservations. Simply break off the Touring Plan and go to the restaurant when the time comes. After lunch pick up the Touring Plan where you left off.

11. Proceed to France. See the film *Impressions de France*.

12. Bypass Morocco and Japan; proceed to the American Adventure and see the show. If you do not have restaurant reservations, you might consider having a burger or hot dog at the Liberty Inn, to your right as you exit the presentation.

13. Bypass Germany and Italy; go next to China. See the film *Wonders of China*.

14. Bypass Norway for the moment and go to Mexico. Ride El Rio del Tiempo unless the line is long.

15. As you leave Mexico, go to the Odyssey Restaurant; pass through its main service area (without stopping) and go back outside. Cross the bridge into Future World.

16. Bypass The World of Motion for the moment and proceed directly to Horizons and ride.

17. After Horizons go, next door and to the right, to the Wonders of Life pavilion. First, see *Cranium Command* (at the back of the pavilion) and, then, if the wait is not prohibitive (ask the attendant), *The Making of Me*. *The Making of Me* is a movie about conception and birth which has proved popular beyond EPCOT Center's wildest dreams, and certainly beyond the tiny capacity of the theater where it is shown.

18. After you enjoy the Wonders of Life pavilion, exit to your right and proceed to the Universe of Energy.

19. If you bypassed Spaceship Earth earlier in the day, try it again now. If the lines are still too long, you will have another shot later.

20. Go next to The Living Seas. For maximum efficiency, try to be one of the last people to enter the theater (where you sit) from the pre-show area (where you stand). Take a seat as close to the end of a middle row as possible. This will put you in position to be first on the ride which follows the theater presentation. After the ride, enjoy the various exhibits of Sea Base Alpha.

    NOTE: Be aware of the time in respect to your dinner reservations. Simply break off the Touring Plan and go to the restaurant when the time comes. After dinner, check your daily entertainment schedule for the showtime of IllumiNations, EPCOT Center's superb laser and fireworks spectacular. This is not to be missed; give yourself at least a half hour after dinner to find a good viewing spot along the perimeter of the World Showcase Lagoon. For additional information on the best viewing spots, see page 200.

21. Leave The Living Seas to the right and return to The Land. See *The Kitchen Kabaret* and/or *Symbiosis*, a wonderful film shown in the Harvest Theater.

22. Leave The Land and walk straight ahead, passing through both hemispheres of CommuniCore, and proceed to The World of Motion. Ride.

23. Return to the World Showcase via the Odyssey Restaurant. Proceed to Norway. Ride Maelstrom.

24. Walk counterclockwise around the World Showcase Lagoon to Canada. See *O Canada!*

25. If there is still time before closing and you have some energy remaining, stroll the streets of the World Showcase nations or

check out the exhibits in CommuniCores East and West. Of special note is Expo Robotics in CommuniCore West. Another fun exhibit is The Image Works upstairs in the Journey into Imagination pavilion.

26. On busy nights, more than 40,000 people will leave EPCOT Center at the conclusion of IllumiNations. Instead of joining the throng as they mob the monorail and the parking lot trams, continue to enjoy yourself in the almost empty park. Have a pastry in France or some ice cream at The Land. Sit outdoors on the Lagoonside veranda of Mexico's Cantina de San Angel (no reservations required) and sip a frozen margarita. Or if there was something you missed or wished to repeat, try it now.

—— *Author's Selective EPCOT Center One-Day Touring Plan* ——

FOR: **All parties.**

ASSUMES: A willingness to experience major rides and shows.

This Touring Plan is selective and includes only the very best EPCOT Center has to offer according to the author. The absence of a particular attraction in the itinerary should not be construed as negative relative to the attraction's worth.

Before You Go

1. Call (407) 824-4321 the day before you go for the official opening time.
2. Purchase admission prior to your arrival. You can either order tickets through the mail before you leave home, buy them at the Walt Disney World Information Center off I-75 near Ocala if you are driving, purchase them at the Disney store in the Orlando airport, or buy them at Walt Disney World resort hotels.
3. Make lunch and dinner reservations before your arrival if you are lodging in a Walt Disney World property. Call (407) 828-4000 between 8 A.M. and 9 P.M. to make EPCOT Center lunch and dinner reservations from one to three days in advance. You do not have to wait until you check in, but can make your reservations from home.

At EPCOT Center

1. Arrive 45–50 minutes prior to opening time. Wait to be admitted at the *farthest left, manned turnstile.*
2. When admitted to the park, move as quickly as possible (jog if you are up to it—but do not run) around the left side of Spaceship Earth to Earth Station (the round building directly behind and adjoining the big globe) to make lunch and dinner reservations. If a couple of members of your group are swift

and energetic, send them ahead to take care of the reservations while the remainder of the group goes directly to Step 4 or Step 5.

If you do not wish to make restaurant reservations, or have made them already by phone, the entire group should skip ahead to Step 4 or Step 5.

3. When you arrive at Earth Station, an attendant will direct you to one of many two-way television monitors to make your reservations for lunch and dinner.

Lunch Situation A. If your group is small (four persons or less) and you follow this Touring Plan walking at a moderately fast pace throughout the morning, make reservations for Germany at 12:30 P.M.

Lunch Situation B. If your group is large (five persons or more), **or** you follow this Touring Plan walking at a slow and leisurely pace throughout the morning, make reservations for Germany at 1 P.M.

Author's Recommendation for Dinner: You can eat your evening meal in any of EPCOT Center's restaurants without interrupting the sequence and efficiency of the Touring Plan. We recommend a 7 P.M. reservation during periods of the year when it gets dark early and an 8 P.M. reservation during the late spring, summer, and early fall. The timing of the reservation is important if you want to see IllumiNations, EPCOT Center's nightly grand laser and fireworks spectacular, held over the World Showcase Lagoon shortly after dark. Our suggestions for dinner include the premier restaurants in Norway, Mexico, Germany, and Morocco. We also like sashimi at the Matsu No Ma Lounge in Japan followed by dinner in the Tempura Kiku Restaurant.

4. Go next to the Wonders of Life pavilion and ride Body Wars. Body Wars, incidentally, has quite a track record for making people sick. Be sure to check our Touring Tips on pages 183–84 before riding. If the area of Future World where the Wonders of Life pavilion is located is not yet open, ride Spaceship Earth in the interim.

5. While at the Wonders of Life, see *The Making of Me*.

6. Save other attractions at the Wonders of Life pavilion for later, cross Future World and pass through the center of both hemispheres of CommuniCore; enter The Land. Ride Listen to The Land.

7. As you exit The Land, move to the right and proceed to the Magic Eye Theater on the left side of the Journey into Imagination pavilion. See *Caption EO*.

8. After *Captain EO*, leave the Journey into Imagination pavilion and take the first available path to your right. Follow the path out of Future World and into the World Showcase.

9. Bypass Canada and proceed to the United Kingdom. If you need a rest room stop now, the rest rooms on your right as you approach the United Kingdom are most convenient. Explore the streets of the United Kingdom.

10. Proceed to France. See the film *Impressions de France*.

11. Proceed to the American Adventure and see the show.

12. Eat lunch per your reservations in Germany.

13. Proceed to Norway and ride Maelstrom.

14. Bypass Mexico. Go to the Odyssey Restaurant, pass through its main service area (without stopping), and go back outside. Cross the bridge into Future World.

15. Bypass The World of Motion and proceed directly to Horizons and ride.

16. After Horizons go, next door and to the right, to the Wonders of Life pavilion. See *Cranium Command*.

17. After you enjoy the Wonders of Life pavilion, exit to your right, and proceed to experience the Universe of Energy.

18. Next go to Spaceship Earth. If the wait is 20 minutes or less, go ahead and ride. If the wait is longer, save Spaceship Earth for later.

19. Go to The Living Seas. For maximum efficiency, try to be one of the last people to enter the theater (where you sit) from the pre-show area (where you stand). Take a seat as close to the end of a middle row as possible. This will put you in position to be first on the ride which follows the theater presentation. After the ride, enjoy the various exhibits of Sea Base Alpha.

NOTE: Be aware of the time in respect to your dinner reservations. Simply break off the Touring Plan and go to the restaurant when the time comes. After dinner, check your daily entertainment schedule for the showtime of IllumiNations, EPCOT Center's superb laser and fireworks spectacular. This is not to be missed; give yourself at least a half hour after dinner to find a good viewing spot along the perimeter of the World Showcase Lagoon. For additional information on the best viewing spots, see page 200.

20. Leave The Living Seas and backtrack to Spaceship Earth; ride if you missed it earlier.
21. Pass through CommuniCore East; proceed to The World of Motion. Ride.
22. Stroll the streets of the World Showcase nations until time for your dinner reservation.
23. After dinner, enjoy IllumiNations.
24. On busy nights, more than 40,000 people will leave EPCOT Center at the conclusion of IllumiNations. Instead of joining the throng as they mob the monorail and the parking lot trams, continue to enjoy yourself in the almost empty park. Have a pastry in France or some ice cream at The Land. Sit outdoors on the lagoonside veranda of Mexico's Cantina de San Angel (no reservations required) and sip a frozen margarita. Or if there was something you missed or wished to repeat, try it now.

EPCOT Center Two-Day Touring Plan ——

FOR: **All parties.**

This Touring Plan is for EPCOT Center visitors who wish to tour EPCOT Center comprehensively over a two-day period. Day One takes advantage of early morning touring opportunities, while Day Two begins in the late afternoon and continues until the park closes.

Before You Go

1. Call (407) 824-4321 the day before you go for the official opening time.
2. Purchase admission prior to your arrival. You can either order tickets through the mail before you leave home, buy them at the Walt Disney World Information Center off I-75 near Ocala if you are driving, purchase them at the Disney store in the Orlando airport, or buy them at Walt Disney World resort hotels.
3. Make lunch and dinner reservations before your arrival if you are lodging in a Walt Disney World property. Call (407) 828-4000 between 8 A.M. and 9 P.M. to make EPCOT Center lunch and dinner reservations from one to three days in advance. You do not have to wait until you check in, but can make your reservations from home.

Day One

1. Arrive at the park entrance 45–50 minutes prior to opening time. Wait to be admitted at the *farthest left, manned turnstile*.
2. When admitted to the park, move as quickly as possible (jog if you are up to it—but do not run) around the left side of Spaceship Earth to Earth Station (the round building directly behind and adjoining the big globe) to make lunch and dinner reservations. If a couple of members of your group are swift and energetic, send them ahead to take care of the reservations

while the remainder of the group goes directly to Step 4 or Step 5.

If you do not wish to make lunch or dinner reservations, or have made them already by phone, the entire group should skip ahead to Step 4 or Step 5.

3. When you arrive at Earth Station, an attendant will direct you to one of many two-way television monitors to make your reservations for lunch and dinner. Most guests complete Day One of the Touring Plan by about 4 P.M. or 5 P.M., so you may prefer just to book lunch and save dinner for Day Two.

Lunch Situation A. If your group is small (four persons or less) and you follow this Touring Plan walking at a moderately fast pace throughout the morning, this is approximately where you will be during the lunch hours:

If You Want to Eat at	*You Will Be Near*
11:00–11:30 A.M.	United Kingdom, France
11:30–12:00 noon	France, Morocco, Japan
12:00–12:30 P.M.	Morocco, Japan, Italy
12:30– 1:00 P.M.	Japan, Italy, Germany
1:00– 1:30 P.M.	Italy, Germany, China
1:30– 2:00 P.M.	Germany, China, Norway
2:00– 2:30 P.M.	China, Norway, Mexico

Lunch Situation B. If your group is large (five persons or more), **or** you follow this Touring Plan walking at a slow and leisurely pace throughout the morning, this is approximately where you will be during the lunch hours:

If You Want to Eat at	*You Will Be Near*
11:00–11:30 A.M.	Canada, United Kingdom
11:30–12:00 noon	United Kingdom, France, Morocco
12:00–12:30 P.M.	France, Morocco, Japan
12:30– 1:00 P.M.	Morocco, Japan, Italy
1:00– 1:30 P.M.	Japan, Italy, Germany
1:30– 2:00 P.M.	Italy, Germany, China
2:00– 2:30 P.M.	Germany, China, Norway

Author's Recommendation for Lunch: Regardless of whether you are moving fast or slow, we recommend lunch in Germany.

4. Go next to the Wonders of Life pavilion and ride Body Wars. Body Wars, incidentally, has quite a track record for making people sick. Be sure to check our Touring Tips on pages 183–84 before riding. If the area of Future World where the Wonders of Life pavilion is located is not open yet, ride Spaceship Earth in the interim.

5. While at the Wonders of Life, see *The Making of Me*.

6. Saving other attractions at the Wonders of Life pavilion for later, cross Future World by passing through the center of both hemispheres of CommuniCore, and enter The Land. Ride Listen to The Land.

7. Save other attractions in The Land for later and move directly to Step 8.

8. Leave The Land and turn right. Proceed to the Journey into Imagination pavilion and take the Journey into Imagination ride. After you exit the ride, go upstairs and explore The Image Works.

9. Return to the ground floor, but do not go back outside; follow the corridor to the Magic Eye Theater and see *Captain EO*.

10. After *Captain EO*, leave the Journey into Imagination pavilion and take the first available path to your right. Follow the path out of Future World and into the World Showcase.

11. Bypass Canada and proceed to the United Kingdom. If you need a rest room stop now, the rest rooms on your right as you approach the United Kingdom are most convenient. Explore the streets of the United Kingdom.

    NOTE: Be aware of the time in respect to your lunch reservations. Simply break off the Touring Plan and go to the restaurant when the time comes. After lunch pick up the Touring Plan where you left off.

12. Proceed to France. See *Impressions de France*.

13. Move counterclockwise and explore Morocco.

14. Continue to move counterclockwise and visit Japan.

15. Proceed to the American Adventure and see the show. If you do not have restaurant reservations, you might consider having a burger or hot dog at the Liberty Inn, to your right as you exit the presentation.

16. Tour Italy.

17. Explore Germany.

18. Go next to China. See *Wonders of China*.

19. Bypass Norway and go to Mexico. Ride El Rio del Tiempo and tour the Mexican pavilion.

20. As you leave Mexico, go to the Odyssey Restaurant; pass through its main service area (without stopping) and go back outside. Cross the bridge into Future World.

21. Bypass The World of Motion and proceed directly to Horizons and ride.

22. After Horizons go, next door and to the right, to the Wonders of Life pavilion. See *Cranium Command*.

23. After you enjoy the Wonders of Life pavilion, exit to your right and proceed to the Universe of Energy.

24. If you have any zip remaining, try Backstage Magic in nearby CommuniCore East.

Day Two

1. If you are lodging at a Walt Disney World property, call (407) 828-4000 one to three days in advance to make dinner reservations.

2. Enter EPCOT Center at about 4 P.M. Pick up a daily entertainment schedule and a park map at Earth Station.

3. While at Earth Station make dinner reservations, if you have not done so by phone. Since it will be well past the usual time for making reservations, you will have to summon a reservationist by using the WorldKey information service terminals (see page 167.)

    You can eat your evening meal in any of EPCOT Center's restaurants without interrupting the sequence and efficiency of the Touring Plan. We recommend a 7 P.M. reservation during periods of the year when it gets dark early, and an 8 P.M. reservation during the late spring, summer, and early fall. The timing of the reservation is important if you want to see IllumiNations, EPCOT Center's nightly grand laser and fireworks spectacular, held over the World Showcase Lagoon shortly after dark. Our suggestions for dinner include the premier restaurants in Norway, Mexico, Germany, and Morocco. We also like sashimi at the Matsu No Ma Lounge in Japan followed by dinner in the Tempura Kiku Restaurant.

    If your preferred restaurants and seatings are filled, try for a reservation at Morocco or Norway. Because the delightful ethnic dishes of these countries are not well-known to most Americans, it is often possible to get a reservation late in the day.

4. Go to The Living Seas. For maximum efficiency, try to be one of the last people to enter the theater (where you sit) from the pre-show area (where you stand). Take a seat as close to the end of a middle row as possible. This will put you in position to be first on the ride which follows the theater presentation. After the ride, enjoy the various exhibits of Sea Base Alpha.

5. Exit The Living Seas to the right and return to The Land. See *The Kitchen Kabaret* and in the Harvest Theater, *Symbiosis*, a wonderful film examining the necessity of man living in harmony with the land.

   NOTE: Be aware of the time in respect to your dinner reservations. Simply break off the Touring Plan and go to the restaurant when the time comes. After dinner, check your daily entertainment schedule for the showtime of IllumiNations, EPCOT Center's superb laser and fireworks spectacular. This is not to be missed; give yourself at least a half hour after dinner to find a good viewing spot along the perimeter of the World Showcase Lagoon. For additional information on the best viewing spots, see page 200.

6. Leave The Land and backtrack to Spaceship Earth and ride.

7. Pass through CommuniCore East and proceed to The World of Motion. Ride.

8. Return to the World Showcase via the Odyssey Restaurant. Proceed to Norway. Ride Maelstrom and tour the Scandinavian Village.

9. Walk counterclockwise around the World Showcase Lagoon to Canada. See *O Canada!*

10. After dinner and IllumiNations, stroll the streets of the World Showcase nations or check out the exhibits in CommuniCores East and West. Of special note is Expo Robotics in CommuniCore West.

11. On busy nights upwards of 40,000 people will leave EPCOT Center at the conclusion of IllumiNations. Instead of joining the throng as they mob the monorail and the parking lot trams,

continue to enjoy yourself in the almost empty park. Have a pastry in France or some ice cream at The Land. Sit outdoors on the lagoonside veranda of Mexico's Cantina de San Angel (no reservations required) and enjoy a cold drink. Or if there was something you missed or wished to repeat, try it now.

PART FIVE—The Disney-MGM Studios and Studio Tours

And Now for Something Completely Different (Again)

Several years ago, the Disney folks decided they wanted to make movies for adults. Figuring that Snow White wouldn't share the set with Bette Midler mouthing four-letter words, they cranked up a brand new production company to handle the adult stuff. Results have been impressive; a complete rejuvenation with new faces and tremendous creativeness, and an amazing resurgence at the box office.

So, as a new era of Disney film and television success begins to crest, what better way to showcase and promote their product than with an all-new motion-picture and television entertainment park at Walt Disney World? The highly successful Universal Studios tour in southern California has demonstrated the public's voracious appetite for peeking "behind the scenes." The new Disney attraction will undoubtedly both satisfy this craving and sell a lot of movie tickets. Smart business.

The MGM Connection

To broaden the appeal and to lend additional historic impact, Disney has obtained the rights to use the MGM (Metro-Goldwyn-Mayer) name, the MGM film library, MGM motion picture and television titles, excerpts, costumes, music, sets, and even Leo, the MGM logo lion. Probably the two most readily recognized names in the motion picture industry, Disney and MGM in combination showcase more than 60 years of movie history.

Comparing Disney-MGM Studios to the Magic Kingdom and EPCOT Center

Such a comparison appears to be an "apples and oranges" proposition at first glance. The Magic Kingdom has modeled most of its attractions from Disney movie and TV themes; EPCOT Center has pioneered attractions and rides as vehicles for learning. Looking more

233

closely, however, there are numerous similarities. Like EPCOT Center, the Disney-MGM Studios is at once fun and educational, and as in the Magic Kingdom, the themes for the various rides and shows are drawn from movies and television. All three parks rely heavily on Disney special effects and AudioAnimatronics (robotics) in their entertainment mix.

The Disney-MGM Studios is about the same size as the Magic Kingdom and about one-half as large as the sprawling EPCOT Center. Unlike the other parks, however, Disney-MGM Studios is a working motion picture and television production facility. This means, among other things, that more than half of the entire Studios area will be controlled access, with guests permitted only on tours and accompanied by guides, or restricted to observation walkways.

When EPCOT Center opened in 1982, Disney patrons expected a futuristic version of the Magic Kingdom. What they got was humanistic inspiration and a creative educational experience. Since then, the Disney folks have tried to inject a little more magic, excitement, and surprise into EPCOT Center. But remembering the occasional disappointment of those early EPCOT Center guests, Disney planners have fortified the Disney-MGM Studios with megadoses of action, suspense, surprise, and, of course, special effects. If you are interested in the history and technology of the motion picture and television industries, there is plenty of education to be had. However, if you feel lazy and just want to be entertained, the Disney-MGM Studios is a pretty good place to be.

—— How Much Time to Allocate ——

A guest really has to scurry to see all of EPCOT Center or the Magic Kingdom (some say it can't be done) in one day. The Disney-MGM Studios are more manageable. There is less walking and much less ground to cover by foot. Trams transport guests throughout much of the backlot and working areas, and the attractions in the open-access parts are concentrated in an area about the size of Main Street and Tomorrowland put together. There will be a day, no doubt, as the Disney-MGM Studios develops and grows, when you will need more than a day to see everything without hurrying. For the time being, however, the Studios are a nice one-day outing.

Because it is smaller, however, the Disney-MGM Studios is more affected by large crowds. Likewise, being the newest Disney theme park, large crowds can be considered the norm for the foreseeable future. To help you avoid the crowds we have developed **Touring Plans** for the Disney-MGM Studios which will keep you a step ahead of the mob and minimize any waits in line. Even when the park is heavily attended, however, you can see most everything in a day.

— *Arriving and Getting Oriented* —

The Disney-MGM Studios has its own pay parking lot and is also serviced by shuttle bus from the Transportation and Ticket Center, from EPCOT Center, and from Walt Disney World hotels. In addition, many of the larger "out-of-the-World" hotels shuttle guests to the Studios. If you drive, Walt Disney World's ubiquitous trams will arrive to transport you to the ticketing area and entrance gate.

As you enter, Guest Services will be on your left, serving as a park headquarters and information center similar to City Hall in the Magic Kingdom and Earth Station at EPCOT Center. Check here for a schedule of live performances, lost persons, lost objects, emergencies, and general information. If you have not been provided with a map of the Studios, pick one up here. To the right of the entrance you will find lockers, strollers, and wheelchair rentals.

For the sake of orientation, about one-third of the entire complex is set up as a theme park. As at the Magic Kingdom you enter the park and pass down a main street; only this time it's Hollywood Boulevard of the 1920s and 30s. At the end of Hollywood Boulevard is a replica of Hollywood's long-famous Chinese Theater. While not as imposing as Cinderella Castle or EPCOT Center's Spaceship Earth, the Theater is nevertheless Disney-MGM Studios' focal landmark and serves as a good spot to meet if your group gets separated.

The open-access (theme park) section of the Studios is situated at the theater end of Hollywood Boulevard and around a lake off to the left of the Boulevard as you face the theater. Attractions in this section of the Studios are rides and shows, which you can experience according to your own tastes and timetable. The remainder of the Disney-MGM Studios consists of the working sound stages, technical facilities, wardrobe shops, administrative offices, animation studios, and backlot sets, which are accessible to visitors via a walking and tram Studio Tour.

—— *What to See* ——

As in our coverage of the Magic Kingdom and EPCOT Center, we have identified certain attractions as "not to be missed." We suggest, however, that you try everything. Usually exceeding your expectations, and always surprising, Disney rides and shows are rarely what you would anticipate.

Open-Access Movie Theme Park

Hollywood Boulevard

Hollywood Boulevard is a palm-lined re-creation of Hollywood's main drag during the city's golden age. Architecture is streamlined *moderne* with art deco embellishments. Most of the theme park's service facilities are located here, interspersed with numerous shops and eateries. Shoppers can select from among Hollywood and movie-related souvenir items to one-of-a-kind collectibles obtained from studio auctions and estate sales. Disney trademark items are, of course, also available.

In addition to the services and commercial ventures, trolleys transport guests who want a lift from the park entrance to the Chinese Theater at the end of the Boulevard, and characters from Hollywood's heyday, as well as roving performers, entertain passers-by. The Boulevard also serves as the site for daily parades and other happenings.

Hollywood Boulevard Services

Most of the park's service facilities are housed along Hollywood Boulevard, including the following:

Wheelchair & Stroller Rental	To the right of the entrance at Oscar's Super Service
Banking Services	An automated bank teller can be found to the right of the entrance turnstiles (outside the park). Only American Express cards and Cirrus system credit cards (look for the Cirrus logo on the back of your card) will work.
Storage Lockers	Rental lockers are located to the right of the main entrance on Hollywood Boulevard on the left side of Oscar's.
Lost & Found	Lost & Found is in the Guest Services Building to the left of the entrance on Hollywood Boulevard.

Live Entertainment/ Parade Information	Available at Guest Services
Lost Persons	Lost persons can be reported at Guest Services
Walt Disney World & Local Attraction Information	At Guest Services
First Aid	At Guest Services
Baby Center/Baby Care Needs	At Guest Services. Oscar's sells baby food and other necessities.
Film	At the Darkroom on the right side of Hollywood Boulevard just beyond Oscar's

The Great Movie Ride

Type of Attraction: Disney mixed-media adventure ride
When to Go: Before 10 A.M. and after 5 P.M.
Special Comments: Elaborate, with several surprises; not to be missed
Author's Rating: ★★★★½
Overall Appeal by Age Group:

Pre-school	Grade School	Teens	Young Adults	Over 30	Senior Citizens
★★★★	★★★★	★★★★	★★★★½	★★★★½	★★★★½

Duration of Ride: About 19 minutes
Average Wait in Line per 100 People Ahead of You: 2 minutes
Assumes: All trains operating
Loading Speed: Fast

DESCRIPTION AND COMMENTS   Entering through a re-creation of Hollywood's Chinese Theater, guests board vehicles for a fast-paced tour through soundstage sets from such classic films as *Casablanca*, *The Wizard of Oz*, *Aliens*, *Raiders of the Lost Ark*, and many more. Each set is populated with new-generation Disney AudioAnimatronics (robots) as well as an occasional human, all assisted by a variety of dazzling special effects. Disney's largest and most ambitious ride-through attraction, The Great Movie Ride encompasses 95,000 square feet and showcases some of the most famous scenes in filmmaking history. Life-sized AudioAnimatronic sculptures of such stars as Gene Kelly, John Wayne, James Cagney, Julie Andrews, and Harrison Ford inhabit the largest sets ever constructed for a Disney ride.

TOURING TIPS The Great Movie Ride is a Disney-MGM feature attraction which draws large crowds (and lines) from the moment the park opens. An interval-loading, high-capacity ride, lines disappear quickly. Even so, waits can exceed an hour after mid-morning (as an aside, actual waits usually run about one-third shorter than the time posted on the "Waiting Sign." If the sign indicates an hour wait, your actual wait will probably be around 40 minutes). Ride before 9:30 A.M. if possible.

SuperStar Television

Type of Attraction: Audience participation television production
When to Go: After 10 A.M.
Author's Rating: Well-conceived; not to be missed; ★★★★½
Overall Appeal by Age Group:

Pre-school	Grade School	Teens	Young Adults	Over 30	Senior Citizens
★★★½	★★★★★	★★★★★	★★★★½	★★★★½	★★★★½

Duration of Presentation: 30 minutes
Pre-Show Entertainment: Participants selected from guests waiting in the pre-show area
Probable Waiting Time: 10–20 minutes

DESCRIPTION AND COMMENTS Audience volunteers (conscriptees) participate in a television production where special effects are used to integrate the actions of the amateurs with footage of well-known stars of past and current TV shows. The combined result, a sort of video collage where the volunteers miraculously end up in the footage with the stars, is broadcast on large-screen monitors above the set. The outcome, always rated in laughs, depends on how the volunteers respond to their dramatic debut.

TOURING TIPS The theater seats 1,000 persons, so it is not usually difficult to get in. If you want to be in the production, however, it is essential that you enter the pre-show holding area at least 15 minutes before the next performance. Participants for the show are more or less drafted by a casting director from among guests of both genders and from all age groups. Those who stand near the director and those who are distinctively (outlandishly?) attired seem to be selected most often.

Star Tours

Type of Attraction: Space flight simulation ride

When to Go: Very first thing in the morning

Special Comments: Expectant mothers are advised against riding; some preschoolers are frightened.

Author's Rating: Disney's absolute best, anytime, anyplace; not to be missed; ★★★★★

Overall Appeal by Age Group:

Pre-school	Grade School	Teens	Young Adults	Over 30	Senior Citizens
★★★★★	★★★★★	★★★★★	★★★★★	★★★★★	★★★★★

Duration of Ride: Approximately 7 minutes

Average Wait in Line per 100 People Ahead of You: 5 minutes

Assumes: All simulators operating

Loading Speed: Moderate to fast

DESCRIPTION AND COMMENTS   This attraction is so amazing, so real, and so much fun that it just makes you grin and giggle. It is the only Disney ride anywhere for which we have voluntarily waited 45 minutes in line, not once, but three times in succession. The attraction consists of a ride in a flight simulator modeled after those used in the training of pilots and astronauts. Guests, supposedly on a little vacation outing in space, are piloted by a droid (android, a.k.a. humanoid, a.k.a. robot) on his first flight with real passengers. Mayhem ensues almost immediately, the scenery flashes by at supersonic speed, and the simulator bucks and pitches. You could swear you were moving at light speed. After several minutes of this, the droid somehow gets the spacecraft landed and you discover you are about ten times happier than you were before you boarded. Speaking strictly for the research team, we would like to see a whole new generation of Disney rides on the order of Star Tours.

TOURING TIPS   This one ride is worth your admission to Disney-MGM Studios. Except for ten minutes or so following opening, lines will be long all day. Since this is Disney-MGM's equivalent of Space Mountain, expect a crazed assault on the order of Pickett's Charge when the park opens. Get in there with the other nuts and run over to Star Tours as fast as you can. If you are not present during the first half hour following opening, expect at least a 40-minute wait.

Monster Sound Show

Type of Attraction: Audience participation show demonstrating sound effects

When to Go: In the first hour the park is open

Author's Rating: Funny and informative; ★★★★

Overall Appeal by Age Group:

Pre-school	Grade School	Teens	Young Adults	Over 30	Senior Citizens
★★★½	★★★★½	★★★★½	★★★★½	★★★★½	★★★★½

Duration of Presentation: 12 minutes

Pre-Show Entertainment: David Letterman and Jimmy McDonald video

Probable Waiting Time: 20–50 minutes except during the first half hour the park is open

DESCRIPTION AND COMMENTS   A live show where guests are invited on stage for a crash course in becoming sound-effects technicians. The results of their training, always funny, are played back at the end of the show for the audience to enjoy.

TOURING TIPS   Because the theater is relatively small, long waits (mostly in the hot sun) are common here. We recommend seeing the show early in the morning. Another thing: the *Sound Show* is periodically inundated by guests coming from a just-concluded performance of SuperStar Television or the *Indiana Jones Epic Stunt Spectacular*. This is not the time to get in line. Wait at least 20 minutes and try again.

Being chosen for participation in the *Monster Sound Show* is pretty much a function of luck. There is not much beyond being accidentally in the right place at the right time to enhance your chances for getting picked.

Indiana Jones Epic Stunt Spectacular

Type of Attraction: Movie stunt demonstration and action show

When to Go: Between 10 A.M. and 11:15 A.M.

Special Comments: Performance times posted on a sign at the entrance to the theater

Author's Rating: Fast-paced and exciting; ★★★★½

Overall Appeal by Age Group:

Pre- school	Grade School	Teens	Young Adults	Over 30	Senior Citizens
★★★★½	★★★★★	★★★★★	★★★★½	★★★★½	★★★★½

Duration of Presentation: 22 minutes
Pre-Show Entertainment: Selection of "extras" from audience
Probable Waiting Time: None

DESCRIPTION AND COMMENTS Professional stunt men and women demonstrate some of Hollywood's most exciting and dangerous stunts in an enlightening and riveting production.

TOURING TIPS The Epic Stunt Theater holds 2,000 people but, owing to the popularity of the presentation, generally plays to capacity audiences. On busy days, you should be able to just walk in 15 minutes prior to showtime for performances scheduled for 11 A.M. or earlier. For shows after 11 A.M., large lines form and on busy days you might have up to a two-and-a-half hour wait. If you want to see *Indiana Jones* after 11 A.M., check out the line about 15 minutes before showtime. If the line reaches the green dinosaur by the lake, you will probably not be admitted to the next show. If the line does not extend that far, go ahead and queue up; most likely you will be admitted. As a footnote, the Disney people could relieve much of the congestion and the discomfort of waiting in the hot sun by simply allowing guests to walk into the theater and sit down. Sea World follows this practice with all their stadium shows, much to their guests' appreciation.

Theater of the Stars

Type of Attraction: Live Hollywood musical performed in the open-air theater at the end of the first block of Hollywood Boulevard
When to Go: In the evening
Special Comments: Performance times posted on a sign at the entrance to the theater
Author's Rating: Excellent; ★★★★
Overall Appeal by Age Group:

Pre- school	Grade School	Teens	Young Adults	Over 30	Senior Citizens
★★★★	★★★★	★★★½	★★★½	★★★★	★★★★

Duration of Presentation: 25 minutes

Pre-Show Entertainment: None
Probable Waiting Time: None

DESCRIPTION AND COMMENTS   *Theater of the Stars* combines Disney characters with singers and dancers in an upbeat and humorous Hollywood musical production. Though the show is excellent, the audience must sit in the wilting Florida sun. During the summer, most guests cannot make it through an entire performance.

TOURING TIPS   You can catch this show at your convenience. To obtain at least partial relief from the sun, try watching the show from the patio of Starring Rolls, a pastry shop situated next to the amphitheater on the left (on the side of the building housing the Hollywood Brown Derby).

Here Come the Muppets

Type of Attraction: Musical stage show featuring the Muppet characters
When to Go: Before 11:30 A.M. or after 3 P.M.
Author's Rating: Warm, fuzzy, funny, and wild; ★★★★
Overall Appeal by Age Group:

Pre-school	Grade School	Teens	Young Adults	Over 30	Senior Citizens
★★★★½	★★★★½	★★★★	★★★★½	★★★★½	★★★★

Duration of Presentation: 14 minutes
Pre-Show Entertainment: Muppets on video
Probable Waiting Time: Before 11 A.M., 12 minutes; after 11 A.M., 20 minutes

DESCRIPTION AND COMMENTS   *Here Come the Muppets* is a lively, well-written, and well-paced musical stage show starring the Muppet characters including Kermit, Miss Piggy, Fozzi, Gonzo, and the Electric Mayhem Band.

TOURING TIPS   *Here Come the Muppets*, because of its location, maintains steady but not overwhelming lines from late morning on. Even on busy days your wait should not exceed a half hour. Usually, performances are scheduled on the half hour until noon, and then run continuously until 5 P.M., when they go back to the half-hour schedule.

Let's Make a Deal

Type of Attraction: Television game show

When to Go: As per the daily entertainment schedule

Author's Rating: Good show and an interesting behind the scenes look at television studio production; ★★★½

Overall Appeal by Age Group:

Pre-school	Grade School	Teens	Young Adults	Over 30	Senior Citizens
★★★	★★★★	★★★★	★★★★	★★★★	★★★★

Duration of Presentation: A half hour for attraction version, and about an hour for the NBC network version

Pre-Show Entertainment: Let's Make a Deal information on video

Probable Waiting Time: 35 minutes

DESCRIPTION AND COMMENTS   *Let's Make a Deal* is located in Soundstage Two. You can reach it by walking through the Studio Gate Arch, making an immediate left at the Muppet Theater, and continuing down the street for about 100 yards to the Soundstage entrance on the right. The show is the same familiar game show, recently resurrected for NBC, with contestants in bizarre outfits wheeling and dealing for what lies behind doors one, two, and three.

There are two versions of *Let's Make a Deal* produced at the Disney-MGM Studios. Most common is the half-hour "attraction" version, where the show is produced for the entertainment of the Studios' guests. This version runs up to ten times daily according to the entertainment schedule. Contestants are chosen at random from among the audience. The other version is the actual taping of *Let's Make a Deal* for later broadcast on NBC. This version takes about an hour or so longer because some segments usually need to be retaped before final editing. The real version usually tapes once a day on weekdays. Contestants are provided by the producer, Dick Clark Productions. Prizes are real in both versions.

TOURING TIPS   Get in line at least 35 minutes before showtime for the NBC version and 10–15 minutes before the attraction version. If you want to be a contestant on the attraction version, get in line early and wear something weird. When admitted to the theater take a seat as close to the stage as possible. To be a contestant for the NBC version call (407) 560-8225 as far in advance as possible. If you go to the

NBC version, be sure to hit the rest rooms before you get in line. The wait plus the taping will tie you up for at least an hour and a half (once taping begins in the studio nobody is permitted to enter or leave). If you go to the attraction version, steer clear of a show which follows an NBC taping. The NBC show almost always runs overtime and will lengthen your wait.

Kermit the Frog Presents MuppetVision 3-D

Type of Attraction: 3-D movie starring the Muppets
When to Go: Before noon and after 3 P.M.
Author's Rating: Not open when *The Unofficial Guide* went to press
Projected Overall Appeal by Age Group:

Pre-school	Grade School	Teens	Young Adults	Over 30	Senior Citizens
Not open when *The Unofficial Guide* went to press					

Duration of Presentation: 17 minutes
Pre-Show Entertainment: Muppets on television
Probable Waiting Time: 12 minutes

DESCRIPTION AND COMMENTS   A zany 3-D movie on the subject of making motion pictures.

TOURING TIPS   Opening in 1991, *MuppetVision 3-D* is sure to draw large crowds. Watch out for huge throngs of people arriving en masse from just concluded performances of the *Indiana Jones Epic Stunt Spectacular, Monster Sound Show*, and SuperStar Television. If you encounter a long line, chalk it up to bad timing and try again later.

Honey, I Shrunk the Kids Adventure Zone

Type of Attraction: Walk-through adventure
When to Go: Before 11:30 A.M. or after 3 P.M.
Author's Rating: Everyone's one-time fantasy; ★★★★
Overall Appeal by Age Group:

Pre-school	Grade School	Teens	Young Adults	Over 30	Senior Citizens
★★★★	★★★★★	★★★★	★★★★	★★★★	★★★★

Duration of Presentation: Varies
Average Wait in Line per 100 People Ahead of You: 5 minutes

DESCRIPTION AND COMMENTS   The idea is that you have been "minia-turized" (i.e. shrunk) and have to make your way through a yard full of 20-foot-tall blades of grass, huge menacing insects, lawn sprinklers, and other oversized wonders.

TOURING TIPS   Though this is a new attraction, crowds usually are manageable until about midday when the park is busy. If the attraction is crowded, bypass it for the time being.

Studio Tours

Disney-MGM Studios Animation Tour

Type of Attraction: Walking tour of the Disney Animation Studio

When to Go: Before 10:30 A.M. and after 5 P.M.

Author's Rating: Next to Star Tours, this is our favorite Disney-MGM attraction; not to be missed; ★★★★★

Overall Appeal by Age Group:

Pre-school	Grade School	Teens	Young Adults	Over 30	Senior Citizens
★★★★	★★★★	★★★★	★★★★★	★★★★★	★★★★★

Duration of Presentation: 36 minutes

Pre-Show Entertainment: Gallery of animation art in waiting area

Average Wait in Line per 100 People Ahead of You: 7 minutes

DESCRIPTION AND COMMENTS   Disney-MGM Studios Animation Tour is where, for the first time, the public is invited to watch Disney artists at work. Since Disneyland opened in 1955, Walt Disney Productions has been petitioned by its fans to operate an animation studio tour. Finally, after a brief three-and-a-half decade wait, an admiring public can watch artists create beloved Disney characters.

The Animation Tour more than exceeds expectations. Much more than watching a few artists at work, the tour is dynamic, fast-paced, educational, and most of all, fun. Upon entering the Animation Building, most guests spend a few minutes waiting in a gallery of Disney animation art. Use your waiting time to enjoy this combination of art and animation history. From the gallery, guests enter a theater where an eight-and-one-half minute introductory film on animation is shown. Starring Walter Cronkite and Robin Williams as your Animation Tour hosts, the film is an absolute delight.

After the film, guests enter the working studio, where they view artists and technicians at work through large plate glass viewing windows. Arranged according to the sequence of creation for an animated production, each work station and task is explained by hosts Walter and Robin via video monitors mounted in each area. Starting with story and character development, guests work sequentially through animation (where the characters are brought to life in rough art), to clean up (where the rough art is refined to finished line drawing), to effects and backgrounds (where backgrounds for the characters are developed), to photocopying, where drawings are transferred from paper to plastic cels prior to being finished with ink and paint. Finally the cels are photographed, put together, and edited.

Having completed the walk-through of the working studio, guests gather in another holding area and view a multi-monitor video presentation in which the Disney animators share their personal perspectives on the creative process. While serving the functional purpose of keeping guests occupied and entertained while awaiting the conclusion of the tour, the presentation is especially warm and endearing, and very worthwhile in its own right.

Finally, guests are seated in a commodious theater to enjoy a concluding film. Pulling together all the elements of animation production, the film features clips from many Disney animation classics.

TOURING TIPS Because the Animation Tour is a relatively small-volume attraction, lines begin to build on busy days by 9:30 and become intolerably long by 11 A.M. Try to line up for the Animation Tour before 10:30 A.M.

After the introductory film, when you enter the working part of the studio, feel free to stay and watch as long as you like. The Cronkite/Williams narrative (on video monitors in each work area) rolls along in sequence at a fairly brisk pace, and most guests try to keep up. Since at each work station the video repeats about every two to three minutes, you can let the better part of your 160-person tour group work past you while you hang out at the first station. Then take your time, watching the artists and technicians as long as you wish. You will most likely catch up with your group. If you don't, no big deal; enjoy the conclusion of the tour with the next group.

Backstage Studio Tour

Type of Attraction: Combination tram and walking tour of modern film and video production

When to Go: Before 10:30 A.M. and after 3 P.M.

Author's Rating: One of Disney's better efforts; efficient, compelling, informative, fun; not to be missed; ★★★★★

Overall Appeal by Age Group:

Pre-school	Grade School	Teens	Young Adults	Over 30	Senior Citizens
★★★★½	★★★★★	★★★★★	★★★★★	★★★★★	★★★★★

Duration of Presentation: About 1½ hours (one hour if you skip Post Production and the Disney previews)

Pre-Show Entertainment: Musicians in the entrance plaza and a video in the tram boarding area

Average Wait in Line per 100 People Ahead of You: 2 minutes

Assumes: 16 tour departures per hour

Loading Speed: Fast

DESCRIPTION AND COMMENTS Approximately two-thirds of the Disney-MGM Studios is occupied by a working film and television facility where throughout the year actors, artists, and technicians work on various productions. Everything from TV commercials, specials, and game shows to feature motion pictures are produced here. Visitors to the Disney-MGM Studios can avail themselves of a veritable "behind-the-scenes" education in the methods and technologies of motion picture and television production. The vehicle for this learning experience is a comprehensive tour of the working studios.

At the end of Hollywood Boulevard, to the right of the Chinese Theater (The Great Movie Ride), guests enter the limited-access area through an ornate studio gate (a sort of art deco version of the Arc de Triomphe) leading into a large plaza. In the plaza lines form for the Backstage Studio Tour on the left and for the Animation Tour (described earlier) on the right.

The Tram Segment

As the anchor (though perhaps not the most popular) attraction at Disney-MGM, the Backstage Studio Tour is fast-paced, informative and well-designed. Divided into riding and walking segments, the tour begins aboard the ever-faithful tram. Departing (on busy days) about once every four minutes, the tour winds among various production and shop buildings and thence to the elaborate backlot sets.

The Backstage Studio Tour stops first at the wardrobe and crafts shops. Here costumes are designed, created, and stored, as are sets and props. From the tram, viewing through large picture windows, guests watch craftsmen at work.

From the shops the tour proceeds to the winding streets of the backlot where western desert canyons and New York City brownstones exist side by side with modern suburban residential streets. The highlight of the backlot tour for many is the passage through Catastrophe Canyon, a special-effects adventure that includes a thunderstorm, an earthquake, an oil-field fire, and a flash flood.

The tram portion of the tour terminates at the Backstage Plaza, where guests can avail themselves of rest rooms, food, and shopping (if they desire) before commencing the walking part of the tour.

The Walking Segment

First stop is a special-effects water tank where technicians explain the mechanical and optical tricks that "turn the seemingly impossible into on-screen reality." Included here are rain effects, a naval battle, and a storm at sea.

Next guests enter a Special Effects Workshop where the arts of enlargement, miniaturization, stop-frame photographic animation, and other technical mysteries are demonstrated and explained.

After Special Effects it's on to the Soundstages, where specially designed and soundproofed observation platforms allow unobtrusive viewing of ongoing productions. After the guide explains the basics of whatever productions are in progress (if any), guests view a video featuring Warren Beatty which explores the technical and artistic aspects of soundstage work.

Next guests enjoy a four-minute movie, *The Lottery*, starring Bette Midler, that was produced in its entirety at the Disney-MGM Studios. In addition to being amusing *The Lottery* provides an example of a finished production. At the next stop guests inspect the sets and props used in *The Lottery* and watch a video explaining how the film was produced. After all of the behind-the-scenes secrets are revealed, guests walk among the sets, props, and special-effects equipment for a closer inspection.

Post Production and Disney/Touchstone Film Previews

At this juncture guests can elect to continue the tour into Post Production where sound, computer effects, and editing are examined, or leave the tour to return to the nonrestricted theme park section of the Disney-MGM Studios. Post Production, in keeping with the foregoing parts of the tour, is interesting and worth seeing. At the conclusion of Post Production, guests are shown previews of new Disney/Touchstone film releases.

TOURING TIPS   Do not be discouraged if the line appears long when you arrive. Trams depart (on busy days) about every four minutes and each tram can hold as many as 200 guests. Even so, we suggest lining up for the Backstage Studio Tour before 11 A.M.

Not to Be Missed at the Disney-MGM Studios

Star Tours
Backstage Studios Tour
Animation Tour
Indiana Jones Epic Stunt Spectacular
The Great Movie Ride

Eating at Disney-MGM Studios

Dining in the Disney-MGM Studios is more interesting than in the Magic Kingdom and less ethnic than at EPCOT Center. Disney-MGM has two reservations-recommended restaurants, The Hollywood Brown Derby and the 50's Prime Time Cafe:

The Hollywood Brown Derby

Seating Capacity: 250

Popularity: Fills its reservations early every day

Critic's Rating: The Brown Derby receives a passing grade. The food does not knock you off your feet, but it is good. Presentation is very nice, service is spotty.

Fare: Cobb salad, fresh seafood, veal, chicken, pasta, desserts, full bar

Atmosphere: Nicely appointed, but somewhat cavernous. Interesting, but not what you would call intimate or romantic. Line drawing caricatures of movie stars decorate the walls.

Entree Prices: Lunch, $6.95–$13.75   Dinner, $13–$22

Entertainment: None

Reservations: Make reservations at the door on your way into the park or, for Walt Disney World lodging and campground guests only, call (407) 828-4000 between noon and 9 P.M. at least one day but no more than three days in advance. If you want to try the Brown Derby and do not have reservations, try walking in at about 3–4 P.M.

Comments: This, the flagship restaurant of Disney-MGM Studios, shares its rest rooms with the enormous, 560-seat, fast-food Soundstage Restaurant around the corner. Even at 3 or 4 P.M. on a busy day, female diners must wait in line (sometimes up to 15 minutes) to use the rest room. If you encounter such a line, the Catwalk Bar (upstairs from the Brown Derby and Soundstage

253

restaurants) has its own rest rooms which are usually not as crowded.

50's Prime Time Cafe/Tune In Lounge

Seating Capacity: 226

Popularity: Fills its seatings early each day

Critic's Rating: Large portions of undistinguished, often overcooked food

Fare: Meatloaf, pot roast, chicken, and other homey fare

Atmosphere: This is like eating out in your own kitchen, 50's style

Entree Prices: Lunch, $7–$15   Dinner, $11–$17

Entertainment: Vintage sitcoms on TV

Reservations: Make reservations at the door on your way into the park, or for Walt Disney World lodging and campground guests only, call (407) 828-4000 between noon and 9 P.M. at least one day but no more than three days in advance. If you want to try the 50's Prime Time Cafe and do not have reservations, try walking in at about 3–4 P.M.

Comments: No problem here finding something the kids will eat

Other Disney-MGM Studios Restaurants

A cut below the headliner restaurants is the Cafeteria of the Stars featuring baby-back ribs, steaks, prime rib, rotisserie chicken, and a variety of salads. Lunch entrees run $6–$11, with dinner running $8–$15. Beer and wine are available.

For the masses, the Studios provides several bulk loaders: the 560-seat Soundstage Restaurant, the 600-seat Backlot Express, and a number of small sandwich and pastry vendors. Menu offerings are varied and interesting, running the gamut from down-home cooking to California *nouvelle cuisine*. Beer and wine can be purchased at the Soundstage and Backlot Express.

The Disney-MGM Studios has two bars, the large Catwalk Bar situated upstairs over the Soundstage Restaurant, and the smaller Tune In Lounge, part of the 50's Prime Time Cafe.

Entertainment at
Disney-MGM Studios

As at the other Disney theme parks, the streets are alive with music and entertainers. Each day a celebrity visits Disney-MGM as the "Star Today," appearing on stage at SuperStar Television and leading a vintage motorcade down Hollywood Boulevard at about 2 P.M. On nights when the park is open late, there is a fireworks and laser display called Sorcery in the Sky.

Theater of the Stars is an amphitheater production (located on your right at the end of the first block of Hollywood Boulevard) where Disney characters combine with singers and dancers in an elaborate Hollywood musical. A schedule of daily entertainment offerings can be obtained at the Guest Services Building.

Shopping at Disney-MGM Studios

Shops throughout the park carry movie-oriented merchandise and, of course, lots of Disney trademark souvenir items. Most of the shopping is concentrated on Hollywood Boulevard and features movie nostalgia goodies ranging from Jujubes (if you are over 40, you still probably have some stuck in your teeth) to black-and-white postcards of the stars.

Unusual shops include Casting Call (identified in the Studios' guidebook as "Pacific Electric Pictures" and in the daily entertainment program as "Calling Dick Tracy") where guests star in their own video. Costumes, sets, props, a plot, and even a director are provided. Even if you do not try it yourself, it is quite a stitch to watch others. Along similar lines, Sights and Sounds offers the opportunity to record a music video. Direction and backup music are provided. The Animation Gallery, located in the Animation Building, markets reproductions of "cels" from animated features and other animation art.

Disney-MGM Studios One-Day Touring Plan, for Visitors of All Ages

Because it offers a smaller number of attractions, touring Disney-MGM Studios is not as complicated as touring the Magic Kingdom or EPCOT Center. In addition, all Disney-MGM rides and shows are essentially oriented to the entire family, thus eliminating differences of opinion regarding how to spend the day. Where in the Magic Kingdom Mom and Dad want to see the *Hall of Presidents*, Big Sis is revved up to ride Space Mountain, and the preschool twins are clamoring for Dumbo, the Flying Elephant, at Disney-MGM Studios the whole family can pretty much see and enjoy everything together.

Since there are numerically fewer attractions at Disney-MGM than at the other parks, the crowds will be more concentrated. If a line seems unusually long, ask a Disney-MGM attendant what the estimated wait is. If the wait is too long try the same attraction again while a show at the Epic Stunt Theater is in progress or while a parade or some special event is going on. All of these activities serve to draw people away from the lines.

The following Touring Plan assumes a willingness to experience all major rides and shows.

1. Call Walt Disney World Information at (407) 824-4321 the night before you go for opening and closing times. If you are lodging in Walt Disney World, you may be eligible for early admission to the Disney-MGM Studios. Inquire at your hotel desk or ask the concierge.

2. Unless you are a Walt Disney World hotel or campground guest and have been given alternate instructions, arrive one hour and ten minutes before the stated opening time, buy your admission, and wait to be admitted to the park.

NOTE: We do not recommend a full-service restaurant meal as part of this Touring Plan. If, however, you want to try either the 50's Prime Time Cafe or the Hollywood Brown Derby, make your reservations at the door of the selected restaurant on your way down Hollywood Boulevard. If you are a guest at a Walt Disney World hotel or campground, you can make advance reservations for the Hollywood Brown Derby Restaurant or the 50's Prime Time Cafe. Call 828-4000 between noon and 9 P.M. at least one day but no more than three days ahead.

3. Upon admission, move as fast as is safe and practical to Star Tours. As at Space Mountain in the Magic Kingdom, you may well find yourself in a footrace, so be prepared. The fastest route to Star Tours is to turn left at the first intersection on Hollywood Boulevard, and then, keeping the lake on your right, head for the far left corner of the park. Ride Star Tours.

4. Having experienced Star Tours, walk across the park past the *Monster Sound Show* and SuperStar Television to The Great Movie Ride, located at the end of Hollywood Boulevard in the Chinese Theater. Ride The Great Movie Ride.

5. After The Great Movie Ride, pass through the large arch marking the entrance to the studios and take the tram segment only of the Backstage Studio Tour. At the end of the tram segment, head down the walkway that serves the shops and restaurants in the Backstage Plaza. Proceed via the backlot to the theme park section of Disney-MGM Studios (if the backlot is under construction return to the theme park section by walking up Mickey Avenue). Pay attention to your route; you will return later to finish the Backstage Tour.

6. Having reentered the theme park section of Disney-MGM Studios proceed to the *Monster Sound Show*. This worthwhile attraction has limited seating and great popularity, thus occasioning bottlenecks and long waits later in the morning.

7. Following the *Monster Sound Show*, do not linger at Sound-Works (a hands-on sound-effects exhibit). Instead, leave the building and turn left. Stop next door and check the next show-time for SuperStar Television. If a performance is 12 minutes or less from starting, go ahead and see the show. If the wait until the next performance exceeds 12 minutes, skip to Step 8.

8. Pass through the Studio Gate Arch and on to the animation building (ahead and to the right). Take the Animation Tour.

9. When you complete the Animation Tour, cross the plaza, and see *Here Come the Muppets*.

10. Check your entertainment schedule for the next performance of the *Indiana Jones Epic Stunt Spectacular*. If a show is scheduled to begin within 35 minutes, go ahead and see it. If you arrive at the Epic Stunt Theater and there is standing room only, stay and see the show anyway. If a show is not scheduled within 35 minutes skip to Step 11.

11. After the *Stunt Spectacular*, proceed to the backlot area and see *Kermit the Frog Presents MuppetVision 3-D* (if it has opened). If not open yet, skip to Step 12.

12. Check your daily entertainment schedule for the next performance of *Let's Make a Deal*. If a show is scheduled to begin within 20 minutes, go ahead and take it in. Otherwise, skip to Step 13.

13. Experience the Honey, I Shrunk the Kids Adventure Zone.

14. This is a good time to stop for lunch if you are hungry.

15. Return to where you disembarked from the tram portion of the Backstage Studio Tour. Take the walking portion of the Backstage Studio Tour.

16. After you see the special-effects studio, the soundstages, and the sets for *The Lottery*, you will exit onto an outside walkway. If you missed *Let's Make a Deal* earlier, turn right and try again. Otherwise, turn left and tour Post Production.

17. After Post Production, see the *Indiana Jones Epic Stunt Spectacular*, SuperStar Television, or any other attraction you missed earlier.

18. Tour Hollywood Boulevard. Consult your daily entertainment schedule for afternoon parades and performances at the *Theater of the Stars*.

19. This concludes the Touring Plan. Eat, shop, enjoy live entertainment, or revisit your favorite Disney-MGM attraction as desired. When ready to leave the park, you can walk (the Disney-MGM parking lot is not all that big) or take a tram to your car. Buses to the other theme parks are available but you can get there faster in your car.

The New Old Kid on the Block: Universal Studios Comes to Florida

Universal City Studios, Inc. has been running a studios tour and movie-theme tourist attraction for more than 25 years, predating all of the Disney parks except Disneyland. In the early 1980s, Universal announced plans to build a studios/theme park complex in Florida. While Universal labored over its new project, however, the Disney organization jumped into high gear and rushed its own studios/theme park onto the market, beating out Universal by a year and a half.

Universal Studios Florida opened its doors to the public in June of 1990. At that time it was almost four times the physical size of the Disney-MGM Studios (Disney-MGM having expanded somewhat subsequently), with much more of the total facility accessible to the visiting public. Like its sister facility in Hollywood, Universal Studios Florida is spacious, beautifully landscaped, meticulously clean, and delightfully varied in its entertainment offerings. Yet, in certain important, almost critical ways, the Florida complex is quite different from Universal Studios Hollywood.

Universal Studios Hollywood is one of the most well-conceived and well-executed tourist attractions in the world. It accommodates large numbers of guests with practically no waiting in line. While Disneyland, several miles away, was testing new techniques in queuing management (how to keep guests happy standing in a line for 45 minutes), Universal Studios was operating a park where lines were the exception, not the rule.

After buying admission to Universal Studios Hollywood, each guest is assigned a reservation for the Tram Tour, a well-paced, multi-segmented tour of Universal's famed film and television studios. Educational, dramatic, and exciting, the Tour is a clinic in television and motion picture art and is the feature attraction of the park. Guests are

relieved of the drudgery of waiting in line for the tour by simply showing up at the embarkation point at their appointed reservation time.
Many surprises are built into the tour including an attack by "Jaws,"
an earthquake, and an encounter with King Kong. In addition to being
a wonderful experience, the Tram Tour is also easy on the feet.

All other attractions at Universal Studios Hollywood are extra-large
theaters featuring various movie- and TV-theme presentations which
are performed according to a show schedule (provided to each guest on
admission). Once again there are no lines. As showtime approaches,
guests simply enter the empty theater and take a seat, first come first
serve. No lines, no standing, no bother, plus you get to wait for the
show sitting down in the theater.

As Universal Studios Hollywood has engineered one of the most
guest-considerate and stress-free theme attractions in the world, it is
only logical to expect that Universal Studios would build on these same
proven, successful techniques when designing a second generation
mega-attraction in Florida. Right? Think again.

Incredibly, at Universal Studios Florida, the Universal planners and
designers trashed most of the formats and techniques which made the
Hollywood park so exceptional, electing instead to develop an attraction in the Disney style with hours of waiting and miles of walking.
In Hollywood, Universal created a superior product by going in a different direction, marching to their own beat. In Florida, unfortunately,
Universal has tried to "out Disney" Disney, and the results have been
mixed.

Gone in Florida is the Hollywood Tram Tour and the much appre-
ciated reservation system. Gone, also, is any sort of integrated educational presentation on movie and television production. True, there are
individual shows on costuming and make-up, set construction, special
effects, film making, and post production, but it is unlikely that each
patron will see them all or that the presentations will be viewed in any
sort of logical sequence. Worst, in California a guest gets all the above
during the Tram Tour with no wait; in Florida a guest must wait in line
for each different show.

Then, there are the rides. In Hollywood, there is one ride, the
Tram Tour. Everything, from earthquakes to avalanches to an attack by
"Jaws," happens while you ride the tram. At Universal Studios Florida
the rides are more in the Disney mold, i.e., totally separate ride/ad-
venture experiences. On the bright side, the Universal Florida rides

are exciting and innovative, and as with many Disney rides, focus on familiar and/or beloved motion picture characters or situations.

On Universal Studios Florida's E.T. ride, you escape the authorities on a flying bike and leave the earth for a visit to E.T.'s home planet. In Kongfrontation, King Kong tears up a city with you in it. In Jaws, the persistent great white makes a heart-stopping assault on your small boat, and in Earthquake, The Big One, special effects create the most realistic earthquake simulation ever produced. The Funtastic World of Hanna-Barbera places you in a bucking rocket simulator for a high-speed chase with Yogi Bear and the Flintstones. Finally, beginning in 1991, guests will ride a Delorean in yet another chase, this one based on the film *Back to the Future*.

While many of these rides represent prototypical state-of-the-art technology and live up to their advance billing in terms of excitement, creativity, uniqueness, and special effects, they unfortunately lack the capacity to handle the number of guests who frequent major Florida tourist destinations. If a ride has great appeal, but can accommodate only a small number of guests per ride or per hour, long lines will form. It is not unusual for the wait to exceed an hour and a quarter for the E.T. ride, and 50 minutes for the Hanna-Barbera ride. The Back to the Future ride, when it opens, might well be the most inventive and extraordinary theme park ride on earth, but if advance information is correct, it will accommodate less than 800 people an hour, a number certain to insure long waits.

Happily, most of the shows and theater performances at Universal Studios Florida are situated in good-sized theaters which accommo-date large numbers of people. Since performances run continuously (except at the *Animal Actor's Stage*) waits usually do not exceed twice the performance time of the show (about 40 minutes). Many shows are multi-segmented, with the audience moving to three or more staging areas during the course of the presentation.

—— *Arriving and Getting Oriented* ——

Universal Studios Florida is located on Kirkman Road, acces-sible from I-4 via exits 29 or 30B. The parking lot holds about 7,000 cars and is filled each day starting with those areas most distant from the gate. A tram transports guests to the ticket booths and entrance.

One-Day and Two-Day Tickets are available at about $32 and $52 respectively for adults, $25 and $42 for children.

The studios are laid out in an upside down "L" configuration. Beyond the main entrance, a wide boulevard stretches past a number of rides and shows down to a New York City backlot set. Branching off this major pedestrian thoroughfare to the right are five streets which access other areas of the studios and which ultimately intersect a promenade circling a large lake.

The studios are divided into six sections: The Front Lot, Now Shooting, Production Central, Hollywood, On Location, and CineMagic Center. None of the areas, except Hollywood, are clearly demarcated and none have particular relevance to the visitor. Guests tend to orient themselves more by major rides or sets, referring to the "Jaws area," "New York," "the waterfront," or "over by E.T." Overall, the area of Universal Studios Florida open to guest visitation is about the same size as EPCOT Center.

Universal Studios Florida offers all the services and amenities you would expect from a major theme park including: stroller and wheelchair rental, lockers, diaper-changing and infant-nursing facilities, car assistance, and foreign language assistance. Most of the studios are accessible to disabled guests and TDD's are available to the hearing impaired. Almost all of the Universal Studios Florida services are located in The Front Lot, just inside the main entrance. For specific requirements or for general information call (407) 636-8000.

—— *Universal Studios Florida Attractions* ——

The Funtastic World of Hanna-Barbera

Type of Attraction: Flight simulation ride

DESCRIPTION   A flight simulation ride in the same family as Disney's Star Tours and Body Wars except that all the visuals are cartoons. Guests accompany Yogi Bear in a high-speed chase to rescue a child snatched by kidnappers.

COMMENTS   This wild, funny, and thoroughly delightful ride is also, unfortunately, a cycle ride (the whole ride must shut down during loading and unloading). Consequently, large lines build early in the day and move very slowly.

"Alfred Hitchcock: The Art of Making Movies"

Type of Attraction: Mini-course on filming action sequences and a testimonial to the talents of Alfred Hitchcock

DESCRIPTION   Guests view a film collage featuring famous scenes from Hitchcock's films and then exit to an adjoining soundstage where the stabbing scene from *Psycho* is recreated using professional actors and audience volunteers. Finally guests move to a third area, where the technology of filming action scenes on a soundstage is explained.

COMMENTS   The Hitchcock "greatest hits" film is disjointed and pretty confusing unless you have a good recollection of the movies and scenes highlighted. The soundstage reenactment of the shower scene from *Psycho* is interesting and entertaining, as are the special sets and film techniques demonstrated in the third staging area. Because of its location, just beyond the main entrance, lines form early for the Hitchcock attraction.

"Murder, She Wrote!" Post Production

Type of Attraction: Multi-sequence mini-course on the post production techniques of sound effects, editing, background music, and dubbing

DESCRIPTION   Guests move from theater to theater in this multi-sequence introduction to post production.

COMMENTS   Informative, worthwhile, and usually not a long wait.

Production Tour

Type of Attraction: Guided behind-the-scenes tour

DESCRIPTION   A guided look at set construction, soundstages (including the Nickelodeon set), wardrobe, lighting, filming, and post production.

COMMENTS   Boring with little substance. A major disappointment.

"Ghostbusters"

Type of Attraction: Theater presentation featuring special effects from *Ghostbusters*

DESCRIPTION   An elaborate set and a thin story line are used to demonstrate a variety of pretty incredible special effects.

COMMENTS   The special effects are great, the presentation upbeat.

Kongfrontation

Type of Attraction: Theme adventure ride

DESCRIPTION   One of Universal Studios Florida's headliner attractions, guests board an aerial tram for a ride from Manhattan to Roosevelt Island. Enroute news reaches the group that the giant ape has escaped. The tram passes evidence of Kong's passage and finally encounters the monster himself. In the course of the journey, King Kong demolishes buildings, uproots utility poles, swats helicopters, and hurls your tram car to the ground.

COMMENTS   A truly amazing piece of work. Not to be missed.

Phantom of the Opera Horror Make-Up Show

Type of Attraction: Theater presentation on the art of make-up

DESCRIPTION   A lively, well-paced look at how make-up artists create film monsters, realistic wounds, and other unmentionables.

COMMENTS   An excellent and enlightening, if somewhat gory introduction to the blood and guts art of cinematic monster-making.

Earthquake, The Big One

Type of Attraction: Combination theater presentation and theme adventure ride

DESCRIPTION   Guests view a film on how miniatures are used to create special effects in earthquake movies, followed by a demonstration of how miniatures, blue screen, and matte painting are integrated with live-action stunt sequences (starring audience volunteers) to achieve a realistic final product. Next, guests board a subway enroute from Oakland to San Francisco and experience a simulated earthquake.

COMMENTS   Special effects ranging from fires, runaway trains, exploding tanker trucks, and tidal waves make the ride one of Universal's most compelling efforts. Not to be missed.

Jaws

Type of Attraction: Theme adventure ride

DESCRIPTION   Guests on an excursion boat outing encounter and do battle with the shark from *Jaws.*

COMMENTS   Another extremely high-tech ride with realistic special effects. Not to be missed.

Back to the Future (opens 1991)

Type of Attraction: Theme thrill ride

DESCRIPTION   Guests in Doc Brown's lab get caught up in a high-speed chase through time that spans a million years.

COMMENTS   This attraction is billed as the thrill ride of the century and will probably be to Universal what Space Mountain is to the Magic Kingdom. Expect heavy-duty lines all day except when the studios open and just before closing.

E.T. Adventure

Type of Attraction: Theme adventure ride

DESCRIPTION   Guests board a bicyclelike conveyance to escape with E.T. from earthly law enforcement officials and then journey to E.T.'s home planet.

COMMENTS   A very nice ride, similar to Peter Pan's Flight in the Magic Kingdom, only longer with more elaborate effects and based on E.T. We thought it worth a 20–30 minute wait, but nothing longer. Guests who balk at the idea of sitting on the bicycle conveyance can ride in a comfortable gondola.

Animal Actor's Stage

Type of Attraction: Trained live animals in an amphitheater performance

DESCRIPTION   A humorous presentation demonstrating how animals are trained for film work. Well-paced and informative, the show features cats, dogs, monkeys, birds, and other creatures.

COMMENTS   One of Universal's better efforts.

Stunt Spectacular

Type of Attraction: Simulated filming of a movie stunt scene

DESCRIPTION   Performed several times each day on the lagoon according to the daily entertainment schedule. Stuntmen demonstrate a variety of spectacular stunts and special effects. The plot involves lawmen trying to intercept and apprehend drug smugglers.

COMMENTS   On a par with Disney-MGM's stunt show, the Universal version is staged on the open lagoon with the audience taking positions along the encircling rail, thus no waiting in line.

Street Scenes

Type of Attraction: Elaborate outdoor sets for film making

DESCRIPTION   Unlike Disney-MGM Studios, Universal Studios Florida backlot sets are all open to guest inspection. Sets include New York City streets, the San Francisco waterfront, the house from *Psycho*, Rodeo Drive and Hollywood Boulevard, and a Louisiana bayou, among others.

—— *Disney-MGM Studios vs. Universal Studios Florida* ——

Two-thirds of Disney-MGM Studios is off-limits to guests except on guided tours, but virtually all of Universal Studios Florida is open for patron exploration. In contrast to Disney-MGM, Universal Florida's open area includes the entire backlot where guests can walk at their leisure among elaborate sets.

Universal Studios Florida hammers on the point that it is a working motion picture and television studio first, and sort of incidentally a tourist attraction. Whether this assertion is a point of pride with Universal Florida or an apology to the tourist is unclear. It is true, however, that guests are more likely to see film or TV production in progress at Universal Florida than at Disney-MGM. On any given day, several production crews will be shooting on the Universal Florida backlot sets in full view of any guests who care to watch.

The fact that Universal Studios Florida is so large, and that almost all of it is open to the public, eliminates most of the crowding and congestion so familiar in the streets and plazas at Disney-MGM. At Universal Florida, there is plenty of elbow room.

The quality of the attractions is excellent at both parks though in general, the Disney-MGM Studios rides and attractions are engineered to move people more efficiently. This advantage is somewhat offset, however, by the fact that there are more rides and shows at Universal Studios Florida. At Disney-MGM there are three rides, six covered theater shows, two walking tours, one walk-through attraction, and one uncovered outdoor production. At Universal Florida there are five rides (six when Back to the Future comes on line in 1991), seven covered theater shows, one walking tour, and one uncovered outdoor production.

Amazingly, and to the visitor's advantage, each of the studios offers a completely different product mix, so there is little to no redundancy for a person who visits both. Disney-MGM and Universal Florida each offer a good exposure to the cinematic arts, though Disney-MGM's presentation is crisper, better integrated, and more coherent.

Stunt shows are similar at both parks. The Disney version, for which guests sometimes endure long waits, is in a huge theater that allows a good view of the action. The Live Action Stunt Spectacular at Universal Studios Florida is staged in a large lagoon with patrons simply taking up viewing positions along the railing. On the positive side, there is no waiting in line to see the show. On the negative side, the lagoon (which provides a huge and realistic setting) is so large that sometimes the action is hard to see or follow.

Our recommendation is to try one of the studios. If you enjoy one you will probably enjoy the other. If you have to choose between the studios, consider the following:

1. ***Touring Time.*** If you tour efficiently, it takes about six to seven hours to see the Disney-MGM Studios (including a lunch break). Because Universal Studios Florida is larger and contains more (and often less efficiently engineered) rides and shows, touring time, including lunch, runs about eight to nine hours.

2. ***Convenience.*** If you are lodging along International Drive, the I-4 Corridor N.E., the Orange Blossom Trail (US 441), or in Orlando, Universal Studios Florida will be closer. If you are lodging along FL 192, in Kissimmee, along US 27, or in Walt Disney World, the Disney-MGM Studios will be more convenient.

3. ***Endurance.*** Universal Studios Florida is larger and requires more walking, but at the same time is much less congested than Disney-MGM so the walking is easier. Wheelchairs are available, as is handicapped access at both Studios.

4. *Cost.* Both parks are about the same for admission, food, and incidentals. All attractions are included in the price of admission.

5. ***Best Days to Go.*** Sunday mornings (except on holiday weekends) and Fridays are the best days to visit either of the studios, followed by Mondays and Saturdays. Wednesdays, Thursdays, and Tuesdays, in that order, are the most crowded days.

6. ***When to Arrive.*** For Disney-MGM Studios arrive, ticket in hand, one hour and ten minutes before the official opening time. For Universal Studios Florida, arrive about 35 minutes before the official opening time.

7. ***Small Children.*** Both Disney-MGM Studios and Universal Studios Florida are relatively adult entertainment offerings. By our reckoning half of the rides and shows at Disney-MGM, and about 65% of the rides and shows at Universal Florida, have significant potential for frightening small children.

—— One-Day Touring Plan for Universal Studios Florida ——

This plan is for all visitors. If there is a ride or show listed which you prefer not to experience, simply skip that step in the plan and proceed to the next. Try to move from attraction to attraction quickly, and if possible, not stop for lunch until after Step 12.

The Hard Rock Cafe is a fun place for lunch or dinner if you enjoy rock 'n' roll. The food is good (though they tend to overcook their burgers) and the service, once you are seated, is usually also good. If you go, get your hand stamped for reentry (the restaurant is technically located outside of the park), and be prepared for a wait. We arrived at the Hard Rock Cafe at 3 P.M. on a Wednesday and had to wait in 4 different lines for a total of 35 minutes before getting seats. On another occasion, at 8 P.M. on a Thursday, we waited in 11 different lines (no kidding! and all in the same restaurant) for a total of an hour and a half before getting a table.

Touring Plan

1. Call (407) 363-8000 the day before your visit for the official opening time.
2. On the day of your visit, eat breakfast and arrive at the Studios 35 minutes before the stated opening time.
3. At the front gate, purchase your admission and line up at the turnstile. Be sure to pick up a studios map and the daily entertainment schedule. Ask the ticket seller or any other attendant whether the Back to the Future Ride is operating and inquire if any rides or shows are closed that day. Adjust the Touring Plan accordingly.
4. When the park opens, move quickly to The Funtastic World of Hanna-Barbera, a rocket simulation ride.
5. After the Hanna-Barbera ride, take a right on Hollywood Boulevard, first passing Mel's Diner (on your left) and then Cafe La Bamba on your right; go through the Central Park set into the CineMagic section of the park.

6. If the Back to the Future Ride is operating, ride now. If not proceed to Step 7.

7. In the CineMagic section, ride the E.T. Adventure.

8. Keeping the lagoon on your left, cross the bridge into the On Location section of the park. Ride Jaws.

9. Once again, keeping the lagoon on your left, proceed to Earthquake, The Big One. Ride.

10. Having survived the earthquake and keeping the lagoon on your left, depart the waterfront and the San Francisco set, and turn right into the New York street set. Proceed to Kongfrontation and ride.

11. If you are still in one piece after the Flintstones, a bike ride to another galaxy, a shark attack, an earthquake, and an encounter with King Kong, you may as well take on some ghosts. Cross the Gramercy Park set and see "Ghostbusters." The line will appear long, but should disappear when guests are admitted inside.

12. After "Ghostbusters," keep the big props lot on your right and head back toward the studios' main entrance. On your left see "Alfred Hitchcock: The Art of Making Movies."

13. This is a good time for lunch if you have not already eaten.

14. At this point you have four major attractions left to see:
    a. *Phantom of the Opera Horror Make-Up Show*
    b. "Murder, She Wrote!" Post Production
    c. *Animal Actor's Stage*
    d. Live Action Stunt Spectacular
    The animals and the Stunt Spectacular are scheduled several times each day as listed on the daily entertainment schedule. Plan the remainder of your itinerary according to the next listed show times for these presentations. *Phantom of the Opera* and "Murder, She Wrote!" run continuously and are situated on opposite sides of Mel's Diner. Work these last two in as time permits.

15. We found the Production Tour unremittingly dull and largely uninformative. It is our recommendation that you skip it entirely.

16. This concludes the Touring Plan. Spend the remainder of your day at Universal Studios Florida revisiting your favorite rides and shows, or inspecting any of the sets and street scenes you may have missed earlier.

PART SIX—

The Water Theme Parks

Typhoon Lagoon

Designed to be the ultimate swimming theme park, Typhoon Lagoon is four times the size of River Country, Walt Disney World's first splash-and-sun attraction. Nine water slides and streams, some as long as 400 feet, drop from the top of a one-hundred-foot-high man-made mountain. Landscaping and an "aftermath of a typhoon" theme impart an added adventurous touch to the wet rides. Features include the world's largest inland surf facility, with waves up to six feet in height in a lagoon large enough to "encompass an oceanliner," and a saltwater snorkeling pool where guests can swim around with a multitude of real fish.

Beautifully landscaped, Typhoon Lagoon is entered through a misty rain forest emerging into a ramshackle tropical town where concessions and services are situated. Disney special effects make every ride an odyssey as swimmers encounter bat caves, lagoons and pools, spinning rocks, dinosaur bone formations, and countless other imponderables.

Typhoon Lagoon provides water adventure for all age groups. Activity pools for young children and families feature geysers, tame slides, bubble jets, and fountains. For the older and more adventurous there are two speed slides, three corkscrew body slides, and three tube/rapids rides (plus one children's rapids ride) plopping off Mount Mayday. For slower metabolisms there is Castaway Creek, a scenic, relaxed, meandering, 2,100-foot-long tube ride that winds through a hidden grotto and a rain forest. And, of course, for the sedentary, there is usually plenty of sun to sleep in.

What sets Typhoon Lagoon apart from other water parks is not so much its various slides, but the Disney attention to detail in creating an integrated adventure environment. The eye (as well as the body) is deluged with the strange, the exotic, the humorous and the beautiful. In point of fact, faster, higher, and wilder slides and rapid rides can be found elsewhere. But no other water park comes close to Typhoon Lagoon in diversity, variety, adventure, and total impact.

Typhoon Lagoon has its own 1,000-car pay parking lot and can also be reached by shuttle bus from Walt Disney World and Walt Disney World Village hotels and campgrounds. There are no lodging accommodations at Typhoon Lagoon.

Typhoon Lagoon Touring Tips

When it comes to water slides, unfortunately, modern traffic engineering bows to old-fashioned queuing theory. It's one person, one raft, or one tube at a time, and the swimmer "on deck" cannot go until the person preceeding him is safely out of the way. Thus the hourly carrying capacity of a slide is nominal compared to the continuously loading rides of EPCOT Center and the Magic Kingdom. Since a certain interval between swimmers is required for safety, there are only two ways to increase capacity: (1) make the watercourse longer so that more swimmers can safely be on the slide or rapids ride at the same time, and (2) increase the number of slides and rapids rides.

The best way to avoid standing in lines is to visit Typhoon Lagoon on a day when it is less crowded. Because of the park's popularity among Florida locals, weekends can be tough. We recommend going on a Monday or Tuesday when most other tourists will be visiting the Magic Kingdom, EPCOT Center, or the Disney-MGM Studios, and the locals will be at work. Fridays are also a good bet since auto travelers commonly use this day to get a start on their trip home. Sunday morning is also a good time to go.

—— *Typhoon Lagoon Touring Plan* ——

Though large and elaborate, Typhoon Lagoon actually has fewer slides than Wet & Wild (its main Orlando area competitor) and on crowded days long lines can develop for the chutes coming off Mount Mayday. Thus to have a great day and beat the crowd, we recommend the following:

1. ***Getting Information.*** Call (407) 824-4321 the night before you go to inquire when the park opens.

2. ***To Picnic or Not to Picnic.*** Decide whether or not you want to bring a picnic lunch. Guests are permitted to bring lunches and beverage coolers to Typhoon Lagoon. No alcoholic beverages are allowed. Glass containers of all kinds (including may-

onnaise, mustard, peanut butter, and pickle jars) are likewise forbidden.

3. ***Getting Started.*** Get up early, have breakfast, and arrive at Typhoon Lagoon a half hour before opening time. If you have a car, we recommend driving instead of taking a Walt Disney World bus.

4. ***Attire.*** We suggest that you wear your bathing suit under shorts and a t-shirt so that you do not need to use lockers or dressing rooms. Lockers are available, but are very small, and will cost you 25 or 50 cents (depending on the size of the locker—small or tiny) each time you use them. Additionally, the lockers are located in an out-of-the-way place relative to where you will be spending your time, making them even more inconvenient.

    Be sure to wear shoes. The footpaths at Typhoon Lagoon are relatively easy on bare feet, but there is a lot of ground to cover. If you have tender feet, we recommend wearing your shoes as you move around the park, taking them off whenever you raft, slide, or go into the water.

5. ***What to Bring.*** Things you will need include a towel, suntan lotion, and of course money. Since wallets and purses just get in the way, lock them safely in your trunk, carrying your money in a plastic bag along with your Walt Disney World hotel ID (if you have one). Though no place is completely safe, our folks felt very comfortable hiding our plastic money bags among our chaise lounges, coolers, and swimming paraphernalia once we settled in. Nobody disturbed our stuff and our cash was much easier to access than if we had had to run across the park to a locker. If you are really carrying a wad or you tend to worry about money anyway, get the locker.

6. ***What Not to Bring.*** Personal swim gear (fins, masks, rafts, etc.) are not allowed in Typhoon Lagoon. Everything you will need is either provided or available to rent. If you forget your towel, you can rent one. If you forget your swimsuit or lotion, these can be purchased.

7. ***Admissions.*** Purchase your admission about a half hour before opening time. If you are staying at a Walt Disney World lodging

property, you may be entitled to an admission discount so bring your hotel or campground ID. For guests on an extended stay at Walt Disney World, unlimited admission to Typhoon Lagoon is included in the 5-Day PLUS Super Pass.

8. ***Getting Oriented.*** Typhoon Lagoon is a circular park with the surf lagoon right in the middle. In terms of a clock face, you enter at the six o'clock position, and Mount Mayday (with the boat on top) is straight across the lagoon at twelve o'clock. A narrow canal, Castaway Creek, carves a wide circle around the lagoon and its adjoining beach area. Shark Reef, all the slides and raft rides, the children's area, and all services and concessions are situated around the outside perimeter of Castaway Creek. As you enter, tube rentals are to your left at seven o'clock, dressing rooms and lockers are to your right at four o'clock.

9. ***Tube Rental.*** When the park opens, walk straight ahead until you get to Castaway Creek. Turn left (without crossing) and head for the tube rental shack. Rent a tube for bobbing in Typhoon Lagoon.

NOTE: Rafting in the lagoon has been discontinued. The lagoon now alternates between "bobbing" waves (small, non-breaking waves) and large, breaking waves for body surfing. During body surfing periods, tubes are not allowed in the lagoon.

A $1 deposit is required per renter (the person who signs the rental agreement). Thus, Mom can plunk down one deposit and rent tubes for the whole family. We recommend a tube for each member of the family over four years of age. Single (one person) tubes rent for $5 a day and double (two person) tubes for $10 a day. Swim fins for body surfing are also available at $1 an hour.

As you might expect, signing rental agreements and checking out equipment is a little time-consuming. That is why you want to rent your tube first thing. If you decide to wait, thinking to save a few bucks on the rental fee, you will probably find yourself in a long slow line. If you want to be super-efficient, have one person in your party rent tubes while others pick a nesting spot.

Many readers have written complaining that their tubes were

stolen by other guests. If this should happen, you will be issued another tube at no charge, but of course will have to suffer the inconvenience. We recommend taking a length of rope and tying your tube(s) to a chair or chaise lounge. This of course is essentially a symbolic gesture, but one that will keep all but the most brazen away from your tube(s).

10. ***Lockers, Dressing Rooms, Towel Rental, Restrooms.*** These are situated to the right of the entrance, back upstream along Castaway Creek.

11. ***Getting Settled In.*** Establish your base for the day. There are many, many beautiful sunning and lounging spots scattered around Typhoon Lagoon. The breeze is best along the beaches of the lagoon (surf pool). If there are children under six in your party, you might choose an area to the left of Mount Mayday (with the ship on top) near the children's swimming area.

Arriving early, you can just about have your pick. There are flat lounges (unadjustable) and chairs (better for reading). There are grass shelters for those who prefer shade and even a few hammocks. Our research crew of seven staked out an area that had a shelter plus some sunny beach on the breezy side of the lagoon. There were picnic tables nearby.

The best spectator sport at Typhoon Lagoon is the surfing action in the lagoon. The second-best thing to being out there yourself is watching the zany antics of the other guests. With this in mind, you might choose a nesting spot with a good unobstructed view of the surf pool.

If you are a locker person, set up camp on the right side of the lagoon, along the beach. This will make it more convenient to visit your money.

12. ***Shark Reef.*** After settling in and stowing away your rented rafts for later use, walk around the right side of the lagoon to Shark Reef where you can snorkel in a saltwater pool with some live fish. Fins, mask, snorkel, and wetsuit vest are provided at no charge in the wooden building flanking the diving pool. Having obtained proper equipment (no forms or money involved), you are directed to take a shower and then to report to a snorkeling instructor. After a few minutes of instruction, you swim approximately 60 feet to the other side of the pool.

You are not allowed to paddle about aimlessly, but must traverse the pool more or less directly.

Shark Reef is fun early in the morning. Equipment collection, shower, instruction, and, finally, the quick swim can be accomplished without too much hassle. Also, owing to the small number of guests present, the attendants are more flexible about lingering in the pool and minor departures in your charted course.

Later, as crowds build, it becomes increasingly difficult and time-consuming to provide the necessary instruction. The result: platoons of would-be frogmen (should I say "frogpersons"?) zippily attired in their diving regalia, all restlessly awaiting their snorkeling lesson. Guests are formed into impromptu classes with the entire class briefed, and subsequently launched, together. What takes four or five minutes shortly after opening can take over an hour by 11 A.M.

By far the most prevalent and exotic species to be viewed in the pool are the dual-finned *homo sapiens*. Other denizens of the deep to be seen include small colorful tropical reef fish and a couple of diminutive rays (rays are members of the shark family and were the only members we saw). In terms of numbers, it would be unusual to swim the length of the pool and not see some fish. On the other hand, you are not exactly bumping into them all the time either.

It is very important to fit your diving mask on your face so that it seals around the edges. Brush hair away from your forehead and take a couple of sniffs with your nose, once the mask is in place, to create a vacuum. Be advised that mustaches often prevent the mask from sealing properly. The first indication that your mask is not correctly fitted will be saltwater in your nose.

If you do not want to swim around with fish early in the morning or fight crowds later in the day, you can avail yourself of an underwater viewing chamber, accessible anytime without waiting, special equipment, showers, instruction, or water in your nose.

13. ***Body Slides.*** Moving counterclockwise around the surfing lagoon in the direction of Mount Mayday, go next to the body slides on the right side of the mountain. Here you will find three corkscrew slides, the Storm Slides, and two steep speed slides called Humunga Kowabunga.

The corkscrew slides are pretty good, twisting off the mountain through arches in the rock and terminating in a pool. One line feeds all three slides. While each corkscrew is a little bit different, they all have pretty much the same feel.

The aggravating thing about the Storm Slides is the walkway to reach them. Obviously designed to handle a line of several hundred waiting guests, the concourse winds and dips all over the side of the mountain. For most folks it is sufficiently arduous to simply scale the vertical distance from pool level to the top of the slide. The walkway does not simply ascend to the top, but instead undulates, dropping down two steps for every three steps up, so that you must climb almost twice as many steps as would ordinarily be necessary to attain the same height.

Humunga Kowabunga (located next to the Storm Slides) offers dual-speed slides dropping about three stories at a pitch just short of vertical. While there is no minimum height requirement for the Storm Slides, riders for Humunga Kowabunga must be four feet tall. Pregnant women and those with back problems and various other health deficits are warned against riding any of the body slides.

We recommend riding each of the three Storm Slides once and then trying the speed slide (which looks worse than it is). If you want to sample remaining park attractions before the lines get heavy, this is about all the time you can afford to spend here.

Coach's Note: To go as fast as possible on a body slide, cross your legs at the ankles and cross your arms over your chest. When you take off, arch your back so that almost all your weight is on your shoulder blades and heels (the less contact with the surface, the less resistance). You can steer by shifting most of your upper body weight onto one shoulder blade. For max speed, weight the shoulder blade on the outside of each curve. If you want to go slow (what's the point?), distribute your weight equally as if you were lying on your back in bed.

14. ***Raft Rides.*** From the body slides continue counterclockwise, passing via a tunnel through Mount Mayday. On the left side of the mountain are three so-called raft rides: Gangplank Falls, Mayday Falls, and Keelhaul Falls.

Of the three, only Gangplank Falls actually involves rafts; the other two use inner tubes. All three are nicely done but are relatively tame as flume rides go. Each courses down a convoluted spillway replete with waves, eddies, chutes, and reversal currents. On Gangplank Falls, guests share round inflatable rafts resembling children's backyard wading pools. A sign at the entrance to the queueing area indicates a three-person minimum to ride. If your party numbers less, not to worry. Simply proceed to the loading point where an attendant will team you up with others.

On Mayday and Keelhaul Falls, you ride single-person inner tubes instead of a raft. Of the two, Mayday Falls is the more exciting, Keelhaul Falls being almost tame. Minimum height for Mayday and Keelhaul is four feet. There is no height requirement for Gangplank Falls.

15. ***Repeat Rides.*** Having completed the raft rides, you will have experienced all of Typhoon Lagoon's attractions which develop lines. If you arrived early and kept up a good pace you should be able to repeat some of your favorite rides without a prohibitive wait. In any event, now is the time to try. The park will only become more crowded as the day goes on.

16. ***Options.*** By the time you finish repeating your favorite slides the park will have become noticeably more crowded. Fortunately, the two remaining untried Typhoon Lagoon features, Typhoon Lagoon surf pool and Castaway Creek, accommodate large numbers with no waiting. Expressed differently, you can structure your own schedule from this point on. The only lines you will encounter will be for food. If you are worn out, relax on Castaway Creek, curl up in a hammock, or grab a bite. If you are still full of energy, head for the surf pool.

17. ***Surf Pool.*** The surf lagoon (along with the beautiful landscaping) is what makes Typhoon Lagoon truly special. We have to tell you that you will experience larger waves in the Typhoon Lagoon surf pool than most folks have ever encountered in the ocean. The surf machine puts out a wave about every 90 seconds (just about how long it takes to get back in position if you caught the previous wave). Perfectly formed and ideal for riding, each wave is about five to six feet tall from trough to crest. Before you throw yourself into the fray, watch two or three waves from some vantage point onshore. Since each wave breaks in almost the same spot you can get a feel for position

and timing. Observing the technique of other surfers will help also.

The best way to ride the waves is to swim out about three-fourths of the way to the wall at the wave machine end of the surf pool. When the wave comes (you will both feel and hear it), swim vigorously toward the beach, attempting to position yourself one-half to three-fourths of a body length below the breaking crest. The waves are so perfectly engineered that they will either carry you forward or bypass you (unlike an ocean wave, they will not slam you down).

The primary hazard in the surf pool is collision with other surfers and swimmers. If you are surfing, the best way to avoid collision is to paddle out pretty far (as described above) so that you will be at the top of the wave as it breaks. This tactic eliminates the possibility of anyone landing on you from above while assuring maximum forward visibility and steerage for collision avoidance with those between you and the beach. A corollary to all this is that the worst place to swim is in the area where the wave actually breaks. As you look up you will see a six-foot wall of water carrying eight-dozen screaming surfers bearing down on you at 90 miles an hour. This is the time to remember every submarine movie you've ever seen . . . Dive! Dive! Dive!

When the surf pool changes to bobbing waves, it's time to grab your tube. If you do not have a tube, you can still have fun swimming or floating in the gentle waves, but you will feel like the only kid on the team without a uniform. It's only five bucks a day; just do it.

Finally, an additional warning: Typhoon Lagoon surf has an uncanny knack for loosening watchbands, stripping jewelry, and sucking stuff out of your pockets. Don't take anything out there except your swimsuit (and hold on to it).

18. ***Castaway Creek.*** Castaway Creek is a great idea. It is a long, long tranquil inner-tube ride that gives the impression that you are doing something while you are being sedentary. For wimps, wussies, and exhausted people of all ages, Castaway Creek is the answer to a prayer. Flowing ever so slowly around the whole park, through caves and beneath waterfalls, past gardens, shipwrecks, and bridges, Castaway Creek offers a relaxing, foot-saving alternative for touring the park.

Castaway Creek can be reached from a number of put-in/

take-out points distributed around its circumference. There are never any lines; just wade out into the creek and plop into one of the inner-tubes floating by. Ride the gentle current all the way around or get out at any exit. If you lay back and go with the flow, it will take about 30–35 minutes to float the full 2,100-foot circuit.

As you might anticipate, there will be other guests on whom the subtlety of Castaway Creek will be lost. They will be the ones racing, screaming, and splashing. Let them pass, stopping in place for a few moments if necessary to put some distance between yourself and them.

19. ***Children's Swimming Area.*** To the left of the raft rides is Ketchakiddie Creek, a delightful children's swimming area featuring mild slides, bubble jets, waterfalls, and a variety of "hands-on" play structures. Spacious and attractive, Ketchakiddie is designed to stimulate young imaginations as well as young bodies.

20. ***Lunch.*** If you did not bring a picnic lunch, you can of course purchase food. Portions are adequate to generous, quality is comparable to chain fast food, and prices are (as you would expect) a bit high.

21. ***More Options.*** If you are really a water puppy, you might consider returning to your hotel for a little heat-of-the-day siesta and returning to Typhoon Lagoon for some evening swimming. Special lighting after dusk makes Typhoon Lagoon an enchanting place to be. Crowds also tend to be lighter in the evening. If you leave the park and want to return, be sure to hang on to your admission ticket and have your hand stamped. If you are staying in a hotel serviced by Walt Disney World buses, older kids can return on their own to Typhoon Lagoon, giving Mom and Dad a little private quiet time.

River Country

River Country is aesthetically among the best of the water theme parks—beautifully landscaped and immaculately manicured with rocky canyons and waterfalls skillfully blended with white sand beaches. The park is even situated to take advantage of the breeze blowing in from Bay Lake. For pure and simple swimming and splashing, River Country gets high marks. For its slides, however, River Country does not begin to compete with its big sister, Typhoon Lagoon, or with its nearby competitors. Where Wet 'n Wild (on International Drive) features in excess of 16 major slides and tube rides, River Country has one tube ride and two corkscrew-style slides. Few slides and many swimmers add up to long lines. If slides are your thing, and you are allergic to long lines, hit River Country as soon as it opens in the morning or alternatively in the hour before closing. You can come and go throughout the day simply by obtaining a reentry stamp.

Sunbathers will enjoy River Country, particularly if they position themselves near the lakefront to take advantage of any cooling breeze. Be forewarned, however, that the chaise lounges are basically flat with the head slightly elevated, and do not have adjustable backs. For a comfortable reading position or for lying on your stomach, therefore, they leave a great deal to be desired.

Access to River Country by car is a hassle. First you are directed to a pay parking lot, where you leave your car, gather your personal belongings and wait for (what else?) a Disney tram to transport you to the water park. The tram ride is rather lengthy, and pity the poor soul who left his bathing suit in the car (a round-trip to retrieve it will take about a half hour).

There are no lodging accommodations at River Country. Food is available or you can pack in a picnic lunch to enjoy in River Country's picturesque, shaded lakeside picnic area. Access is by bus from the Transportation and Ticket Center (junction and transfer point for the EPCOT Center and Magic Kingdom monorails) or from the River Country parking lot on Vista Boulevard (see map, page 45). River

285

Country can also be reached by boat from any of the Bay Lake or Seven Seas Lagoon resort hotels. Combination passes, which include both River Country and Discovery Island, are available and represent the best buy for anyone interested in the minor Disney theme parks. For guests staying at Walt Disney World for five or more days, the 5-Day PLUS Super Pass includes unlimited admission to both River Country and Typhoon Lagoon.

—— Orlando/Kissimmee Area
Water Theme Parks ——

Just for the record, if you are into water theme parks, here's how the area's offerings compare:

	Typhoon Lagoon	River Country	Water Mania	Wet 'n Wild
Theme presentation	Yes	Yes	No	No
Beautiful scenery/landscaping	Yes	Yes	No	No
Large general swimming area	Yes	Yes	No	Yes
Children's swimming area	Yes	Yes	Yes	Yes
Snorkeling pool	Yes	No	No	No
Wave pool	Yes	No	Yes	Yes
Vertical-drop thrill slide	2	No	2	2
Graduated-drop thrill slide	No	No	2	2
Corkscrew body slide	3	2	3	4
Corkscrew tube/raft/mat slide	No	No	No	6
Whitewater rapids ride	3	1	No	1
Tranquil/scenic tube ride	1	No	No	1
Knee waterski	No	No	No	Yes

Typhoon Lagoon vs. Wet 'n Wild

Wet 'n Wild has Typhoon Lagoon beat in the slide department. Wet 'n Wild has more slides, wilder slides, and more direct ramps and walkways which cut down travel time back up to the top. The headliner at Wet 'n Wild is an attraction called the Black Hole where guests descend on a two-person tube down a pitch black corkscrew slide. It's a wet version of Space Mountain only much darker. Our research team thinks this is the single most exciting slide offered at any Florida swimming theme park.

Typhoon Lagoon wins hands down in landscaping and aesthetic beauty, and has the better surf pool of the two parks. Typhoon Lagoon also has a superior children's area. Both parks feature unique attractions. Wet 'n Wild has a ride where guests kneel on water skis and Typhoon Lagoon has Shark Reef where guests can snorkel among live fish.

Prices for one-day admission are about the same, though Wet 'n Wild stays open until 11 P.M. while Typhoon Lagoon generally closes at 6 P.M. or 7 P.M. We think their closing time is a great plus for Wet 'n Wild. Warm Florida nights are a great time to enjoy a water theme park. There is less waiting for slides and the pavement is cooler on your feet. Additionally, Wet 'n Wild features live music on its wave pool stage many evenings.

PART SEVEN—Nightlife
& Special Tours

Behind the Scenes at Walt Disney World

Interested adults (16 and over) can book guided walking tours exploring respectively the architecture of the international pavilions of EPCOT Center (Hidden Treasures of World Showcase), and/or Walt Disney World's gardens (Gardens of the World), horticulture, and landscaping. Each tour lasts three-and-a-half hours. Cost is about $15 plus an EPCOT Center admission ticket. For reservations call (407) 345-5860.

A shorter tour along similar lines is the Harvest Tour, which takes guests behind the scenes to tour the vegetable gardens in The Land pavilion of EPCOT Center. The tour requires same-day reservations made on the lower level of The Land (to the far right of the fast-food windows). There is no charge for the Harvest Tour, which lasts 30–45 minutes.

Another tour for adults (16 and up) is Innovations in Action, a behind-the-scenes exploration of the Magic Kingdom. Currently available only to groups of 15 or more, information and reservations can be obtained by calling (407) 828-1500.

For children 10–15 years there are a number of behind-the-scenes special learning programs available. In addition to being educational, these six-and-a-half hour programs also give Mom and Dad a little time to themselves. The Entertainment program takes a look at what goes into a Walt Disney World live-theater performance. The Art program looks both at Disney character art and at the architecture of EPCOT Center. Finally, a Nature program examines the various zoological exhibits at Discovery Island. Each program costs about $75 but includes admission to any attraction visited and lunch. Enrolled students meet instructors at the Transportation and Ticket Center. Call (407) 345-5860 well in advance of your visit for information and reservations.

Walt Disney World at Night

The Disney folks contrive so cleverly to exhaust you during the day that the mere thought of night activity sends most visitors into anaphylactic shock. For the hearty and the nocturnal, however, there is a lot to do in the evenings at Walt Disney World.

In the Parks

At EPCOT Center the major evening event is IllumiNations, a mixed-media laser and fireworks show at the World Showcase Lagoon. Showtime is listed on the daily entertainment and special events schedule.

In the Magic Kingdom there is the ever-popular Main Street Electrical Parade and Fantasy in the Sky Fireworks. Consult the daily entertainment schedule for performance times.

The Disney-MGM Studios feature a laser and fireworks spectacular called Sorcery in the Sky on nights when the park is open late. Consult the daily entertainment schedule for showtimes.

At the Hotels

At waterside at each of the hotels connected by monorail is the Bay Lake and Seven Seas Lagoon Floating Electrical Pageant. For something more elaborate, consider one of the dinner theaters described on the next page. Finally, if you want to go honky-tonkin', many of the hotels at the Disney Hotel Plaza (adjacent to Walt Disney World Village) have lively bars with rock bands and other entertainment.

At Fort Wilderness Campground

A campfire program is conducted each night at the Fort Wilderness Campground. Open only to Walt Disney World resort guests, the event begins with a sing-along led by Disney characters Chip and Dale, and progresses to cartoons and a Disney feature movie. There is no charge.

At Pleasure Island

Pleasure Island, Walt Disney World's nighttime entertainment complex, features seven nightclubs for one admission price. Dance to rock or country, or take in a showbar performance, or see a movie. Pleasure Island is located in Walt Disney World Village and is accessible from the theme parks and from the Transportation and Ticket Center by shuttle bus. For a detailed description of Pleasure Island, plus Touring Plans, see page 297.

At Disney's Boardwalk

Disney's Boardwalk is situated along the walkway connecting EPCOT Center with the Swan Hotel. Modeled after the Coney Island and Atlantic City boardwalks in their days of glory, Disney's version features game arcades, amusement park rides for all ages, bright lights, music, and food. Disney's Boardwalk is accessible on foot from EPCOT Center or from any of the EPCOT Center resort hotels (Swan, Dolphin, Yacht Club, Beach Club) and by bus from other Walt Disney World destinations. Guests who walk over from EPCOT Center after IllumiNations can catch a bus directly back to the EPCOT Center parking lot to retrieve their car at the conclusion of the evening.

—— Walt Disney World Dinner Theaters ——

There are several dinner theater shows each night at Walt Disney World. Reservations can be made on the day of the show at any of the resort hotels, or by calling (407) 824-8000 for *Broadway at the Top* and *Polynesian Revue* and (407) 824-2748 for the *Hoop Dee Doo Revue*. Visitors with reservations for a Walt Disney World lodging property can make reservations prior to arrival by calling the same numbers. Getting reservations for *Broadway at the Top* and *Polynesian Revue* presentations is not too tough. Getting a reservation to the *Hoop Dee Doo Revue* is a trick of the first order.

Broadway at the Top

Broadway at the Top, situated atop the Contemporary Resort Hotel, features a creative menu with entrees such as roast duck, shrimp brochette and steak combination, seafood catch of the day, prime rib, and veal with sausage. Unlike most other dinner theaters, the pace is unhurried and the menu provides plenty of variety. The food is good and nicely presented, and the service is excellent.

The entertainment consists of dinner music and dancing to a live orchestra (playing primarily easy-listening standards), followed by a lively stage show featuring showtunes from Broadway and limited choreography. The presentation is professional and straightforward, but not particularly imaginative or compelling. *Broadway at the Top* appeals to a more mature audience and we do not recommend the show for children under twelve. Cost is about $40 per person plus drinks and tips. Gentlemen are required to wear jackets (but not ties).

The Polynesian Revue

Presented nightly at the Polynesian Village, the evening consists of a "Polynesian style" all-you-can-eat meal followed by south seas island native dancing. The dancing is interesting and largely authentic, and the dancers are comely but definitely PG in the Disney tradition. We think the show has its moments and that the meal is adequate, but that neither are particularly special. Cost per adult is about $30. If you really enjoy this type of entertainment, and experience a problem getting a reservation for the Polynesian Revue, Sea World presents a similar dinner and show each evening.

Also at the Polynesian Resort's Luau Cove is *Mickey's Tropical Revue*, where Disney characters are tossed into the regular entertainment show. This show starts at 4:30 P.M. when it is too early to be hungry and too hot to be sitting around outdoors. Cost is about $25 for adults, $20 for Juniors (12–20), and $11 for children (3–11).

Hoop Dee Doo Revue

This show, presented nightly at Pioneer Hall at Fort Wilderness Campgrounds, is by far the best of the Disney dinner shows. The meal, served family-style, consists of barbecued ribs, fried chicken, corn on the cob, and baked beans, along with chips, bread, salad, and dessert. All of these are most satisfactory. Portions are generous and service is excellent.

The show consists of western dancehall song, dance, and humor, much in the mold of the *Diamond Horseshoe Jamboree* in the Magic Kingdom, only longer. The cast is talented, energetic, and lovable, each one a memorable character. Between the food, the show, and the happy, appreciative audience, the *Hoop Dee Doo Revue* is a delightful way to spend an evening. Cost per adult is about $30.

Now for the bad news. The *Hoop Dee Doo Revue* is sold out months in advance to guests who hold lodging reservations at Walt Disney World properties. If you plan to stay at one of the Walt Disney World hotels, try making your *Hoop Dee Doo* reservations when you book your room. If you have already booked your lodging call as far in advance as possible. For those with accommodations outside of Walt Disney World:

1. Call (407) 824-2748 thirty days prior to visiting. If that does not work:
2. Call (407) 824-2748 at 9 A.M. each morning while you are at Walt Disney World to make a same-day reservation. There are three performances each night, and for all three combined, only three to twenty-four people, total, will be admitted on same-day reservations. If no reservations are available:
3. Show up at Pioneer Hall (no easy task in itself unless you are staying in the Campgrounds) 45 minutes before showtime (early and late shows are your best bets) and put your name on the standby list. If someone with reservations fails to show, you may be admitted.

If all of this sounds too much like work, try the show at *Fort Liberty*, a non-Disney attraction on FL 192. Call (407) 351-5151 for reservations.

—— *Other Area Dinner Theater Options* ——

There are a number of dinner theaters within twenty minutes of Walt Disney World. Of these, *Fort Liberty* is a good substitute for the *Hoop Dee Doo Revue*. *Medieval Times*, featuring mounted knights in combat, is fun and most assuredly different, and *King Henry's Feast* is a fun variety show on the theme of King Henry's birthday celebration. The food at all three of these dinner theaters is both good and plentiful and all three shows are highly recommended. Cost per adult is around $25–30, but discount coupons are readily available at brochure racks and in local tourism periodicals found in motel lobbys. *Fort Liberty* and *King Henry* reservations can be made by calling (407) 351-5151. Call (407) 239-0214 for *Medieval Times*.

A fourth dinner theater, *Mardi Gras*, stages a better Broadway-style show than does Disney's *Broadway at the Top*. Unfortunately, and in contrast to *Broadway at the Top*, the food is mediocre. In addition, *Mardi Gras* guests are literally packed at their tables. The tariff at *Mardi Gras* is about $25 for adults not counting the bar tab. For information or reservations call (407) 351-5151.

Pleasure Island

Pleasure Island, which opened in 1989, is a six-acre nighttime entertainment complex situated on a man-made island in Walt Disney World Village. The complex consists of seven theme nightclubs, a ten-theater movie complex, restaurants, and shops. While some of the restaurants and shops are open during the day, Pleasure Island does not really come alive until after 7 P.M. when the nightclubs open.

Admission Options. One admission (about $11) entitles a guest to enjoy all six nightclubs (the Baton Rouge Lounge on the Empress Lily steamboat is not part of Pleasure Island per se, but is so close that we include it in our discussion and Touring Plan as a seventh club). Admission is restricted to guests 18 or older after 7 P.M. unless accompanied by a parent. Unlimited 7-day admission to Pleasure Island is also included in the 5-Day PLUS Super Pass.

Alcoholic Beverages. Guests not recognizably older than 21 are required to provide proof of their age if they wish to purchase alcoholic beverages. To avoid repeated checking as the patron moves from club to club, a color-coded wristband indicating eligibility status is provided. All the nightclubs on Pleasure Island serve alcohol. Those under 21, incidentally, while allowed in all of the clubs except Mannequins, are not allowed to purchase alcoholic beverages. Finally, and gratefully, you do not have to order any drinks at all. You can go into any club, enjoy the entertainment, and never buy that first beer. You won't be hassled a bit.

Dress Code. Casual is in. Shirts and shoes are required.

New Variations on an Old Theme. The single-admission nightclub complex was originated in Florida at Orlando's Church Street Station, still very much alive and well in historic downtown Orlando. Starting fresh, the Disney folks have been able to eliminate some of the problems which have haunted Church Street Station and a lot of other nightspots over the years.

Summertime, and the Parking Is Easy.   To begin, Pleasure Island has its own vast parking lot so, unlike Church Street downtown, parking is easy. Pleasure Island's parking lot is confusing, however, unnecessarily convoluted, and not well-marked. If you drive, study all landmarks and other identifying objects near your parking space so you will be able to locate your car when you are ready to leave.

Good News for the Early to Bed Crowd.   If you are not nocturnal by nature or if you are tired from a long day in the theme parks, you do not have to wait until 11 or 12 P.M. for the Disney nightspots to get revved up. There is no waiting till the wee hours for Pleasure Island to hit its stride. All bands, dancers, comedians, and showmen come on like gangbusters from the very beginning of the evening. For *real* night people, it feels weird to be dancing to "Shout" at 8:15 P.M. But that's the way it is at Pleasure Island; there are no "best sets" or grand finales, it's full tilt all the time.

It's Possible to Visit All the Clubs in One Night.   Where a performance in most nightclubs might be an hour or more in duration, at Pleasure Island the performances are shorter but staged more frequently. This allows a guest to move around from club to club without missing much. Since you can experience the essence of a given club pretty quickly, there is no need to hang around for two or three drinks just to see what is going on. This format enables a guest to have a complete and satisfying experience in a brief time and then, if desired, to move on to sample another club.

The music clubs (XZFR Rock & Roll Beach Club, Cage, the Neon Armadillo, the Baton Rouge Lounge, and Mannequins) go non-stop. Sometimes there are special performances within the context of ongoing club entertainment. The Adventurers Club and the Comedy Warehouse offer scheduled shows. All shows are of short duration, leaving plenty of time to sample other Pleasure Island offerings.

We are very high on Pleasure Island. The cover is a little pricey and the drinks are not cheap, but the entertainment is absolutely top-notch. And if you arrive by 9 P.M., you will have time to sample all of the clubs.

Pleasure Island First Timers' Touring Plan

This itinerary is for first-time visitors to Pleasure Island who want to check out all of the clubs.

1. Arrive by 7:30 or 8 P.M. if you intend on eating at a Pleasure Island restaurant. If you eat before you go, try to arrive by 9 P.M.

2. Purchase your admission or enter using your 5-Day PLUS Super Pass.

3. *Comedy Warehouse.* Bearing left from the admission windows, proceed to the Comedy Warehouse. If a show is scheduled to begin within a half hour, browse the shops (some are great entertainment in their own right) until about ten minutes before showtime. Then head back to the Comedy Warehouse for the show. If showtime is more than 30 minutes off, check out the country and bluegrass music at the Neon Armadillo, located pretty much across the street from the Comedy Warehouse. Use your own judgment about whether you have time to buy a drink. Return to the Comedy Warehouse ten minutes before showtime.

4. *Adventurers Club.* After the show at the Comedy Warehouse cross the street to the Adventurers Club. Another comedy presentation, this show does not run on a posted schedule (but should). Patterned after a rather stuffy English gentlemen's club, the Adventurers Club is a two-story turn-of-the-century affair with big armchairs, walls covered with animal heads (some of which talk), and other artifacts.

   Many guests will stroll through the Adventurers Club, inspect the ridiculous decor, and then leave, not realizing that they missed anything. The main attraction at the Adventurers Club is a show in the club's private library. About once every 30 or 40 minutes all the guests present will be ushered into the library for a show. Nobody informs the guests that a show is upcoming; they either must hang around long enough to be invited in, or alternately intuit that with Disney, what you see isn't what you get.

When you arrive at the Adventurers Club, ask an attendant when the next show in the library will be starting. If showtime is 20 minutes or less away, go on in and have a drink. If it's a long while until the next show, the Neon Armadillo is right next door.

5. ***Neon Armadillo Music Saloon.*** Located next door to the Adventurers Club, what you see here is definitely what you get: first-class country and bluegrass music. If you have not spent some time here counting down to showtime for one of the comedy presentations, go ahead and visit the Neon Armadillo now.

6. ***Mannequins Dance Palace.*** Backtrack toward Pleasure Island's front entrance to Mannequins. Mannequins is a ritzy, contemporary rock dance club with incredible lighting and special effects. Music for dancing is recorded but the sound system is superb. Those under 21 are not permitted in Mannequins.

7. ***Cage.*** When Pleasure Island opened in 1989 this club was an under-21 club called Videopolis East. For various reasons it was closed and reopened as Cage. The decor is the same (steel beams, catwalks, and metal mesh with video monitors hung in strategic locations), but the entrance is now in front (instead of around the back) and it is an adult club featuring what Pleasure Island terms "alternative music." The music is not so much music as it is endless, repetitive percussion, and we think "alternative" applies to what you need after spending about five minutes at Cage. The music at Cage, like that at Mannequins, is recorded.

8. ***XZFR Rock & Roll Beach Club.*** The next stop is XZFR, featuring oldies rock. The bands here are always first-rate and they raise the roof beginning early in the evening. A variety of games are available at XZFR (pronounced zephyr—zeff-fur) for those who do not wish to dance.

9. ***Baton Rouge Lounge.*** The last club on the itinerary is the Baton Rouge Lounge situated on the stern of the main deck of the *Empress Lily* riverboat. Located at the far end of Pleasure Island, the *Empress Lily* can be reached by walking out the main

entrance and turning left before crossing the bridge over the canal. The Baton Rouge Lounge features light musical comedy and is a great place to mellow out after the hard-driving music of the other clubs.

10. ***Pleasure Island Restaurants.*** There has been a lot of attention paid to menu creation at Pleasure Island's eateries. Unfortunately, as with almost all Disney restaurants, most of the fun is in the anticipation, the real item not quite living up to its billing.

The Empress Room on the *Empress Lily* is the island's flagship restaurant, but probably not its best. Serving Continental cuisine, what Disney calls subtle, we call bland. The Empress Room is pricey and reservations are required (407) 828-3900. Coats are required for gentlemen. In addition to the Empress Room, there are two somewhat less sumptuous dining rooms on the *Empress Lily* (Steerman's Quarters and the Fisherman's Deck), each serving steak and seafood as well as New Orleans specialties. Attire at these latter is more casual, reservations are taken but not required, and prices are somewhat more reasonable. With all three restaurants, however, the riverboat ambience is a decided winner over the table fare. There is no show or entertainment in any of the three eateries. Finally, and having nothing to do with nightlife, there are two seatings each morning in the Steerman's Quarters and the Fisherman's Deck for a Disney Character Breakfast (a breakfast buffet with Disney characters in attendance).

Onshore across from the riverboat is the Portobello Yacht Club, serving fresh seafood, pasta, and pizza. Casual, palatable with good variety, and reasonably priced.

The Fireworks Factory specializes in barbeque, with several types of ribs available. Slaw and cornbread are some of the best we have had anywhere. Appetizers (catfish, buffalo wings, barbequed shrimp) are disappointing. If you stick to ribs and chicken and skip the appetizers, you can have a good meal here.

Merriweather's Market offers fast food at upscale prices. In addition to the restaurants described, some of the clubs offer snacks and light eats.

If you want to eat dinner at a Pleasure Island full-service restaurant, we recommend arriving by 6:30 P.M. and eating early or waiting until after 10:00 P.M. An alternative, of course, is to eat sandwiches and munchies in the clubs. It is not necessary to buy any sort of club admission to eat at Pleasure Island restaurants. Many of the restaurants are open during the day as well as in the evening.

11. ***Pleasure Island Shopping.*** Pleasure Island features some shops which are entertainment attractions in themselves. At Cover Story, guests don costumes prior to being photographed for the mock cover of a major magazine. Want to see yourself on the cover of *Cosmo*? Here's the place. In a similar vein, Super-Star Studio provides the opportunity to star in your own music video. Props, including keyboard, drums, and guitar are available. Video technicians record your lip sync (or you can actually sing), varying camera angles and making you look good. Post Production adds background to your tape for added realism. Work alone or make up a whole group with your friends. If you do not want your own magazine cover or rock video, drop in and watch others; it's a hoot of the first order.

It is not necessary to pay any sort of admission to shop at Pleasure Island during the day. In the evening, all of Pleasure Island except the restaurants, however, is gated.

—— *Pleasure Island vs. Church Street Station* ——

Both Pleasure Island and Church Street Station are worthwhile attractions. Pleasure Island has a plastic, trendy, brand-new (translate Disney) feel. Church Street Station is situated in a restored city block of historic old Orlando adjacent to the railroad tracks. Both sites have their strong points, but architecturally Church Street is much more interesting.

As discussed previously, parking is a minor problem at Church Street, but no problem at all (if you can remember where you parked) at Pleasure Island.

Performances are longer and fewer in number at Church Street making it much more difficult than at Pleasure Island to see all the shows covered in your admission. Also, the timing of performances (starting and ending times) at Church Street mitigates against getting from one show to another or getting a good seat. Pleasure Island's comedy clubs feature shorter shows performed more frequently, and the music clubs run pretty much continuously, so that making the rounds is no particular problem.

Rock music and dancing to rock music is better at Pleasure Island. But when it comes to country music and dancing, as good as the Neon Armadillo is, it cannot compare to Church Street's rollicking Cheyenne Saloon & Opera House. Comedy is good at both places, although different.

Church Street is a more adult night complex. The humor is bawdier, the crowd older, and you don't have to check out the wristband of the girl by the bar to know she's over 21.

Food is a toss-up. Both places serve both good and undistinguished fare at an upscale price. You just have to ask the right questions and pick your way carefully through the menus.

Church Street admission at about $16 per adult (including sales tax); a bit pricey compared to Pleasure Island's $11.

Readers' Questions to the Author

Q: Why were rental rafts discontinued at Typhoon Lagoon?

A: Evidently, there were a number of problems with the rafts. In addition to guests stealing rafts from one another, the rafts took up a lot of room in the Lagoon and caused a great many collisions. The only surfing currently allowed is body surfing.

Q: You go on and on about how much trouble it is to eat in the Magic Kingdom and how mediocre the food is, but never make any constructive recommendations for how to improve the situation.

A: One way to provide dining variety, simplify service, and speed customer processing is to operate a buffet. Guests pay one fixed price on entering, eliminating the need to key in different menu items, and then serve themselves. Instead of a Mom or Dad placing different orders for every member of the family, Mom just walks up to the cashier and says, "Two adults and three kids, please." Many of the Las Vegas casinos operate huge buffets, efficiently serving several thousand patrons every meal. One casino operates four individual, double-sided, serving stations (i.e., eight serving lines) in their buffet, allowing almost 400 people to be serving themselves at once.

Q: When you do your research, are you admitted to the parks free? Do the Disney people know you are there?

A: We pay the regular admission and usually the Disney people do not know we are on site.

Q: How often is The Unofficial Guide *revised?*

A: We do a major revision once a year, but make minor corrections every time we go to press, about three times a year on average.

Q: Do you stay in Walt Disney World? If not, where do you stay?

A: We do stay at Walt Disney World lodging properties from time to time, usually when a new hotel opens. Since we began writing about Walt Disney World in 1982 we have stayed in over forty different properties in various locations around Orlando, Lake Buena Vista, and

Kissimmee. Home bases for our research team are the Howard Johnson Fountain Park Plaza Hotel on US 192 (407-396-1111) and the Star Quality Resort on International Drive (407-351-4100).

Q: How can you write about rides and shows which are new and have not yet opened?

A: We are familiar with some new attractions at Walt Disney World because we have experienced them previously at Disneyland. Several members of our research team are fully credentialed travel journalists who are often invited to preview new Disney attractions before they open. For developments ranging far into the future, we rely on reports to Disney shareholders, and information released to the travel press.

Q: What new attractions are in development at Walt Disney World?

A: A new Circle-Vision 360 presentation is scheduled to open in 1992, initiating the first stage of a renovation of Tomorrowland to be completed in 1996. Splash Mountain, a flume ride already operating in Disneyland, will come to the Magic Kingdom in 1993. In Mickey's Starland, a ride based on *The Little Mermaid* is planned.

In EPCOT Center, a George Lucas 3-D musical movie is planned to replace *Captain EO* by 1994. Journeys in Space will be a new thrill ride in Future World (no projected date of completion). In the World Showcase, a Matterhorn mountain bobsled ride is planned, as is a Soviet Union pavilion. No opening dates have been established for either.

At Disney-MGM Studios a 3-D Muppet movie is due to premier in 1991, followed by the Muppets Movie Ride in 1993. A new area, Sunset Boulevard, will be developed during the 90s and will be home to several rides based on *Who Killed Roger Rabbit?* and *Dick Tracy*.

Q: What is your favorite Florida attraction?

A: What attracts me (as opposed to my favorite attraction) is Juniper Springs, a stunningly beautiful canoeing stream about an hour north of Orlando in the Ocala National Forest. Originating as a limestone aquifer, crystal clear water erupts from the ground and begins a ten-mile journey to the creek's mouth at Lake George. Winding through palm, cypress, and live oak, the stream is more exotic than the Jungle Cruise, and alive with birds, animals, turtles, and alligators. Put in at the Juniper Springs Recreation Area on FL 40, 36 miles east of Ocala. The seven-mile trip to the FL 19 bridge takes about four and a half hours. Canoe rentals and shuttle service are available at the recreation area. Phone (904) 625-2808 for information.

Q: *Why are there no photographs in* The Unofficial Guide*?*

A: Disney has copyrighted many identifiable buildings and structures in Walt Disney World. Any recognizable photo of Walt Disney World which we publish without Disney's permission, even if we take the picture with our own camera, could constitute copyright infringement, according to Disney's legal representatives. Walt Disney World will not grant *The Unofficial Guide* permission to publish photographs because of its relationship with Steve Birnbaum's *Official Guide to Walt Disney World.*

Q: *What are your recommendations for non-hotel restaurants outside of Walt Disney World?*

A: Unfortunately, we are not able to eat many meals outside of Walt Disney World, and a couple of our favorite off-World spots have dropped in quality lately. Restaurants we can recommend include Numero Uno (cheap) for Cuban food and Siam Orchid (expensive) for Thai food. Caruso's Palace on International Drive is an excellent restaurant and a good value with multi-course dinners for big eaters. Only half of the specialties, however, are Italian.

Scott Joseph, the wine and food critic of the *Orlando Sentinel*, has recently published a guide to the Orlando area dining in which he recommends the following restaurants:

American	Chatham's Place; 7575 Dr. Phillips Blvd., Orlando; Moderate to expensive
	Pebbles; 12551 State Road 535, Crossroads Shopping Center, Lake Buena Vista; Moderate to expensive
Beef	Butcher Shop Steakhouse; Mercado Mediterranean Village, 8445 International Drive, Orlando; Moderate
Chinese	Ming Court; 9188 International Drive, Orlando; Moderate
Cuban	Numero Uno; 2499 S. Orange Avenue, Orlando; Inexpensive
Indian	Darbar; 7600 Dr. Phillips Blvd., Orlando; Moderate to expensive
	Passage to India; 5532 International Drive, Orlando; Moderate

Italian	Capriccio; 9801 International Drive, Orlando; Moderate to expensive
	Christini's; 7600 Dr. Phillips Blvd., Orlando; Expensive
Japanese	Ran Getsu; 8400 International Drive, Orlando; Moderate to expensive
Middle Eastern	Phoenician; 7600 Dr. Phillips Blvd., Orlando; Inexpensive
Seafood	Banana Bay Grille; 2948 Vineland Road, Kissimmee; Moderate
	Calico Jack's; 5648 International Drive, Orlando; Inexpensive
	Hemingway's; 1 Grand Cypress Blvd., Hyatt Regency Grand Cypress Resort, Orlando; Expensive
Thai	Siam Orchid; 7575 Republic Drive, Orlando; Moderate to expensive

To order a copy of *The Orlando Sentinel Restaurant Guide*, by Scott Joseph, send $9.95 to Sentinel Books, P.O. Box 1100, Orlando, FL 32802. Or call 1-800-3474-6868, extension 5521, for credit card orders.

—— *About the Author* ——

Bob Sehlinger is a theme park design and operations consultant and author of five successful books on travel and recreation.

Index